Paths to Transnational Solidarity

Trade Unions Past, Present and Future

Edited by Craig Phelan

Volume 24

PETER LANG

Oxford • Bern • Berlin • Bruxelles • Frankfurt am Main • New York • Wien

Paths to Transnational Solidarity

Identity-Building Processes in European Works Councils

Hermann Kotthoff and Michael Whittall

PETER LANG

Oxford • Bern • Berlin • Bruxelles • Frankfurt am Main • New York • Wien

Bibliographic information published by Die Deutsche Nationalbibliothek.
Die Deutsche Nationalbibliothek lists this publication in the Deutsche National-
bibliografie; detailed bibliographic data is available on the Internet at
http://dnb.d-nb.de.

A catalogue record for this book is available from the British Library.

Library of Congress Control Number: 2014932443

ISSN 1662-7784
ISBN 978-3-0343-1775-7

© Peter Lang AG, International Academic Publishers, Bern 2014
Hochfeldstrasse 32, CH-3012 Bern, Switzerland
info@peterlang.com, www.peterlang.com, www.peterlang.net

This publication has been peer reviewed.

Printed in Germany

Contents

Preface

Previous research into European Works Councils (EWC) has principally concerned itself with the functioning and outputs of this new representative institution. One of the main outcomes has been the sober realization that in many instances EWCs have not, in practice, succeeded in becoming collective actors with a capacity to generate unique outputs as their members have not managed to form a cohesive group with a European perspective that can be brought to bear on this area of activity.

This central focus of this study is the process through which an EWC becomes able to emerge as an actor: that is, how a set of strangers can cohere into a cooperative team able to offer mutual support and with the capacity to engage in the common European task of company-level interest representation. It is based on five companies selected on the ground that they exemplified best practice. We then explored and analysed the conditions for the possibility of transnational solidaristic behaviour in a series of case studies. The research took place during 2009 and 2010. In 2012 the results were fed back to the EWCs concerned and discussed with them.

We are grateful to the Hans Böckler Foundation, which financed the research project originally submitted by Hermann Kotthoff and which provided us with the opportunity to pursue the question of the conditions for the constitution of EWC in a direct and concentrated fashion. We are also grateful to the project's advisory board for their support in our project of making 'soft facts' hard.

Our method of intensive interviews and participant observation necessitated acquiring a high degree of familiarity with the internal worlds and histories of the EWCs that we studied. We are very grateful to these EWCs for their openness in this respect. In particular we would like to thank EWC chairs and steering committee members as well as the representatives of national and European trade union confederations for granting us extremely informative interviews.

We would also like to thank Frau Zöller-Wolff for transcribing those interviews conducted in languages other than German, and Frau Amelot for the German-language transcriptions.

As authors we came together through our common interest in developing an approach that is centred on theorising solidarity and identity in a way that can be summarized, drawing on Richard Hyman, as follows: 'We are shaped by our experiences, immediate milieu, and specific patterns of social relations'.

The empirical work for the study was conducted jointly by the authors. Michael Whittall wrote Chapter 6, on trade unions. The other chapters were written by Hermann Kotthoff.

Hermann Kotthoff

Michael Whittall

Saarbrücken and Munich, October 2013

CHAPTER I

Introduction

This study follows on from earlier work by one of the present authors that looked at the first decade of the development of European Works Councils (EWC) following the adoption of the European Works Council Directive in 1994 (Kotthoff, 2006a). This research noted a high degree of variability both in the forms of EWC activity and in EWCs' effectiveness as an instrument for employee interest representation. Five types of EWC were proposed.[1] Although a small minority of EWCs were found to have approached the standard of representation characteristic of German works councils, a much larger proportion proved to be either relatively inactive or were only symbolic in nature. A similar degree of variation has also been identified by other researchers (Lecher et al., 1999; Marginson et al., 2004; Weiler, 2006). Where there was a low level of effectiveness, this was not primarily a function of the modest scope provided by the EWC Directive and nor was it principally attributable to management resistance. Rather, the main factor was seen to lie in the fact that different national contingents had little sense of mutual dependence and only a limited notion of what value a transnational representative body might offer. There was often little cross-national communication between country contingents and only a meagre awareness of any obligation to provide mutual support. They were, and remained, largely alien to each other. Precisely the converse was the case in those few EWCs that had attained a substantive degree of effectiveness. As a consequence, one of the central conclusions of the

---

[1]   These were as follows. Type 1: 'Active participant: the EWC as a functioning forum'. Type 2: 'Advocate for the diaspora: German works council chair as intercessor'. Type 3: 'Information analyst: sparring with management'. Type 4: 'Stuck in neutral: the EWC as a toothless tiger'. Type 5: 'The marginalised EWC: a false start'.

study was that differences between EWCs could be explained in terms
of the cognitive preconditions, specifically in the field of social morality,
that prevailed within these forums, and in particular the degree of 'felt
interdependence' (Kotthoff, 2007) and progress in overcoming 'otherness'.

As yet, exploring these preconditions has not played a central role in
EWC research. This raises the very question that the present study aims to
answer. Namely, what preconditions need to be met to enable EWC members to develop a sense of mutual transnational interdependence, recognize
their common interests, cooperate with each other on the basis of solidarity
to pursue these interests, and identify with the EWC as an institution that
is acknowledged by all? How successfully can they manage the challenge
of balancing national and supra-national solidarity? Michael Whittall
(2007: 10) also posed this very same question at around the same time:
'Can they establish solidarity links with colleagues from other European
countries in a fashion similar to the one they are used to within local and
national settings?'

The central concern in this study is, therefore, to elaborate and develop
a research perspective that engages with the prerequisites for effective representation at the European company level in terms of the consciousness
of the actors. This distinguishes our approach from the focus of much
previous work that has been predominantly concerned with measuring
outputs, conceptualised in terms of the results of EWC activity. In our
view, we now need to look inwards, as it were, and consider the emotional,
social and cultural determinants and conditions of the possibility of any
such positive output.

Both the legal construction of the EWC Directive, as well as EWC
research, have operated on the assumption that the EWC, as an actor
willing and able to think and act in European terms, already exists as a
finished entity. In practice, however, EWCs do not spring into existence
fully formed. We therefore need to consider the process through which
they emerge. This raises a number of further, and fresh, questions. How is
the capacity to act constructed and organized? How much social integration is necessary for this? How do EWC members from different countries
understand and interpret common interests and objectives? How do they
respond to the national styles and *habitus* of workplace representatives from

other countries? What constitute legitimate forms of interaction with top management? How do they see themselves, and how do they see others? How do roles become differentiated during the process of group formation? How are internal dominance, authority and professionalism dealt with? Are there selective solidarities, in which internal coalitions emerge that run across the lines of national delegations? Who are the true driving forces and promoters of the process through which the EWC is formed?

On the issue of the question of the structural factors that operate at the level of the EWC as an actor, EWC research has focused on the characteristics of industrial relations systems, and in particular the 'home-country effect', under which the industrial relations regime at a company's national base exercises a profound influence both on its EWC's internal structure and relationships to management and trade unions. A branch effect has also been noted. In contrast, mainstream EWC research has tended to devote less attention to the organizational and managerial structures of individual companies, and in particular the degree of centralization or decentralization – factors that arguably would have a direct impact on the interdependence of local operations. The principal exceptions to this are Marginson et al. (2004) and Kotthoff (2006a). Both these studies suggest that the minority of EWCs found to exhibit a high level of representative effectiveness are mainly located in companies with highly internationalized organizational and managerial structures centralized at the European level. Such 'Eurocompanies' are characterized by a distinct and centralized European-level of management, integrated and interconnected production operations (such as a platform strategy in the car industry), a unified sales and distribution system, and a centralized approach to rationalization. All these factors exercise a major influence on the 'objective' interdependence of local operations, and with that on the employment conditions of their workforces.

In contrast to Marginson et al. and Kotthoff, who view organizational structure as one factor among several within the context of an overall industrial relations approach, Hauser-Ditz et al. (2010) adopted a strategy of isolating the structural element and, in a process of critical distancing from an industrial relations approach, grounded their study on the assumption of a direct correspondence ('organizational fit') between types of EWC and organizational types, derived from the typology of international enterprises originated by Bartlett and Ghoshal (1989). EWCs are also categorized using the Bartlett and Ghoshal framework ('multinational', 'focal', 'global', 'transnational') and EWC activity then represents a facsimile of the international organizational structure of the corresponding company (structural determinism), although this relationship could only be confirmed in some of the case studies researched by the group (Hauser-Ditz et al., 2010: 384). This suggests that objective interdependence is not the same as felt interdependence: rather, it must be subjectively interpreted and socially embedded, and also be rendered culturally 'connectable'.[2]

Taking as her starting point the macro-economic regulation theory of global value chains, Hürtgen (2011) also offers a similarly highly deterministic and structure-based account of EWCs, focused on the relative power distribution between country delegations and how the home-country delegations of a dominant country, based on economic strength, extend their claim to represent workforce interests from their own immediate constituency to other countries. In line with Gramsci's notion of 'cultural hegemony', economic dominance is held to generate hegemony on the part of its institutions and patterns of interpretation. These two factors then constitute a *regime* – that is, a relatively stable and persistent formation. As far as relationships between German and Central European EWC members are concerned, Hürtgen noted that the primacy of the German element in European value chains had been undermined by the fact that Central European operations had advanced into high-tech fields, but at low wage levels, weakening the foundations of the hegemony of the German members within EWCs, at least in relationship to those from Central Europe (Hürtgen, 2011).

An alternative path to an approach anchored in cultural sociology and phenomenological perspectives has recently been elaborated by Klemm et al. (2011a and 2011b), who focus on the preconditions, in terms of the sociology of knowledge, for interest-related communication, which they graphically

---

2   For an overview of current EWC research, see Müller and Hoffmann (2001); Kotthoff (2006a); Hertwig et al. (2009); Bleses (2009).

denote as 'cultural toolboxes'. In their study, these embrace mutual patterns of interpretation (images of the self and others) and expectations of solidaristic behaviour on the part of German and Eastern European EWC members in three German automotive companies against a background of transfers of production to Eastern Europe. In this context, issues of equality in internal EWC relationships and the nature of their behavioural style (*habitus*) towards management are seen to play a major part. The images of the other, as ascertained through empirical research, proved to be largely characterized by mistrust and wariness. Eastern European delegates saw German EWC members as arrogant and as engaged in a suspiciously close relationship to top management, from which they drew their power. In reality, behind their 'cheap calls for solidarity', the Germans were seen as covertly advancing their own interests. Conversely, German delegates saw Eastern European members as 'underdeveloped' in terms of representation and as having no interest in forging solidarity as a means of overcoming competition over allocations of production since they did not want to sacrifice their status as 'winners' in the relocation game.

Klemm et al. viewed each of these mutually disappointed expectations of solidarity as representing nationally homogeneous patterns of interpretation with their origins in significant historical experiences, and in particular different industrial relations systems and routines.

This approach, which engages with patterns of interpretation and categorization, is very close to our own concern to examine those prerequisites for EWC activity that are related to the consciousness of the participants. However, the 'images' and knowledge that the specific parties have of each other should also be related to the actual experiences that each has had over the course of their mutual relationships. And they also need to be located in the context of the structural conditions of specific companies.

In this study, we offer a more open and pragmatic variant of the interactionist-interpretive approach. We are also interested in the 'cultural' preconditions for solidarity as the 'a priori' of mutual understanding and communication within the EWC. However, we wish to locate these within the real history of these relationships and the process of group formation, as well as the framework conditions of the company. At the same time, we do not want to isolate any theorization of the constitution of EWCs from the flow of activity; rather, this represents an integral part of what happens at the level of both action and outputs. In turn, this complex formation of actors is embedded in two more overarching structural contexts: firstly, in the structure of management and organization of the company; and secondly in the history and culture of human resource and personnel policies and industrial relations in the company's home country as well as – inasmuch as we can establish this historically – between this and other European countries. We are not committed to a monocausal approach and do not, therefore, see any antithesis between an agency perspective and a structural perspective: rather, we situate actors in the context of their structurally pre-given circumstances, limits and opportunities.

The EWC literature cites a number of factors that inhibit EWCs from effective activity as representative bodies through processes of information, consultation and, possibly, negotiation. These are:

- differences between national systems and cultures of interest representation;
- dominance of home-country representatives within the forum, as a result of which the representatives of other countries are marginalized and demotivated;
- competing interests between countries and operations;
- disinclination on the part of central management to accept the EWC as a partner for dialogue;
- lack of resources;
- low level of support and participation on the part of trade unions.

The main internal factors hampering EWC activity are seen as:

- language barriers;
- low level of knowledge about the practice of interest representation in other countries;
- low frequency of meetings and low density of communication;
- overformalized agenda setting, which hinders internal discussion.

Only a small proportion of those EWCs so far studied – we estimate it at no more than a fifth – has developed to a stage where consultation, and on occasions negotiation, has taken place with management. In these instances, EWCs have been able to surmount, circumvent or neutralize these obstacles to a sufficient degree to enable such activities to occur. It is almost inconceivable that this would have been possible unless progress had been made in constructing solidaristic forms of behaviour. In order to examine and analyse the conditions under which such forms of behaviour can emerge and spread, our approach has been to step inside the laboratory constituted by this minority.

One frequently encountered paradigmatic *indicator* of solidarity, both for researchers and practitioners in the field of interest representation, is that of transfers of production – and, as a consequence, of jobs – to other European countries and operations. The central demand for solidarity in such instances is the achievement of consensus between EWC members on issues of allocations of production and resolving inter-site competition. The norm of solidarity is that either the status quo should be retained or that a 'pain-sharing' strategy should be adopted: the central prescription is that there should be no winners or losers. The dramatic increase in inter-plant competition as a result of globalization and associated changes in value chains has made the issue of relocation and the allocation of investment and production into the paramount challenge confronting EWCs. Identifying the capacity to achieve a consensual resolution of this problem as the hard and central indicator of solidarity is not only a reasonable decision in the light of these developments, but also one dictated by the logic of international interest representation. However, adhering to this norm at the current stage of EWC development, and for the foreseeable future, evidently constitutes a profound collective challenge for EWCs in that there is barely one example in which this has been achieved on a sustainable basis. As a consequence, if we retained this as *the* sole criterion then in all likelihood we would have to abandon our research before we even began.

The principal *nature and form* of solidarity identified by researchers and practitioners are those types of industrial action, such as strikes, demonstrations and other protest activities, aimed at a common objective or as support for fellow-workers at an operation under threat. This form for expressing solidarity is also one that is logically required, but is also no less a challenge than that of achieving solidarity on the issue of international allocations of production. To our knowledge, as yet there has been only one company in which coordinated European mass protect action has taken place, at GM Europe. This not only applies at the transnational (European) level, but also very frequently nationally. Overcoming competition over allocations of production and striking on behalf of colleagues at other sites at risk from company decisions are also rarities within national borders. There is a wide gulf between expectations and reality.

Our expectations of solidarity are not tied solely to the very demanding indicator of whether EWCs have been able to resolve conflicts prompted by the distribution of work but range more widely in that we are also interested in unearthing any traces of processes of solidarity that might represent precursors for future development. Overall, the core task of an EWC is to obtain information on the strategies and policies of European central management – from business strategy, rationalization plans, HR policies to health and safety – and analyse this in terms of its impact on the workforce, disseminate this to national-level employee representatives and individual operations, develop common positions, and counter any negative effects through active consultation with central management, in particular in the case of strategies aimed at playing different national workforces off against each other.

EWCs are also expected to act as an advocate with central management for the concerns of employee representatives from individual operations or countries who cannot obtain a hearing with their local managements. One of the specific tasks of an EWC is to serve as a partner for dialogue with and a counterpart to European central management within the company and represent the overall body of national representatives to it. In order to do this it must, as a forum, develop into an effective union of these representatives: that is, a body capable of collective action on matters of European company policy. This capacity is not present as a matter of course when an EWC is established as, up to that point, there will have been no pre-existing amalgamation of representatives able to pass on such a capacity as a dowry, as it were. On the contrary, local and national workforce representatives are usually unfamiliar with each other and have no common bonds.

Constituting the forms and images of a new collective actor on the transnational stage, without which it is impossible for the problems outlined above to be resolved, poses the central challenge. EWC members will only be able to embark on establishing such a union once they stop attending meetings with the sole aim of 'getting something' for their own operation and complement this objective with the more fundamental perspective of taking on responsibility for the whole. As yet, the assumption that EWCs already exist as transnational actors has meant that research has tended to overlook the process of how EWCs constitute themselves institutionally to be able to assume this role.

Searching for traces means directing attention towards early signs and potential prospects of impulses towards solidarity, but which have not yet fully matured. Detecting such potentials requires detailed investigation of specific circumstances, courses of action, histories and patterns of interpretation, set against the background of their contexts and framework conditions, and establishing connections between these. Our case studies consist, therefore, of detailed individual portraits of EWCs that *ex ante* share only one common characteristic: based on our prior knowledge, and the views of the experts we consulted, they number among that minority of EWCs that manifest a comparably high degree of development in terms of their capacity for action. As a consequence, we have not designated those traces of solidarity action that we found as 'types', which suggest something already structurally consolidated, but rather as 'patterns of development'.

One regulatory obstacle to constructing an institution located at EU-level is that that EWC members are not elected and legitimated transnationally by the European workforce as a whole but are delegated by national bodies. Legitimation can be achieved where there is national level representation of the entire national workforce, as with central works councils in Germany, which represents a recognized and significant representative institution. The German example indicates that it is possible to establish an effective overarching representation, in particular by establishing a division of labour (that is, internal professional specialization and experience of office-holders with multiple roles). One example can be seen in the multitude of 'hats' worn – and balanced – by local works council chairs, who are also chairs of general works councils, supervisory board members, and EWC chairs.

Turning to the issue of the capacity of the EWC as an effective union of representatives, the question arises as to where the directing organ is located within the anatomy of the whole. The forum overall, usually made up of unfamiliar individuals lacking a common language, experiences and general lifeworld, and meeting once a year or at most twice, is a fleeting phenomenon, and it would be unreasonable to expect too much from it in terms of focus, capacity and initiative. The converse was the case with the steering or select committees that we encountered in our case studies, the members of which meet regularly and communicate intensively. The EWC's capacity to act, and hence its potential for solidarity, is therefore located to a greater degree in the steering committee than in the forum as a whole. This is not to say that the forum as a whole is any the less important as it is the body that legitimates initiatives taken by the steering committee through voting and exercising oversight, and acting, in particular, as the mediator between different levels. The fact that the steering committee is the factually active body means that it plays a prominent role in our case studies. Although such an internal hierarchy is not formally provided for by the EWC Directive, in practice it is both very characteristic and of great significance. As such there is an institutional tension between the text and the reality of the constitution of EWCs.

Solidarity is a complex and many-faceted concept with a wide range of meanings, and one that requires further specification to acquire sufficient rigour for use in social research. The notion of 'international solidarity', in particular, is often drawn on rather superficially, sometimes even glibly, within trade union discourse. As a consequence, our own study presupposes a more precise definition of what we mean by 'solidarity'.

In the broadest terms, we see solidarity as pro-social, altruistic and cooperative behaviour: both helping strangers in distress as well as mutual support and obligation within a social association; humanitarianism; mutual commitment; placing one's own interests behind those of a collective (common good); a feeling for community and action related to community. Two criteria are of particular relevance in order to establish a further conceptual distinction: first, the motivation for such behaviour;

and second, the context of the relationship between the giver and receiver of support. The following conceptual distinctions draw heavily on the work of Bayertz (1999) and Mau (2009).

(1) *Solidarity out of enlightened self-interest*

This represents a rational utilitarian form of solidarity guided by the principle that individuals are dependent on each other and have complementary interests ('all in the same boat') and that cooperative and mutually supportive action will ultimately also therefore serve self-interest. It rests on the notion that immediate and short-term interests should be set aside (or given lower priority) to satisfy more significant (long-term) interests. The concern is to produce a collective good that no individual is capable of creating in isolation but which all will benefit from. There is no postulate of any pre-existing trait of sociability: rather, the argument asserts that individuals will engage in selfish instrumental (egoistic) activity, but that this runs into a dilemma where it depends on others to meet individuals' own interests. This is a calculative form of solidarity, as found in the relationships between business partners.

This is the explanation for solidarity that can be found in rational choice theory and individual theories of morality (such as contractualism or Kantianism). Solidaristic behaviour is not a fundamental theoretical category. On the contrary, it is simply an outcome, and frequently only found in a weak form, of the dead-end into which individualistic calculative behaviour leads. From this standpoint, system integration can function without social integration. This is the sober and disenchanted functionalist notion of solidarity. Its strength is that it appears to correspond to the reality of pluralistic and individualistic societies in which 'strong' communities are eroded.

When applied to the process of European unity, it would imply that greater economic integration raises the interdependence of interests, promoting the emergence of self-interested solidarity. The expectation is that economic integration will drag political integration along in its wake. The relationship between actors is determined by reciprocity ('do ut des'). It is the solidarity of risk insurance: I pay into a joint fund in order to be able to draw out of it in the event of a possible loss.

The difficulty for this approach is that individuals can enjoy the benefits of a collective good without having contributed ('free riding', opportunism). Redistribution – that is, a 'forfeited' contribution that benefits those in need based on overarching norms of justice – cannot reasonably be anchored on this form of solidarity.

Applied to the case of EWCs, the question is then: are delegates from a specific country genuinely convinced that they are in the same boat as other countries and that they will only be able to advance their local (plant or operational) interests with the help of delegates from another countries? Do they perceive and feel themselves actually to be dependent on the other countries, in the sense of 'felt interdependence' (Kotthoff, 2007)? Or do they have no expectations of a 'value added' from the EWC and simply attend as a formality and a matter of routine?

(2) *Community solidarity*

This is the basic category of solidarity in sociological theory. It is the form of solidarity that arises from feelings of belonging and attachment (cohesion, 'we-feeling', identity), similarity and familiarity (social proximity) in an established community of a manageable scale. For the 'founding fathers' of sociology, in particular Tönnies and Durkheim, a 'community' bound by common values and a common destiny is the cement that holds society together. Mutual support is a moral obligation, a norm, lack of compliance with which is punishable. In traditionally segmented societies it rests on ethical and religious homogeneity ('mechanical solidarity'); in modern functionally-differentiated societies with a division of labour, it is based on mutual reliance (interdependence; 'organic solidarity' in Durkheim), and the complementary interests and increased density of communication and interaction on which these rest. The centrepiece of this theorization is the metamorphosis of interests into emotions. In the case of organic solidarity, Durkheim draws on the idea of cooperation resting on the self-interest of the first type of solidarity, based on agreed contracts, but then endows it with moral force and theorizes it in terms of social integration in that he argues that contractually-based mutual interests (self-interested solidarity) are precarious unless supported by a moral duty to abide by contracts: that is, are based on social or group solidarity. Conversely, this solidarity always has some admixture of desired (self-interested) consequences.

One notable feature of group solidarity is its particularity: that is, the distinction between insiders and outsiders, those 'who belong' and those who do not. As such, it constitutes a form of social selectivity based on feelings of belonging, since a feeling of association with a community is the most important source of personal identity, as Bayertz (1999) has argued against analysts of a world society based either on a universalist system theory approach (see Stichweh, 2000) or a communication theory approach (see Habermas, 2004).

In small-scale lifeworlds, contexts such as the family or clan represent the prime stage for group solidarity; in modern large-scale societies it is primarily the nation. From a political standpoint, a larger community can be conceptualized as an association based on domination (*Herrschaftsverband*), in particular the state. Commonality in this context is principally the result of common submission to the same ruling force (government, the law) together with significant common historical experiences.

This category of solidarity, which occupies the boundary between in and out, seems unsuited, at least at first sight, for helping to develop an understanding of transnational relationships, where the key issue is to transcend borders and where the central problem is how strangers can become friends. How can an EWC, composed of national delegates, come to form the sort of close association that goes beyond a simple business partnership? Solidarity that is intended to remain stable – and this is core proposition – needs social networks and a feeling of belonging. The strongest form of emotional community at the level of large-scale political and organizational structures remains that of nationality. What, therefore, might lead delegates to build networks that cross national borders and establish a new set of affinities at transnational level? What might appear initially as an illusory or romantic category of solidarity will, nonetheless, occupy a key place in our research – meriting, at the least, a 'second look'.

(3) 'Solidarity-in-struggle'

This refers in this context to solidarity between workers or class solidarity, and, as such, is the prime referent for the concept of solidarity in the trade union sphere. Workers' solidarity arises out of experiences of injustice and oppression and consists in joining together to build an organized and disciplined countervailing power to overcome this condition. It can be applied to any group ('movement') that seeks to achieve certain objectives and interests through collective organization in the face of resistance from dominant groups or individuals. In contrast to the view advanced by Marx and Engels, it does not emerge of necessity out of objective class interests but presupposes a subjective class consciousness ('class for itself' vs 'class in itself'). As Bayertz (1999) has emphasized, it is constituted *morally* on the basis of community solidarity (type 2). Solidaristic behaviour within their own group is a moral duty for members of a 'movement', as such behaviour 'cannot be reduced to prudence. Wherever there is good reason to expect it [that is, solidarity], its absence is not only regretted but also morally disapproved of: non-solidary behaviour [such as strikebreaking: *author's note*] is considered not only imprudent but shabby and reprehensible' (ibid: 18). Solidarity has a 'genuine' – and ineliminable – 'moral dimension' (ibid).

As a consequence, workers' solidarity has arisen primarily in circumstances where there is pre-existing group solidarity within a moral community, as in the early period of industrialization amongst the miners of the Ruhr Valley, who Moore characterized as being 'embedded in the system of corporate paternalism' (Moore, 1978: 233) with their recognized status in the German social order' (ibid: 234), and which he contrasted with the first generation of steelworkers from the same region, who migrated individually from rural areas, or it has arisen where solidaristic relationships were created in an organized form by workers, as in workers' housing settlements (*Wohnkolonien*), workers' associations for sport and education, and consumer cooperatives.

The main obstacle to forging solidarity in these contexts is also that of free-riding. Mancur Olson (1965: 57f.) saw this as an insuperable problem in large groups and organizations due to the difficulties in enforcing effective control and discipline. In contrast, Albert Hirschman (1982) argued that participation in a struggle for a just cause was sufficient to satisfy the need for community, generating trust and social solidarity and mitigating the problem of free-riding. For Hirschman (1982: 85) 'public-oriented action belongs, in this as in other respects, to a group of human activities that includes the search for community, beauty, knowledge, and salvation'. On this interpretation, the feeling of community, of jointly pursuing a just cause, satisfies the human need for community. Being able to participate in the pursuit of an objective is in itself part of the reward for the effort expended. This is an understanding of solidarity-in-struggle based not on instrumentalism but rather anchored in recognition theory.

This emphasis on the quality of participation and the nature of the experience represents an original contribution by Hirschman that links solidarity-in-struggle with group solidarity. It will play a major part in our own approach to analysing EWCs as it was coined specifically to deal with the context of a demanding set of tasks in which the exercise of the capacity for mutual dependence released socially integrative forces. It articulates the dimension of enthusiasm and sacrifice directed at attaining a significant and important objective that, just as with 'beauty' and 'redemption' (Hirschman), rarely merits attention in the sociological literature. However, for historians of the labour movement the enthusing effect of common action is a very familiar phenomenon.

The most concise definition of this type of solidarity can be found in Bayertz (1999: 23): 'Solidarity is the willingness of an individual or group to help another individual or a group to secure their rights'. This contains the core observation that this does not simply entail purely economic interests ('bread and butter issues') but is primarily an objective with moral legitimacy, a 'struggle for recognition' (Honneth).

Astonishingly, the sociological literature on solidarity has given little emphasis to the operational performative conditions for solidarity-in-struggle. One exception is Claus Offe (2007), who characterizes the cooperation called for in trade unions, parties and associations as 'constitutive or organization-building solidarity' and 'solidaristic disciplining' and unity as their central operational requirements. Internal discipline is subordination 'for the sake of collective goals and goods ... for the sake of some "common cause"' (Offe, 2007: 117). This aspect of the specific organizational performance involved in constituting an organization and the establishment of its capacity both to act and to prevail through the possession of internal discipline, together with self-subordination and solidarity within a group of actors (group-constituting behaviour), will play a major part in our analysis of EWCs. One particular focus of our research is on actors, and in particular the main actors within EWCs.

The extraordinarily high degree of solidarity generated by such commitment to solidarity-in-struggle within the labour movement is well attested to within labour history. However, as yet, this has only been the case in a very restricted sense in an international context. And because 'international workers' solidarity' is often paid no more than lip service, many observers remain sceptical about the scope for solidaristic behaviour within EWCs ('Euro-pessimists'). Is this because there are no complementary interests? Are there such interests, but they have not been recognized? Or does the explanation lie in the fact that mutual unfamiliarity and the lack of any sense of group cohesion and collective identity mean that engaging in a struggle for a common aim has never begun?

(4) *Civic solidarity*
This is the type of solidarity that accords with the republican model of the role of the citizen. Based on their membership of a polity, citizens are granted a legal status by the state that entitles them to solidaristic support from the generality, but which also entails a duty of solidarity towards this collective. This support is not provided on the basis of affective affiliation or social proximity but because of the notional status of the individual as an acknowledged full member of a legal community (that is, a citizen).

This historical status has been extended over the course of history to that of 'social citizenship' (the welfare state), 'industrial citizenship' (trade union rights) (Marshall, 1950), and, in countries with statutory institutions at company and workplace level, 'workplace citizenship' (see Müller-Jentsch, 2008; Kotthoff, 1994).

In this instance, asserting interests is not viewed as a struggle by pressure groups, as with solidarity-in-struggle, and nor is the acknowledgement of employees' interests left to the voluntary discretion of management. Rather, solidarity is a legal entitlement anchored in the recognition of the individual and the principle of equality before the law.

Citizenship is a legal construction that remains abstract unless it is demanded, appropriated and invested with life by workplace citizens. A number of authors have noted that the actual assertion of these rights, and the assumption of the corresponding duties, is more likely where this is closely bound to group or community solidarity (Mau, 2009; Münch, 2008, Bayertz, 1999).

The EWC Directive – albeit in rudimentary form – represents an extension of the concept of workplace citizen to the European level.

(5) *'Humanitarian' or 'charitable' solidarity*
This is a form of solidarity that rests on charity, concern and compassion. It is a humanitarian stance, sometimes referred to in the literature as 'fraternal' (Rawls), that is directed towards others, including strangers, in specific situations of distress as there is, as a rule, no real social connection, no attachment, between those who give and those who receive. Rather, contact between them is spontaneous and specific. The relationship is asymmetric and unreciprocated. There is no expectation that the recipient will return the generosity on another occasion. The fact that this form of solidarity does not presuppose any attachment, but flows from common humanity, means that it is not particularist but tends to be universalist in conception. This feeling of solidarity is present in contexts other than that dealt with here, and we do not draw on it in this study to guide our research.

The literature on solidarity is characterized by two competing notions. For utilitarians, the starting point is the premise that solidarity based on enlightened self-interest is both the only appropriate and the most theoretically succinct explanation of solidaristic conduct in functionally differentiated modern large-scale societies. Conversely, the moralists, following Durkheim, argue that social attachment, and the norms and sense of obligation that rest on this, are the basis for solidaristic conduct, not only in traditional but also in modern societies, with an admixture of desired consequences (solidarity based on self interest). Even in social contexts in which self-interest becomes predominant, as in business relationships, cooperation – that is the long-term flourishing of the relationship – is only possible if it is embedded in a value-based perspective (such as the 'honest merchant'). In contrast, for utilitarians, attachments and norms of solidarity, inasmuch as these can be registered at all empirically, represent an emotional vestige and moral accessory that are not needed to actualize conduct.

In this study, we consider the question: what type of solidarity is required for the effective operation of an EWC that wishes to meet its statutory mission?

Given the high degree of unfamiliarity and difference between delegates from different countries that represents the starting point of internal relationships within EWCs as a supranational representative institution, there is a good case to be made that cooperation will principally take place on the utilitarian basis of solidarity rooted in enlightened self-interest. In view of the disappointing experiences encountered by 'proletarian internationalism', with its high ambitions but also its formulaic quality, this would seem to be a realistic expectation. It implies that the main determinant will be growing awareness of an interest dilemma: namely, that local or national interests can be met only in cooperation with delegates from other European countries – via the roundabout path of the EWC as a public good. This is a cognitive process – recognition of a common interest – that motivates A to support B, so that B will subsequently do the same for A.

In our view, this is indeed a precondition for an EWC. Our hypothesis is that this process of recognition is not an isolated and single initial step by forum members but rather that it presupposes, as a type of 'a priori', a simultaneous social relationship, personal mutual acquaintance, intensive communication, and the growth of trust – in short, the social integration of the members – in order for 'enlightened self-interest' to be recognized. Our premise is that enlightened self-interest and group solidarity are not mutually exclusive, and in the case of EWCs emerge in parallel and are closely interconnected.

The central challenge for EWCs is that socially integrating transnationally composed groups is not a given, but is a process that must be formed and created. This process of group formation, and the role of solidarity in this, constitutes the core of this study. Given the unfamiliarity and difference of delegates from different countries, and the sobering conclusions of previous research on the extent of 'strong' EWCs, it would be advisable not to entertain overly optimistic expectations of solidarity and, as a consequence, to widen the net to look at weaker expressions as phenomena with a potential for future development.

Trade union solidarity-in-struggle and civic solidarity would appear to be the forms that fit most appropriately to the EWC context and we therefore make extensive use of these as analytical tools. In contrast to social and self-interest based solidarity, which are the focus of a theoretical debate between individual and collective approaches, our concern here is the specifically social field. Both these forms presuppose a solidarity of the first type (enlightened self-interest), as the recognition of such an interest is the precondition for solidarity-in-struggle as well as the realization that actively exercising workplace citizenship at European level is also in the enlightened self-interest of local employee representatives. One of the guiding hypotheses of this study is that any of these three forms of solidarity (self-interest, struggle and civil) depends on the emergence of group solidarity within the forum of the EWC, which, as a consequence, constitutes the fundamental and original basis for all other types of solidarity. If this is the case, as we believe, then we need to develop a particular sensitivity to the growth of such group solidarity and loyalty in conducting research.

In summary, our research aim can be characterized as follows. The object is to understand the emergence of the institution of the EWC into a forum that enables employees' industrial citizenship to be asserted at the level at which European management is located and in a manner able to exercise influence through having developed the capacity for information, consultation, and possibly negotiation. This process includes developing an awareness of mutual interdependence (long-term interests take priority over short-term interest) and a willingness to contribute to the development of the forum – in particular in the form of time for active cooperation, open and honest communication, and group discipline. Both of these – growing consciousness and building the forum – are more likely to flourish on a foundation of social attachment and personal loyalty that can emerge as a result of ongoing communication and time spent together: that is, through an element of a shared lifeworld.

Our research focuses on the scope for activity, and on the dynamics and bearers, of transnational employee representation, with a particular concern for elements and processes of solidarity, understood as their driving force. This approach implies that solidarity cannot simply be read off from an action, as if it were emblazoned on its forehead, but must be teased out of it, decoded, inductively.

CHAPTER 2

Summary of main results

We identified four patterns of solidarity in EWCs. These were:

1. The EWC as a working group in dialogue with management – solidarity as an extension of workplace citizenship.

CASE STUDIES: UNILEVER AND KRAFT FOODS

In this pattern of development, the EWC steering committee constitutes a well-integrated working group whose members share a common transnational perspective. Its work consists in engagement in producing a public (collective) good (solidarity as enlightened self-interest). The public good consists in the exercise of the citizen role within the enterprise (solidarity as civic solidarity): that is, participation in the political process through dialogue and consultation, and, in some cases, via negotiation with management. Management will have a co-constitutive role in developing this type of solidarity. However, the process can only begin once group solidarity has been established – that is, mutual social obligation, attachment and a 'we-feeling', especially within the steering committee. Trust within a core group is the foundation for all the other forms of solidarity.

One structural prerequisite for the emergence of this pattern is that the undertaking has the organizational and operational form of a Eurocompany: that is, there is a high degree of real interdependence that is transmitted and mediated through the formal organization. The output of this pattern is structured dialogue at a high level together with an acknowledgement of employees' status as workplace citizens. 'The EWC is in a position such that it is granted attention' (Interviewee).

2. Integration of the EWC into strong codetermination arrangements at
    the German headquarters – 'subsidiary solidarity'.

CASE STUDY: FORD OF EUROPE

In this case, the EWC's European members have secured a foothold in the
German system of codetermination. The EWC and steering committee are
not as evident in terms of independent activity as is the case at Unilever and
Kraft Foods, but are nonetheless highly effective – as witnessed by the conclusion of a number of substantive European Framework Agreements. The
steering committee meets relatively infrequently and its internal cohesion
is, as a consequence, fairly modest. It does not represent a standing working
group and confines itself to dealing with a small number of emergency situations, to which it must then respond immediately with the strongest form
of activity available – negotiating agreements. For the most part, employee
representatives at local operations act independently. If they need support, the head of the German central works council, who is also the EWC
chair, will engage with central management in Germany on their behalf.
Everyday contact is maintained via an organizational 'relay station', the
EWC secretary, who is a professional European specialist ('Mister Europe')
located within the central works council and who maintains intensive and
close relations, based on a high level of trust, with senior employee representatives at non-German operations. This is a highly efficient model of
representation, in which a good deal is achieved with limited inputs. The
forms of solidarity that it generates are civic solidarity and solidarity based
on enlightened self-interest.

3. Penetration of a Southern European model of representation into the
    EWC of a German company – 'protest solidarity' versus 'participative
    solidarity'.

CASE STUDY: BURGER-MILLER

In this instance, the protagonists generate a high level of activity, typified
by solidarity based on self-interest. However, it is activity that is directed

externally. Given that management pays little attention to the EWC, rather than attempting to establish dialogue with management (consultation), the EWC's efforts are increasingly aimed at building a grass-roots oriented countervailing power to management. The core concept of solidarity is 'networking', not (only) between EWC members but also directly between local employee representatives. This can culminate in protest actions that are not simply intended as occasional accompaniments to dialogue with management but can also take on a different tenor. This is the path of voluntaristic and pluralistic trade union 'actionism' and is expressed in such phrases as 'That's the way we do it in France' (French EWC delegate) and 'To show the colleagues in local operations – we're with you in the struggle'.

Solidarity, in the sense of internal social ties, is also a prerequisite in this case, but is precarious as there are repeated disputes over the course to adopt. This pattern of European employee representation can be contrasted with the mature culture of codetermination at the company's German headquarters.

One reason that a form of solidarity inspired by the French culture of representation has gained traction in a traditional German company is that those employee representatives who are embedded in the established codetermination arrangements that prevail at the group's German headquarters remain sceptical about the rapid internationalization of the group, and the associated incursion of new employment relationships into formerly stable patterns. This aversion on the part of German representatives is compounded by central management's refusal to transpose the spirit and culture of German codetermination into the group's foreign operations. In contrast to Ford, European EWC members have secured only a very slender foothold within the German system of codetermination.

4. The EWC as an information analyst – solidarity as a gesture of sympathy.

CASE STUDY: SANOFI

In this case, the forum is well resourced with a high level of activity, but in contrast to pattern (3) is less concerned with specific issues related to employee interests and is also less effective. Top management avoids dialogue with the EWC, which, for its part, does not pursue it. Its activities are focused, on the one hand, on rituals of information analysis, aimed at forcing disclosures out of an incommunicative management by confronting it with the results of tenaciously-conducted research; and on the other, on French trade union organizational and political concerns through processes intended to smooth over and accommodate French inter-union competition. The EWC has developed only a limited degree of 'constitutive solidarity'. Instead of developing solidaristic activities, it transmits *gestures* of solidarity to representatives and workforces at endangered operations. In contrast to what might be expected at this markedly French company, and unlike Burger-Miller, the EWC's repertoire does not include protests or other militant activities. Based on the allocation of seats, the forum is polarized between French delegates and a German contingent (formerly Hoechst AG), in which the French dominate and determine procedures.

CHAPTER 3

Methodology and structure of the report

3.1 Methodology

The aim of the study is to investigate the conditions for the possibility of EWC effectiveness, based on the premise that solidaristic behaviour, through which the group becomes socially constituted, represents a crucial precondition for such a development. As a consequence, and in order to undertake comparative research, we initially decided to choose four 'best case' EWCs from a larger number of those that had demonstrated a capacity to undertake a range of activities, and hence representative effectiveness, and proceeded to carry out intensive case studies on these. Our aim was to identify companies in which the EWC had attained a developed practice of information and consultation, possibly extending to negotiation. We also wanted to select companies from four different industrial sectors (metals, chemicals, food, and services), with their corporate centres in four different countries. In order to identify 'best candidates' for inclusion, we undertook an extensive prior search process in which we drew on the advice of other EWC researchers and trade union officials active in the EWC field. Our own previous fieldwork, involving case studies of two EWCs, was also included when assembling the list of EWCs that met the criteria. The initial long list contained eight EWCs, and these were then subject to further exploratory interviews. This process yielded a final total of five candidates, and we decided to retain all five, rather than the four initially envisaged. They are:

- Unilever (food: Netherlands/UK)
- Kraft Foods (food: USA)

- Ford (automotive: USA)
- Burger-Miller (anonymous: Germany)
- Sanofi (pharmaceuticals: France).

With hindsight, it became clear that the views of our advisers were not entirely apposite in one of these cases, where there were few signs of solidaristic processes. This also revealed that it is not easy for an external observer, however well informed, to obtain an accurate impression of the internal workings of an EWC.

We conducted initial interviews in each company with nearly all members (between five and seven) of the EWC's steering committee, with two 'ordinary' EWC members (that is, not on the steering committee), with one or two local employee representatives who were not members of the EWC, and one to two full-time trade union officials. Overall, between ten and thirteen interviews were conducted for each case. As a rule, interviews took around two hours. Interviewees originated from ten different countries, with the bulk (some three-quarters) from Germany, the UK and France.

Interviews were conducted by the authors. All the German and most of the British and French interviews were conducted locally at interviewees' workplaces. Other interviews were conducted at the locations in various countries where EWC or steering committee meetings were held. Interviews conducted in French were conducted by a research colleague with French as their mother tongue in the presence of one of the researchers. Interviews in other languages, carried out on the margins of EWC meetings, were conducted using the services of one of the professional interpreters at the meeting. Overall, these arrangements proved to be successful and enabled us to conduct a large number of fruitful and informative interviews.

In addition to the interviews, we also observed two meetings of the steering committee in each of the five case-study companies, and in two of the companies we observed a training session for the whole EWC that extended over several days. These participant observations and informal discussions held in the context of these meetings also allowed us to gain deeper insights into processes of group dynamics.

Our original intention was to interview a number of employees from different countries in each company. In practice, this proved possible to only a limited extent, as the steering committee members were only able to secure interviews with a small number of employees on the subject of the EWC. The level of interest was low. Those interviews that did take place also confirmed this impression: lack of familiarity with the issue and meagre interest. We replaced the smaller number of employee interviews, with additional interviews with 'normal' EWC members.

Given that our aim was to focus on internal EWC processes, we did not envisage conducting interviews with managers – although this was certainly a disadvantage in terms of obtaining an overall picture of how the institution functions. As a consequence, our understanding of the shift in how central managements perceived the EWC, evident in all five case-study companies, had to be based on inferences drawn from statements made by EWC members. Empirical work for this study was carried out during 2009–2010.

3.2 Structure of the report

This study focuses on the activities of EWCs, and in particular steering committees, in terms of their internal relationships, their relationship to management, and their relationship with national workplace employee representatives. The main outcome was our identification of four distinct patterns of dynamics in terms of how EWCs demonstrated solidarity. These will be described and analysed in each of the detailed case study reports that make up Chapter 4. Two case studies have been combined for the first pattern, as they exhibit close similarities: Unilever and Kraft Foods. The second pattern is represented by Ford; the third Burger-Miller (as already noted, anonymized at the request of the EWC chair); and the fourth Sanofi.

The presentation of each of these patterns follows the same structure, using the sections indicated below:

1. Organizational and operational structure of the company, principally from the perspective of the real interdependencies between countries and the history of industrial relations in the company. Both these factors – the nature and degree of structural interdependence and the history of industrial relations – influence the pattern and extent of solidarity.
2. Structure and development of the EWC, with a focus on EWC resources and organizational potential.
3. Activities and representative effectiveness of the EWC. This involves an overview of the effectiveness of the EWC, its previous achievements, its 'outputs', which issues it had engaged with and with what outcome, and what type of solidarity might be identified.
4. Relationship between EWC and management – also in terms of aspects relevant to solidarity.
5. Steering committee – the protagonists in action. The focus here is on internal social attachments and connections, integration, emergence of a common perspective, the definition of a common set of tasks, the group's social network (sociogram), links between the committee and other EWC members and local employee representatives. This constitutes the main part of the case-study analysis as it allows observation of solidarity phenomena at close quarters.
6. Relationship between the EWC and national/local representative bodies.
7. The role of trade unions in the EWC process.

Chapter 5 compares these patterns of solidarity and offers an overall interpretation.

Chapter 6 combines results from the case studies in an analysis of the contribution of trade unions and considers these in the light of the literature on the role and strategy of trade unions in the process of Europeanizing employee interest representation.

Chapter 7 draws together and summarizes the various themes considered in the research.

CHAPTER 4

Transnational patterns of EWC solidarity: Case studies

4.1 The EWC as a working team in dialogue with management. Solidarity as workplace citizenship

UNILEVER AND KRAFT FOODS

The two cases of Unilever and Kraft Foods closely resemble each other and are therefore grouped within the same pattern of solidarity. The main part of this section consists of a detailed analysis of Unilever, followed by a shorter, complementary, outline of developments at Kraft Foods. The remaining patterns of solidarity are illustrated with one case study in each instance.

4.1.1 Operational and organizational structure

UNILEVER

At the time our research was conducted, Unilever, sometimes referred to as an Anglo-Dutch company, had four business divisions: food (including margarines, soups and sauces, and beverages); food solutions (individual production and supply to large-scale kitchens); ice cream; and home and personal care (including personal care and domestic cleaning agents). The company is a market leader in most of these fields or, as with margarine, ice cream, beverages and personal care, is in second place.

Unilever was created in 1929 through the amalgamation of the British soap manufacturer Lever Brothers and the Dutch margarine producer

Unie. The two companies shared a common basis in the main raw material for their products, edible oils. The company grew rapidly in Britain and Continental Europe through a large series of acquisitions of small and medium-sized food and detergent manufacturers that largely maintained their local autonomy. From the 1950s, the company set about establishing a high degree of vertical integration by acquiring a substantial speciality chemical division, an agricultural division (large fishing fleeting, fish processing, fish restaurants, extensive tea plantations), and its own logistics division. By 1970, Unilever employed 350,000 people worldwide, including 40,000 tea workers in India and Pakistan, and was the largest company in Europe and the fifth largest in the world (at that time, Siemens, the largest German company, was 50th in the global ranking).

Until recently, Unilever did not represent a brand in itself. Rather, the company operated as a conglomerate carrying some 2,000 individual brands, most of which were sold in only one country. This formed the basis for the unusually strong belief within the company in the advantages of a highly decentralized organizational structure. Amongst multinational companies, Unilever arguably was the most devolved in terms of the autonomy granted to local operations and national centres: that is, there was recognition that in the fast-moving consumer goods sector detailed local knowledge was crucial, and that all other business decisions should be subordinated to this principle.

One further structural determinant was the company's bi-nationality, with head offices in London and Rotterdam, and with UK and US businesses reporting to London and Mainland European businesses to Rotterdam. Bi-nationality of the firm's assets also led to a complex organizational structure in which each national part enjoyed equal status. The company was headed not by a CEO but by a three person 'Special Committee', with a British chair, a Dutch chair, and a British (non-voting) vice-chair. This structure led to the highly consensual internal culture that characterized the entire history of the firm and which was observable in the delicate balance maintained between London and Rotterdam. In practice, Unilever was a company without a central directing agent and was held together instead by a strong interpersonal culture within top management that Jones (2005: 27) described as a 'gentlemen's club', an observation anticipated as early as 1960 by *Der Spiegel*, which dubbed the firm 'a highly exclusive men's club'. Great attention was devoted to selecting the top 200 managers, fostering their identification with the firm, and cultivating a corresponding *esprit de corps*. 'Unilever tended to rely on personal relationships and informal contacts rather than formal structures and systems' (Jones, 2005: 38). Senior management was either British or Dutch, with most British managers having an Oxbridge background. A conscious effort was made to distinguish the company's approach from that typical of US management philosophy, with its emphasis on managerial techniques, controls and systems. Unilever did not aim to imitate its principal competitor, Procter & Gamble, which was the corporate embodiment of these principles. Its extraordinary corporate governance arrangements were denoted as 'paternalistic democracy' or a 'decentralized federation', each seen as constituting the secret of its success. In the business literature, the company was fêted as a major global success story and viewed as an exemplar of a firm whose achievements rested on profound knowledge and experience in establishing marketing structures abroad and as a pioneer in the professional development of what was one of the earliest instances of an entirely university-trained executive cadre (Jones, 2005: 15).

In the late-1970s, Unilever – along with its competitors – ran into a serious growth and profits crisis. In contrast to these, however, Unilever did not make a full recovery and has continued to lag behind its rivals. The prime explanation for this has been seen as a function of its previous strengths, namely decentralization and fragmentation. During the 1980s, top management responded with cost reduction programmes and an attempt to focus the business around two core areas – food together with home and personal care – although this was only half-heartedly implemented. The Unilever culture meant that closing underperforming plants and dismissing managers were virtually inconceivable. Finally, from the mid-1990s, a process of centralizing decision-making was inaugurated, but this also failed to overcome weaknesses in performance, leaving the company permanently exposed to criticism both from the business press and investors. After 2000, the company embarked on a wave of strategic restructuring, dubbed 'Path to Growth', which aimed at radically pruning the 1,600 brands carried down to some 400. In 2005, a new top management initiated a further programme of centralization, 'One Unilever', which, according to the German business journal *manager magazin*, represented the largest reorganization in the company's history. A single 'autocrat' was installed in the form of a CEO, and the number of top managers reduced by a third, with local national subsidiaries and operations stripped of their autonomy. Product categories were organized into business units, and some of the larger subsidiaries, such as Bestfoods, Langnese and Lever-Fabergé, consolidated into a single company. A new regional structure was created. For example, in Europe the German-speaking countries (Germany, Austria, Switzerland), were brought together under a regional section termed 'DACH' (the initials of the countries in German, also the German for 'roof'). A further administrative restructuring programme, 'Shared Services', also initiated in 2005, aimed to concentrate and transfer more routine administrative operations in finance and HR to Eastern Europe and India. The most significant step towards centralization took place between 2007 and 2009, under which all plants in the major regions (Western Europe, America, and Asia-Africa) were placed under the control of single regional centres. In Western Europe, the 'Unilever Supply Chain Company' (USCC), located in Schaffhausen, near Zurich (Switzerland), is responsible for the detailed control and oversight of production operations, logistics and performance improvements. In organizational and legal terms, all 75 European manufacturing locations constitute a single plant – an abandonment of Unilever's long-standing and characteristic tradition of decentralization in favour of a very pronounced form of centralization. One article published in January 2007 in *manager magazin* bore the headline 'The Central Authority'.

In Europe, the company's restructuring and strategic overhaul over the past two decades went hand-in-hand with the closure and sale of a large number of plants and a dramatic cut in workforce numbers. As the following overview of key events illustrates, 'normality' for Unilever's employees and their representatives was characterized by a series of such announcements. For example:

- All chemical plants sold to ICI.
- Disposal of the entire agri-business division, except for tea. Sale of the coffee business.

- Sale of the animal feeds division BOCM (25 per cent of the British market).
- Disposal of all fish processing in Europe (15,000 jobs). Disposal of the chain of 'Nordsee' fish restaurants (mainly located in Germany and Austria).
- Sale of the soup and stock brands Unox, Oxo, Royco and Batchelors.
- Sale of the pharmaceutical brand 'Unipath', cleaning and hygiene products 'Diversey Lever', and the personal care brands Elizabeth Arden, Calvin Klein and Atkinsons.
- Disposal of Croklan Oil (palm oil), the baking division, '4P' packaging.
- Closure of two margarine plants in Germany (Kleve, 400 employees; Mannheim, 300 employees).
- Sale of Germany's largest cheese factory at Kempten (with 600 employees), producing Edelweiß, Bresso and Milkana brands.
- Disposal of the oils and fats brands Livio, Bechts, Biskin and Palmin; the semolina brand, Pomps; and the Dextro Energy dextrose plant in Kleve.
- In 2006, sale of the entire deep-frozen products business Iglo to the private equity company Permira (4,000 employees in Europe, of which 2,000 in Germany), including a large deep-frozen vegetable plant in Münsterland and the 'Frozen Fish' plant in Bremen. In 2007, closure of FRIGO in Barcelona.
- Closure of the olive oil business in Italy; six food processing plants in the Netherlands; the Prague margarine factory (700 employees); and Unilever Denmark.

The strategy underlying this transformation was to concentrate the portfolio on profitable margarine brands (especially cholesterol-lowering lines such as Becel, Flora and Lätta); ice cream brands (primarily Magnum); and bodycare products (Dove and Axa). The company used the receipts from disposals for acquisitions, notably, in the mid-1990s, of Bestfoods (at $13.4 billion, financed by the sale of the chemicals division, and at that time the second largest acquisition ever, with 33,000 employees and 120 plants in 63 countries). Unilever also bought the leading US ice cream brands Breyers (from Philip Morris) and Ben & Jerry, Amora-Maille (Dijon mustard), Slim Fastfood; and the body and haircare brands Alberto Culver (for $2 billion). In 2010, the company bought the personal care division of Sara Lee for $1.3 billion, including three plants in Germany.

In Europe, eighty-five of the company's 165 plants were closed or sold between 1996 (the year the EWC was established) and 2009, with a loss of some 60 per cent of jobs in these facilities. The total share of jobs lost in Europe was even higher, at 80 per cent, over the period 1965–2009. This marked a process of retrenchment in Europe in parallel with growth in Asia and America and represents the megatrend for the preceding phase of Unilever's history. At the time this research was undertaken, Unilever had seventy-five plants in Europe, with 42,000 employees. Two-thirds of this employment was located in the UK, Germany, the Netherlands and France, with the remaining third distributed across other Western European countries. Germany had nine plants, with 7,000 employees. The Eastern Europe countries are counted as part of the Asia-Africa region, as are Russia and the Ukraine, but are represented on the EWC in accordance with the requirements of the Directive.

Table 1: Unilever turnover by region (in per cent)

Region	1965	2003	2010
Western Europe	65	40	30
America	13	24	20
Asia-Africa	22	36	50

Table 2: Unilever employment in Western Europe and globally by region (in '000s)

Region	1965	1984	1996	2003	2010
W. Europe	210 (= 70%)	245 (= 45%)	105 (= 35%)	58 (= 25%)	42 (= 24%)
Global	300	320	300	230	175

Table 3: Nestlé and Kraft Foods employment (in '000s)

	1965	1984	1996	2003	2010
Nestlé	100	150	220,000	250	280
Kraft Foods	15	35	50	50	105

Source: Tables 1–3, author's calculation.

Culture of industrial relations

Based on the high level of autonomy of local operations and national subsidiaries, personnel and employment policies – aside from top management appointments – were dealt with exclusively locally. This meant that industrial relations was flexibly adapted to national and local custom-and-practice, an approach reinforced by the fact that plants in Continental Europe reported to Dutch top management in Rotterdam and were subject to the overarching philosophy of consensus that characterized industrial relations in the Netherlands. 'Although sometimes impatient with these constraints, Unilever managers did not necessarily completely object to the system which strongly emphasized consensus-seeking and conflict avoidance in labour relations' (Jones, 2005: 241). Overall, Unilever's approach to personnel management was based on consensus and social responsibility. The company was, and remains, generally welcoming to works councils. Industrial relations in Germany and the Netherlands were both cooperative and trust-based, with a high level of unionization. In addition, HRM at Unilever had customarily enjoyed a high status and influence across the spectrum of management functions.

Data on works councils for Germany and the Netherlands for 1980 indicate that Unilever-Deutschland had 180 works council bodies (including many small ones for the large number of small distribution centres), with 905 individual members, of which fifty-two had full facility time. In the Netherlands, which had approximately the same level of employment as Germany at that time, there were thirty-three works councils (*ondernemensrad*) with 330 individual members, of which only two, however, were granted time off. This is also an indication of the much higher level of resources enjoyed by workplace employee representatives in Germany, despite other similarities in the industrial relations of the two countries.

In contrast to the cooperative style of industrial relations in Germany and the Netherlands, there were major and serious industrial conflicts in the company's British plants during the 1970s and 1980s, mainly as a consequence of pay disputes and (in the 1980s) workforce reductions prompted by rationalization. In stark contrast to the cooperative approach at local and national level, Unilever set its face very firmly against any extension of works council or trade union rights at European level and was an active lobbyist on this issue both with the highest levels of the British government and the European Commission. This marked aversion was based on the company's governance arrangements: the only thing that made a collection of companies within a decentralized conglomerate into Unilever was its joint British-Dutch board, and the delicate balance between London and Rotterdam. The notion that Dutch and British trade unions might sit on the board – a prospect envisaged by Dutch proposals for corporate governance based on the German 1976 Codetermination Act and also toyed with in the UK in the mid-1970s – would have represented a nightmare for Unilever management (Jones, 2005: 240). Having avoided this particular hazard, management regarded the initiative for statutory EWCs as a Trojan horse driven by the same aspiration. There was also little enthusiasm for wage comparisons and for solidarity 'for workers in one country to support those elsewhere' (Jones, 2005: 239). Moreover, the tradition of the strongly decentralized corporate organization also meant that there was little urgent need for an EWC on the employee side. At that time, there was little inter-plant competition within the company and management did not pursue a strategy of social dumping.

The social image of the company has suffered considerably as a result of continuous restructuring and disinvestment in Europe. As we set out below, the demand for growth and investment in Europe lies at the core of the EWC's strategy. In 2008, Unilever appointed its first non-internal CEO, Paul Polman, a Dutchman who had built his career at the company's two greatest competitors, Nestlé and Procter & Gamble, and who brought with him their philosophy of centralization and rationalization – summed by one press headline as 'Polman won't shilly-shally'. Whether by accident or design, in 2010 the company enjoyed its first positive press coverage for many years. The critical advantage over its competitors is that Unilever's sales in emerging markets now account for more than half of its turnover. Based on this, the new CEO has redirected the company's attention back to the old continent. His aim, as reported in the *Frankfurter Allgemeine Zeitung* (16 February 2011), is: more growth in Europe, greater market presence through a widened range of products in different price classes 'in order to take account of differing consumer habits country-by-country'. At the same time, Polman acknowledged that 'as well as a desire to be profitable there was also an obligation to society' in an article with the title 'child of his homeland'. This Dutch view of corporate governance and responsibility, condemned a few years previously as typifying a 'provincial giant', has now enjoyed a renaissance. It appears as if, over a period of twenty years, the Unilever wheel has come full circle. This metaphor should not be pursued too far, however. The company's management structure and system of operational control has changed fundamentally. However, the – reluctantly installed – centralized system seems to have become more flexible and the company more oriented to its European origins, and more locally responsive in its marketing. The EWC, which has constantly called for this, sees itself – as we set out below – closer to its objective, as for a long period it was confronted with a series of changes that had led to a rapid loss of significance for Europe. Its expectation of the company is now: growth and investment in Europe.

Unilever's organization and strategy has meant that plant closures, sales and transfers of production to Eastern Europe and Asia, but also within Western Europe, as well as never-ending rationalization programmes, have been a constant trend in employment at the company, leading to a steady reduction in the workforce in Western Europe. These developments constitute the raw material, as it were, for the ongoing work of the EWC and represent its *raison d'être*.

These changes have progressively diminished the autonomy of national Unilever subsidiaries and their managements virtually to zero, leaving national employee representatives almost devoid of direct influence over both company strategy and employment matters. When executives repeatedly tell the EWC that all production operations in Europe constitute, for the company, one *single* plant, this is not merely a management slogan.

On the other hand, the existence of distinctive national systems of social legislation and collective bargaining, but also particular Unilever-specific features, not all of which are evident at first glance, has meant that plant managers have retained a relatively large scope for autonomy on employment and personnel issues. As a consequence, national and local workplace employee representatives continue to constitute a very relevant level of activity to an extent that surprised us, given the notable internal discourse focused around centralization. Ascertaining the specific relationship between centralization and decentralization processes in employee representation, and hence the relationship between the EWC and local representative bodies, made up an important aspect of our analysis.

The food and personal care industries are not high-tech branches, and transferring output and entire facilities, either on cost or market grounds, carries fewer risks than in such sectors. Frequent changes in the product portfolio, as witnessed at Unilever in the 1980s, are common. The purchase and disposal of brands and product lines, and associated mergers and acquisitions, are everyday events. The link between corporate management and individual plants has always been a fairly weak one, all the more so because of their sheer number. This approach to corporate strategy has taken on a number of new characteristics as a result of the regionalization and centralization of operational control and marketing. This has tended to marginalize production operations and led to an increased focus on marketing and sales. Some of our interviewees were concerned that centralization of the supply chain on Zurich was simply the prelude to a complete outsourcing of all production operations and felt that management's vision was for a pure sales organization that would rule as an imperium over its suppliers – an IKEA or Benetton of the global food industry, in which the feeding of humanity would fall to a handful of giant firms supplied, as with the putting out system of the nineteenth century, by legions of dependent producers.

The fact that one of the core issues for Unilever is to tilt the business towards Asia also suggests that the formation of a unitary operational system in Europe (Eurocompany) – albeit a very profound step – is in essence simply a derived function of the firm's overall global strategy. As a consequence, the EWC's field of activity is not pre-structured solely by Europe but also to a high degree by Unilever's global business activities.

KRAFT FOODS

Kraft Foods is a US company, with some 105,000 employees worldwide (excluding recently-acquired Cadbury), and with Nestlé and Unilever, is one of the largest food companies in the world. Kraft Foods has some ninety production facilities in Europe, with 23,000 employees (including Cadbury, 35,000). There are nine plants in Germany, with 3,500 employees. The German workforce has fallen to its current figure from 12,000 in 1990. The European headquarters was previously in London.

Prior to 2007, Kraft Foods was owned by Philip Morris (later renamed the Altria Group), which acquired the company in 1988: it had no European operations prior to its acquisition of Jacobs Suchard in 1990. Kraft Foods was floated by Altria in 2007. In 2008, Kraft Foods bought Danone's biscuit division, LU, and in 2010 – while this research project was underway – acquired the British chocolate maker, Cadbury, which had 55,000 employees worldwide. The product portfolio is concentrated on a small number of lines (chocolate, biscuits, cheese, coffee) and on a number of transnational brands. In contrast to Unilever, the European business is not a mature company but a recent element in the overall group that has been created through a sequence of spectacular acquisitions.

The European configuration of the company is very similar to that of Unilever, even to the extent that the entire European supply chain is managed from Zurich. Individual plants have largely lost their autonomy, with the company now representing a very concentrated instance of a 'Eurocompany'.

The individual production operations in the twenty-one countries in which the company has facilities are only medium-sized; the largest in Germany, for example, has 500 employees. Plant closures, sales and transferring output to other locations is as common as at Unilever. The most important structural difference is that acquisitions have played a much greater role, with their concomitant problems of integrating workforces into the group, and employee representatives into the EWC (notably the French LU and Cadbury).

Kraft Foods in its current incarnation is a recent product of a highly capital-market driven strategy, organized along centralized US lines: 'Kraft … is a Wall Street driven company' (Huffington Post, 19 January 2010). Its European arms are still in the process of being integrated. The company makes 50 per cent of its turnover in the US and 25 per cent in Europe.

4.1.2 Structure and development of the EWC

UNILEVER

The EWC has thirty-five members: four from Germany; four from the UK, three from France; three from the Netherlands; three from Spain; three from Italy; and three from Poland. Other countries represented have one or two members each. There is an annual plenary meeting, held in Rotterdam. Member turnover is high, in part because members from Southern Europe with multiple trade unions rotate attendance by union affiliation. The chair of the EWC from the outset up until the point when this research was conducted was the chair of the German group works council, Herr G. The EWC role was far from being a sideline, and as a rule took up the bulk of his working time. There is an office with an employed EWC secretary as well as an administrator who works both for the EWC and group works council. The EWC secretary speaks several European languages and is in almost daily contact with members of the steering committee. She acts as the information hub and also undertakes most of the organizational activity for the forum. In 2011, Herr G. retired and was succeeded in both his roles by another German, Herr H., who was already a member of the EWC and who had been groomed as a successor by Herr G., with the agreement of the steering committee – for example, through working for two years in the EWC office. As a consequence, the succession had not only been well prepared and planned for, but the new chair had also had an opportunity to ease themselves into the role. For both the former and current EWC chair, the central perspective for their approach and activity is the European reality of the group. Both individuals can be denoted EWC 'professionals' as employee representation in its European dimension is both their occupation and accounts for a large part of their everyday experience.

The steering committee has eight members. Even those countries with the largest workforces (Germany and the UK) have only one member each. In contrast to the EWC as a whole, the steering committee has had a very stable composition. Four of the six Western European representatives (Germany – EWC chair; UK – deputy chair; Spain and France) have been members since the outset, and the two other Western Europeans (Netherlands and Italy) have served for around ten years. The two East European members (Poland and Romania) have also remained members since the accession of their countries to the EU. The British deputy chair, along with the chair, also left to retire shortly before this research was concluded, and the Spanish member then moved into this role.

The steering committee meets very frequently, with a regular monthly meeting at the company's headquarters in Rotterdam and London. This is not an ad hoc body, but a working team engaged in ongoing activity, as described in our first EWC study (Kotthoff, 2006a). Given the close working relationships between members of the steering committee, surmounting language barriers is extremely important. Both the previous and current chairs speak English (along with the English deputy), as do the Dutch and Romanian representatives. The other members (France, Spain, Italy and Poland) each have an interpreter at steering committee meetings. The interpreters are not present for the numerous 'small talk' contacts that take place in the evenings after the formal meetings, but discussion here is facilitated by the EWC secretary, whose language skills play a major role in helping to integrate the members to ensure that – as all confirmed – no one feels left out at mealtimes or at the bar, when conversation becomes more personal, and more open.

There is also intensive contact between steering committee members via e-mail and telephone between meetings, often as a radial network functioning via the EWC office. E-mail circulars in English can also be understood by committee members who do not speak English, as provision has been made for someone to be available to translate them promptly into national languages.

In 2008, the steering committee achieved a major step forward in organizing its own work when it set up a 'feedback group', consisting of four members (German chair, British deputy chair, Dutch and Spanish representatives), together with the EWC secretary, who ensures that discussion in the steering committee and plenary sessions remains focused on the key issues in order to prepare for full meetings and develop options for decision-making. The original proposal to establish the feedback group was made by the chair and deputy chair, and was born out of frustration with the fact that management would simply deluge the EWC and, on occasions, the steering committee with a huge volume of unsorted and often irrelevant information, and dissatisfaction with the fact that internal discussion was often insufficiently focused. This created a need to avoid meetings drifting into unrelated areas so that strategic issues could be aired and properly debated. One further reason was a need to find a means of dealing with the profound differences in approach between steering committee members from Northern and Southern Europe. In practice, the feedback group has also acquired a further function: it visits plants at which employee representatives are currently confronting major problems with the aim of supporting the position of local representatives. In doing this, it has been surprised to discover that simply turning up in itself constitutes a major event. The group has been received by management, local representatives, and the workforce as a high-ranking delegation, with subsequent reports in the local media. The feedback group has also noticed that their greatest effect in terms of representative activity has consisted in the 'visit' as such, and since then it has regularly structured its appearances to include a meeting with plant management, workplace and local employee representatives and, first and foremost, with the workforce. This meant, they reported, that the EWC, which had previously represented a rather anonymous forum, suddenly acquired a human face. The capacity of the feedback group to trigger this effect also led our interviewees at Unilever to see this institution as the most beneficial innovation made by the EWC in recent years. At the same time, the group also serves as a type of executive sub-committee of the steering committee, a strategic centre, a mobile intervention unit ('fire brigade') when needed, and, primarily, the external face of the EWC in 'Europe at large'.

> We visit plants where there are problems, meet management, and also the local trade union. We explain what the EWC is and does, and we ask about problems. This is a very successful way to operate. It raises the profile of the EWC significantly. (English member of the steering committee)

> The only way to gain recognition for the EWC is by going around. We visit plants so that the people there can ask: who are you? Why are you here? And the press also reports this. This means we are no longer faceless bureaucrats but real people – not just abstract, not just on paper, but people who arrive as individuals with a specific task. And people at the local operation then have to ask: were you are the meeting? If not, who went for you? (Dutch member of the steering committee)

The steering committee is currently working on bringing together local employee representatives at production facilities in the same business area into a working group, chaired by a member of the steering committee, as direct dependence, competition for work, and employment-related problems, as well as the concomitant need for cross-border action, are at their greatest for such plants. At the time of writing, a start had been made with margarine plants in the Netherlands, Germany and Poland. The major business groups of dry soups, ice cream and personal care are intended to follow on. Direct transnational contact between local operations within the same business area would be likely to enable much more intensive networking between the EWC and local employee representatives.

Early in the 2000s, the EWC succeeded in securing the right to hold a second meeting of the EWC, if needed, in addition to the annual session provided for in the agreement. As a consequence, the EWC has developed a practice of using this special meeting every second year as a four-day training event for the entire EWC. These events were judged to be very important by our interviewees, and two regarded them as milestones in the overall development of the EWC. For example, the idea of the feedback group was conceived at one of them and it was initially decided to run this as an experiment.

In autumn 2010, after two years of negotiation between the EWC and European management, a new EWC agreement was signed. The EWC's main aim was to institutionalize those practices it had developed and that had proven to be worthwhile. Management ultimately turned out to be much more accommodating than our respondents had expected and agreement was reached on establishing the feedback group with a travel budget for plant visits; an annual second meeting for the whole EWC, which could be held as a plenum or for training; maintenance of the travel budget, despite the fact that management had pressed for sometime on cost grounds for this to replaced by English language training; and – as the crowning achievement – agreement on a robust definition of 'consultation'. This was significant as the EWC had noted that, although management had become noticeably more cooperative and open over the years, in some instances it had made decisions before discussions could be regarded as having been completed, at least in the view of the EWC. The new agreement stipulated the specific issues that had to be consulted on in the event of factory closures, disposals, or transfers of production and that this consultation should aim at coming to an agreement, a timetable that had to be complied with for consultation, and a provision that these measures could not be implemented before this agreed timetable had elapsed.

The Unilever EWC steering committee is an astonishingly well-organized, tightly networked and highly stable working body with plentiful resources. The efficient organization and the modus operandi of the steering committee in terms of its scope to influence management processes, as well as the organization of the meetings of the EWC as a whole, were the object of repeated profound reflection and innovation. These evident advances in self-organization suggest that this EWC has some 'bite' – that is, it had undertaken growing efforts to be taken seriously – and also indicate that such a growth in transnational self-organization is scarcely imaginable without a growth in solidarity.

At the time this research was concluded, a further innovation in the EWC's operations was under discussion: this would involve arranging the annual plenary meeting as a panel discussion in order to engage management more in discussions rather than allowing them to confine themselves to giving presentations. The – now retired – EWC chair, Herr G. noted:

The flood of presentation documents was becoming impossible to deal with – we were being overwhelmed by information. Out of hundreds of pages, only five or so were of any interest, and the rest could be thrown away. We'll now have a panel discussion – the head of Europe, the European HR head and we'll also make sure the head of marketing comes along, and for our side there'll be my deputy and myself and the chair. This will allow a focused discussion by topic area that we'll set out and fix in advance, otherwise someone will inevitably ask why the cap of the toothpaste tube turns to the left. After the day with management, we'll have a follow-up session where the feedback group can tell us what the key points were from the previous day, and colleagues can then go back home and *not get lost in all the complexity.*

In summer 2010 a generational change took place, with the retirement of both the German chair, G, and the British deputy D., and shortly before that the Dutch representative on the steering committee, J. These three protagonists, who had held their positions since the establishment of the EWC, were the dominant figures in the forum for the first fifteen years of its existence and their departure marked the end of an era. The succession for all three positions was systematically planned and prepared for. As already noted, the new chair is the young German, H., and his deputy is the Spanish member Ms M. The Dutch member in the steering committee is P., who, like his predecessor, works in the head office in Rotterdam and serves as the link to the parent company. This succession arrangement was intended to secure as high a degree of continuity as possible. It represents a significant indicator of the high degree of institutionalization of the EWC at Unilever.

KRAFT FOODS

Following the acquisition of LU but excluding Cadbury, at the time our research was conducted the EWC at Kraft Foods had thirty-eight members from nineteen countries, as follows: France six; Belgium four; Germany, Spain, the Czech Republic and Poland – each three; UK, Italy, and Sweden – each two; and other countries one seat. France and Belgium combined, with a quarter of the seats, were the most strongly represented countries. All the Southern European countries together – including Belgium that has a similar system of plant-based trade union representation – had as many as 45 per cent of all the seats, and the combined Northern European countries just 21 per cent. This might suggest that the style of representation on the EWC is likely to lean towards that of Southern Europe. However, as we show below, this was far from being the case.

The steering committee has seven members, of which two are from France, one each from Belgium, Germany, Norway, the Czech Republic and Lithuania. The chair of the EWC from the outset has been Ms. B., a Norwegian delegate. The committee has a permanent adviser, who is an executive board member of the German food, drink and hospitality union NGG. He participates in all meetings and should be counted in practice along with the elected members as an 'insider', meaning that the committee effectively has two German members.

The development of the EWC was described by the chair as follows:

> At the beginning we didn't really know each other. In the first plenary session I felt like a fish out of water. It was difficult. We talked about what the EWC should do, what its task was, and what its purpose was. When I made a proposal, the room went quiet; hardly anyone took part in the discussion. The main consideration was how to get information out of management earlier. In particular, the Germans and myself put pressure on the company to provide us with information on a quarterly basis. However, this was not successful in the initial years. I had a good relationship with the Germans. In contrast, the British said that it was not our task to be involved in company processes – that's management's job. Things are different now. We have good and lively discussions in the forum as a whole. There are many questions and a great deal of discussion. Members feel more at home than at the start. We work closely together in the steering committee. We've already achieved a good deal.

This trajectory is very similar to that of the Unilever EWC. One difference is that the Kraft Foods EWC has neither its own office nor an EWC secretary or other support staff. The Norwegian chair undertakes all the administrative and organizational work on her own. She is the works council chair for a small plant, and devotes around 80 per cent of her facility time to the EWC.

One priority for the chair is to keep not only the steering committee but also the entire EWC up-to-date with information. She would like to maintain as democratic and egalitarian a structure as possible, and cultivates an open style of leadership, with a high level of involvement by the forum as a whole. However, she has also encountered the same obstacles experienced with the other EWCs and in particular the difficulty in engaging a wide membership with only a single annual meeting. When a new EWC agreement was recently being negotiated, Ms. B. sent the draft to all EWC members with a request for comments. 'Very few came back. I was a little disappointed'.

One structural problem for the EWC is that there is, as yet, no satisfactory joint representation at the level of national operations – that is, no institution comparable with a German central works council.[1] As a consequence, it is very difficult to cascade information down from the steering committee, and conversely to pull in information from local operations. The chair says:

> There are problems in some countries with contact to individual plants, to local works councils and also to local management. If there is no national overall representation, then it is difficult. Information must flow up and down. This works well in Germany, France and Spain but not as well in other countries: for example, there are difficulties in the UK.

The German adviser on the steering committee noted that in part this was due to the fact that in some countries resource problems prevented representatives from travelling and they are not able to visit plants in their own country. The company remains restrictive on that issue.

4.1.3 Scope and effectiveness of the EWC

UNILEVER

In the case of Unilever, it should be borne in mind that, in view of the fact that the EWC meets only once a year, this forum cannot play the role of a true operating team that affects the everyday life of the firm, in contrast,

---

1   The central works council (*Gesamtbetriebsrat*) is the representative body above the level of local individual operations. That is, it is located at the level of central management of a company.

for example, to a German works council. The real European counterpart to such a type of forum is not the EWC but, at most, its executive body – that is, the steering committee. This was also made clear at the outset of our interview with the chair of the Unilever EWC. 'The EWC has made a good deal of progress, but that is all related to the steering committee'.

The steering committee is the principal actor and the source of the EWC's effectiveness in a social sense. The EWC as a whole is certainly significant as the body that is formally empowered to make decisions, but its effect needs to be analysed specifically for each case study in terms of its relationship with the steering committee.

The most distinctive overarching interpretative framework for the protagonists on the EWC was, from the outset, the gulf between the cooperative and constructive stance of Unilever management in industrial relations at national level (in countries with works council arrangements) and its vehement rejection of such relationships at European level. 'Given the positive traditions of cooperation at national level, we did not understand why Unilever rejected any European interest representation out of hand' (previous EWC chair, G.). The chair and fellow campaigners (the British deputy and Dutch representative on the steering committee) set themselves the declared aim of overcoming this discrepancy. They wanted the dialogue that they were used to at national level to be raised to the European level. *'We wanted to be a political counterweight to the group board'* (Herr. G.).

The most notable area of effectiveness of the steering committee at Unilever has consisted in the fact that it has succeeded in achieving its goal of dialogue at European level. The new EWC chair, H., responding to the question of what the biggest gains were over the preceding history of the EWC, said: 'That we are taken seriously. Initially, we were not wanted at all. That is serious progress'. The EWC has been able to induce European management to engage in a regular process of consultation. It is now informed about significant issues, such as business developments, proposed closures, transfers of production, disposals and rationalization. Although these discussions are not always entirely official, there is, at the least, informal contact with the protagonists. Previously, management was deeply sceptical about employee representation at European level as it was concerned that French or British shopfloor trade union militancy might come to dominate. As a consequence, the main background issue in the development of the EWC was the establishment of personal trust on the part of management – and specifically trust that those actors from countries with a stable works council tradition would be able to build a majority for their style of cooperative conflict resolution within the EWC. The next section (4.1.4), on the relationship between the EWC and management, will deal with how the cooperative style that emerged between the steering committee and top management functioned in practice. At this stage, the issue here is to note that the Unilever steering committee is actually involved in a practice of participation. It no longer has to beg for information and is integrated into how company policies are implemented and problems resolved. It is engaged in ongoing dialogue with management. In this respect, it is moving towards the practice typical of a German, Austrian, Dutch or Swedish works council. And the further that it has advanced along this path, the more our interviewees expressed regret that it had not yet attained the power resources of a German works council, with its institutional scope for influence. The German and Dutch members, in particular, lamented the lack of appropriate codetermination rights.

> We have a developed consultation procedure, we're extensively involved. When we called for the EWC in the 1980s our argument was that we did not know what management, in its far-off homeland, had in store for us. This factor no longer applies; we now know what is happening. What we need would be the next step towards more codetermination rights on European social compensation plans, where we would also have some power. We don't have that yet, and so we look like supplicants. (Herr G.)

> The EWC is in the position such that it is now taken into account. We have consultation, where we can challenge management if it's made mistaken decisions. That's new for them. Although it does not stop the decision, it changes the way in which it is implemented. It makes management think. The EWC has already had an effect. We work with – and press – management on the basis of solid and consistent standards. (Former British deputy chair of the EWC, Mr. D.)

> We receive high quality information and consultation is also well advanced. There is no longer any discussion about the fact that we are informed about everything with a European dimension. Getting that took a lot of effort, as Unilever did not accept this initially. (Ms. M., Spanish delegate on the steering committee and new deputy EWC chair)

Based on a scale we adopted for assessing the influence of the EWC within a company (1 = low, 10 = high), the former EWC chair awarded a score of six, that is slightly above the mid-point, but distinguished the indicator 'influence' from that of 'importance', which he considered merited a higher rating. Out of all the steering committee members, he had the highest aspirations for the effectiveness of the EWC in terms of 'full-blooded' codetermination. Despite the success achieved over his fifteen years of office, at the end of his period he remained disappointed that the EWC had still not come sufficiently far. However, he noted, *'Politically one can do a good deal with the EWC if one sets about it in the right way'.*

The previous deputy chair, D. from the UK, gave an even more positive assessment, ranking the EWC's influence at eight or nine on the scale. 'The effectiveness is pretty good, certainly not low'.

The Spanish representative on the steering committee, who also served as the spokesperson for the Southern European cluster (France, Italy, Spain), similarly awarded a score of eight. She was amused by the fact that the EWC at Danone was given an especially high rating by union-friendly publications. She noted: 'They have good agreements and everything is nicely written down, but in practice – and in contrast to us – it doesn't work quite as well. We don't have these fantastic agreements, but we operate in a pragmatic way, *we travel*, we have flexibility, and we can achieve more in practice. Danone has been built up as a poster boy by the trade unions. However, we do need to set down on paper [in an agreement] what we've achieved in practice'.

'Consultation' is a core concept in determining how our interviewees judged effectiveness. This is a complex notion with a number of elements directly relevant to the idea of 'solidarity', expressed, for example, in the expression that *'understanding of contexts and connections has grown'*. Consultation was understood to refer to the scope and capacity of the steering committee to develop a common overarching European perspective on representation, to formulate a joint position on specific issues and problems, and to engage in intensive dialogue with management to find solutions. 'Understanding contexts and connections' implies a relational structure of interaction that only emerges in the interaction between the steering committee and management. The expression 'knowing how the company works' captures one important aspect of this. The first prerequisite for the EWC's becoming effective is the securing of an understanding of the highly international organization of the company – that is, the 'contexts and connections' in terms of corporate strategy, organizational structure, and managerial approaches. Understanding these, in turn, is a prerequisite for a common perspective, and for its part the first step on the long road to achieving solidaristic patterns of behaviour. The key issue is that grasping these contexts and connections also relies heavily on whether management will play its part in terms of being prepared to reveal the internal workings of the company as one aspect of its general approach to information and consultation.

For the German, Dutch and British representatives on the steering committee, this understanding of connections is embedded in their own conceptualization of European employee representation as a kind of co-management exercised through close social partnership. In such a 'productivity coalition' each side aims to view matters from the standpoint of the other – that is, management demonstrates social concern and employee representatives assume some responsibility for the success of the business.

This connection was expressed by the English representative in the following terms.

> One advantage of our EWC is that you're aware of the organizational relationships between the different countries, how production is organized – so that all the operations have a chance to share best practice. This means that we can make the whole company more resilient and more productive. On the other hand, management understands that it's important for the new organization in Zurich that employee representatives understand the function of this organization because this will make the plants more productive and our jobs will be more secure.

The difficult issues for the EWC have been plant closures, plant disposals and transfers of production to other locations both within Western Europe (concentration in larger plants) and, in particular, to Eastern Europe. Its involvement in regulating and resolving these problems constitutes the acid test of its representative effectiveness. Such measures are not a rarity: on the contrary, they are a frequent occurrence within this sector and specifically at Unilever, as noted above. As such, they have been a regular part of the EWC's experience. For example, since 2007 three plants in the Netherlands, two in France, two in Italy, one in Germany, one in Ireland, one in the Czech Republic, and one in Hungary were either closed or sold. In 2011, two closures were imminent in the UK. A number of other plants were at risk of closure, including two in Germany. The EWC has no scope or power to stop the company from withdrawing from a plant. Its priority is 'Sale before Closure': that is, to try and ensure that where Unilever withdraws from an operation this should not simply be in the form of a 'scorched earth' closure but that the facility should be sold and continue to operate under the ownership of another company. The EWC concluded an agreement on this with management in 2002 ('Responsible Restructuring'), although this was more a declaration of intent than a stipulation of binding rules. Instances have occurred in which the principles in this agreement have been complied with, but there have also been others in which there was no sale, and the factory was closed. Interviewees reported that it was hard to prove the contrary if management asserted that no buyer could be found.

The fact that Unilever makes frequent and abrupt changes in its product portfolio means that sales and closures are so common, as with the sector as a whole, that the steering committee considers it illusory to think that they could be prevented entirely: 'It's inconceivable that we can save all jobs'. Rather, the steering committee's approach has been to try to raise the barriers for a closure as a high as possible: that is, to increase the cost to the company through wide-ranging social compensation plans in all countries based on the standards that prevail in countries such as Germany. If a closure only affects a single country, which is often the case, then the social consequences will be regulated at national level and not by the EWC. However, as far as the EWC is concerned, such closures are almost invariably an indirect consequence of a single cross-border corporate strategy and, as such, should be considered as falling within its remit. Management does not share this view. It was also reported that national employee representative bodies also jealously guarded their right to regulate closures themselves. Nonetheless, the EWC can still exercise a major role even in purely national cases, as it will offer its support to national employee representatives, and this can be decisive as it will assume the role of overall coordinator for social plan negotiations and intervene in any local negotiations being undertaken by European management. It will inform local representatives about the standards it should aim for, and will also audit the outcome. If these standards are not met, and national-level negotiations do not lead to a satisfactory conclusion, this can trigger a visit by the feedback group of the type already outlined above. This will then directly call on local management to re-enter negotiations with local representatives to improve on the initial agreement.

One example of this was the most recent visit of the feedback group to the Czech Republic, where a 'large' plant with some 700 employees was closed. The EWC contacted local employee representatives and management with a request for information about how negotiations were proceeding. Management stated that negotiations had been concluded, and that local employee representatives had signed an agreement. However, after having spoken directly to representatives, the feedback group discovered that no negotiations had taken place. During the visit it emerged that by 'agreement' management had referred merely to a confirmation, signed by local representatives, that an information meeting had taken place. One member of the group (the EWC chair) immediately phoned the European HR manager in Zurich and pressed him to intervene in the Czech Republic. This took place on the same day, and succeeded in 'pulling the fat out of the fire'. The fact that this rapid reaction was seen as an especially successful instance led to several interviewees describing the outcome in dramatic terms: 'Just two hours after the call, everything was sorted'. This was intended to imply that European management, which kept local management on a tight leash on logistical and operational matters, should also do the same on social matters. As a result, all the interviewees considered that the high degree of operational centralization in Zurich was advantageous for the EWC.

The social plan subsequently agreed in the Czech Republic was seen as a success. Its main provisions were for a high level of severance pay in national comparison, company support for job search, and training for less-skilled employees.

One 'ordinary' German EWC member stated:

> An attempt was made to carry out a closure on the absolute cheapest terms, but it was then possible, through the steering committee, to substantially improve the conditions by putting pressure on central management and attempting to put the issue into the public domain through a plant visit. The same is now happening in Dijon, where a mustard factory is to be closed: there were problems as management was locked in by the workforce.

The deputy chair, D., from the UK, also noted:

> A factory was closed in the Czech Republic without prior consultation with the local union. However, because of the feedback group there was a major revision of the decision. That's a good example of how the EWC can get active – that is, be determined and get management to rethink its decision.

The intervention of the feedback group also proved to be helpful subsequently in the cases of the proposed closures of the mustard factory at Dijon, a margarine factory in Ireland, an ice cream factory in Sweden, and a ketchup factory in England.

In each of these instances, it was important that the feedback group was recognized as a European authority. As a consequence, as D. added, it was vital that for it to be able deliver a single agreed opinion to central management on behalf of the EWC. 'We'll put an agreed position to Unilever for the case in hand. We then take that to the steering committee and back it up, and then it goes back to the local level, social plans and other things'.

However, there are also instances in which the EWC does not take on this coordinating role during a closure: this is when local employee representatives are sufficiently strong, or feel themselves such, to secure a positive outcome on their own. This applies principally to Germany and the Netherlands, where there is an established, and legally supported, practice of negotiation on social compensation plans. The same also applied in a case in Italy, where the EWC offered its assistance but this was turned down by local representatives who were ultimately able to achieve a satisfactory result themselves. In the case of the closure of a tea factory in the South of France, initially announced in 2010, the EWC also offered help, but this was also turned down by local representatives. This case then developed into a major conflict, and ultimately a political and media cause célèbre, with a nine-week strike, the holding captive of management by local activists, and legal proceedings against some local employee representatives, including the French member of the steering committee. This individual approached colleagues on the steering committee at a later stage of the conflict, which continued into 2012.

When three out of six factories were slated for closure in a single action in the Netherlands, it was evident that although national works councils and trade unions would lead the negotiations, the blow was such a severe one that the steering committee organized the largest protest action in its history in Rotterdam. There was a six-week strike in the Dutch plants, the outcome of which was that an extremely high level of severance pay was achieved in negotiations for the social compensation plan – the actual level of which was only whispered by interviewees as there was another moral aspect to this issue, namely that national employee representatives allowed themselves to be 'bought out' of their aim of employment security through high redundancy payments. One English convenor, who had recently joined the steering committee and who was not familiar with the internal workings of the body, saw this 'buying off' in the event of closures as very objectionable and held a critical view of the effectiveness of the EWC. 'Unilever will do what Unilever wants to do. I don't think you can change that. It's only a decent pay out. For the last plant closure in the UK we [!] paid three times the national level of redundancy pay. They got them a better deal, that's all'.

We have already noted that the EWC tried for several years to conclude an agreement with management that would more clearly stipulate information and consultation procedures, especially in the event of closures. It tenaciously stuck with this objective as its own long-term project. As early as 2004, it circulated a 'Six Point Proposal', later termed the 'Agreement on Socially Responsible Restructuring', and incorporated this into the negotiations on the renewal of the EWC agreement. In autumn 2010, the new EWC agreement was signed, and included, amongst other things, a specific definition of the consultation procedure in the event of closures and rationalization. This was seen as a major step by all involved.

The agreement is a real milestone. Under the new consultation process we will be included at an early stage in the event of closures and rationalization, so that we will be in a position to indicate alternatives and make proposals. In the new agreement, we also achieved official recognition of the feedback group and its scope to be able to visit countries and operations in which closures and rationalization measures are imminent, as well as a second annual EWC meeting. (new EWC chair, H.)

The English deputy chair commented on this:

We wanted a European Framework Agreement on socially-responsible restructuring – so people locally can come up with creative solutions if a plant is closed. The EWC has to look after the effects on other plants, but the details of how the closure will be handled are a matter for local representatives. *But there needs to be someone in the background who says to management: you have to consult with someone. There has to be someone who can put pressure on management and say: this is what we expect. And we were able to achieve that this year.*

In the case of the *factory disposals* that have taken place in recent years, the EWC succeeded in concluding agreements with management on retaining Unilever standards (collective agreements, terms and conditions of employment) for employees transferring to the new company but only in instances where the sale covered factories in several countries. This was the case, for example, with the sale of Nordsee in 2002, and Iglo in 2005 to Permira, when it was possible to agree very advantageous terms for the workforce. This agreement was seen as a particular success in trade union circles. 'They say that you have achieved a good deal in the case of disposals, secured the number of employees and conditions. In the case of the sale of Iglo, employees are now better off than before. These are European successes, that was a good thing' (former EWC chair, G.).

In terms of its response to the enduring topic of *transfers of production*, some years ago the EWC resolved to abide by a code of conduct, under which employee representatives at the receiving plant were to indicate that they would hold up the start of additional output – for example, by refusing overtime or not agreeing to new shift patterns – until any social compensation plan terms at the plant losing the work had been finalized. However, this code has only been consistently complied with in a small number of instances, and in most cases it was only half-heartedly deployed, or not at all, as local employee representatives were always glad – our interviewees noted – to be awarded additional output. As yet, the EWC has not become an institution for regulating a fair or appropriate allocation of production volumes.

The new EWC chair commented:

> No, that's not always kept to. Sadly solidarity does not extend that far. My experience tells me, no – the pressure of competition is simply too great. In Europe, every factory celebrates every ton of output. There are always initiatives to do this differently, such as in strike situations, as in Italy when an ice cream factory was on strike and production was moved to Germany for that period: the German works council boasted about how quickly they had dealt with the extra output. And we then had a solidarity debate here in the central works council in Germany and we said: where was your solidarity? Yes, they said, we couldn't refuse. That was true in that case, as it wasn't done through overtime but in normal shifts. And when a margarine factory was on strike over a closure, the plant in East Germany put on a great show and took on the extra Saturday shift, although we in the EWC had asked them not to. It just doesn't work. I think that any real solidarity stops if you have to give something up in order for others to be able to keep something. That only functions at an abstract level, as with our protest action in Rotterdam.

One other possible path for the steering committee to exercise influence is for it to give an early – confidential – signal to any local works council whose operation might be negatively affected by a change, based on information it receives in confidence on proposed changes, to give local employee representatives an opportunity to prepare themselves.

The previous EWC chair explained as follows:

> We can tell local works council what will happen with their operation in three or four years *as we have the line of communication*. We should keep the EWC for this reason alone. As far as German works councils are concerned, I inform them in writing at all the meetings, they get everything. I report to the group works council, the economic committee,[2] and the operations working party. The comparative metrics for all the sites also allow them to draw the appropriate conclusions for their plants,

---

2   The economic committee (*Wirtschaftsausschuss*) is a special committee of the works council for information and consultation on the company's business situation and strategy.

and they do this. They can see whether they rank highly in production operations or at the bottom. This is a very important point for discussions in the plant. We would not have this without the EWC, and that's a real benefit. They can compare themselves with any operation in Europe on any significant dimension. They see the context, it's possible to explain to them that they have a chance but they've got to be consistent. [*Interviewer: Is this a type of local productivity pact?*] Yes, yes. I always see how occupied my works council colleagues are with this, they set a lot of store by it – that their operation is doing well, that secures the future of the plant. They say, 'That's my contribution'. However, this will only work if management doesn't take it too far, which they could do. You can't just keep trying to screw more out.

The chair of a German works council, not a member of the EWC, confirmed this from his standpoint:

> If there is something on the agenda of the steering committee that affects our operation, then any presentations to be given will be run through directly by H. [*new EWC chair*], and whatever else they might have found out from management about the prospects so that I can get in contact with the local general manager and ask what the implications are for our plant.

The positive effect of the EWC that emerged was that where a plant appeared to be unlikely to meet its targets, the intervention of local representatives who had been informed by the steering committee would give it an opportunity to rectify the position and stay in the race. This could be somewhat crudely designated as remedial coaching. As a rule, the (egoistic) response by an individual plant to improve its competitive chances is seen as a paradigm case of unsolidaristic conduct. However, our interviewees did not categorize such self-interested behaviour as social dumping or unfair competition; on the contrary, they saw it as an act of solidarity with those at risk of being eliminated from the competition. Such a perspective is only understandable against the background of an acceptance of benchmarking and inter-plant competition as economic givens and as an accepted challenge, in which action by local representatives to improve performance and competitiveness was seen as both sensible and desirable and where the key issue was to ensure that any competition took place under fair conditions – including crucially the right to a second chance.

Securing the economic survival of a plant through productivity pacts with local management has represented the main issue for local employee representatives in all the countries. If European management announces the closure of a plant or transfer of production, then they will fight to get this second chance – that is, for scope to improve productivity through cooperation or achieve the required benchmark by relinquishing some elements of pay that are set at plant level in excess of any mandatory industry-level provisions. The EWC sees its task as ensuring a level playing field between countries and plants and offering stragglers a helping hand.

This strategy has a normative basis, as there is a consensus that basic agreed standards should not be sacrificed. The fact that the steering committee has a role in this makes the whole process more transparent and backstairs dealing less likely.

One other effect of the EWC is that, as a result of its existence, in countries in which there are no works council structures or national single employee interest representation in a company (akin to a German central works council), equivalents emerge to meet this role. This has applied in particular in the UK, where representatives saw this as a highly beneficial effect of the EWC. Unilever has six manufacturing sites in the UK, all of which are strongly unionized, and five administrative or sales operations, with a high proportion of white-collar staff and very low union membership. The shop stewards and convenors at the manufacturing plants did not know each other beforehand and had never met. The first step towards creating a unitary representation began with the election of national representatives for the Special Negotiating Body (SNB) required to set up the EWC and, following the conclusion of the EWC agreement, for the election of national delegates to the EWC. It was reported that the representatives at the British Unilever plants met for the first time in Brussels at the EWC meeting. Sporadic cooperation at national level, along with meeting the formal legal requirements for the SNB process, was the starting point for the development of a national umbrella organization of employee representatives into the 'Unilever National Forum' (UNF) – albeit encompassing only manufacturing operations. This change in industrial relations practice at the company in the UK was also supported by national management, which, in stark contrast to the previous approach at Unilever

UK, subsequently developed an interest in cooperating with employee representatives at national level and openly informed and consulted it. The UNF has since become a stable institution with some similarities to a German central works council.

The deputy chair, from the UK, noted:

> In recent years, management started to get things organized with the union group. We now discuss things in a more generic sense. They say: we've got a problem, we don't know how to solve it, but let's talk about a possible solution. And this also involves those affected locally directly. And the role of us British EWC members is to look at things in the round and make sure that management decisions are fair and to make proposals from an overall standpoint ... I've given the shop stewards in the UK a whole lot of information about Unilever, and I've made sure the senior members locally get in touch with each other, and they're much more engaged now. The key union members are now directly involved with national Unilever management. That is the UK Unilever National Forum. The firm has decided to have better contacts with those production locations, which are all highly unionized.

He also reported that initially there was no trust between the British representatives.

> This changed when management in the UK switched to cooperation and UK representatives were able to hold their first national meeting as a pre-meeting to the EWC session. We could prepare ourselves nationally, have an agenda, and give feedback afterwards. Management gave us rooms, travel costs, and conference facilities. For those of us from production operations, this was extremely hard to organize. It was a nightmare for me to communicate with manual staff because of shifts, and that they didn't have e-mails etc.

The EWC chair, G. also commented:

> In England, Unilever is consolidating operations into a few large sites. Management says: we'll come and discuss this with you, let's look for solutions together. And as the steering committee, we were also involved at European level. We support the colleagues there. The feedback group was therefore often over there on this account. But this would be inconceivable for the French, the Spanish, and the Italians. England has completely moved towards the culture that we have in Germany, and management has also moved and says: we will come towards you, we want to resolve this with you through dialogue.

Solidaristic protest actions

When asked what they understood by 'solidarity', virtually all our respondents, including members of the steering committee and other EWC members as well as local employee representatives, said: a strike or other protest action to support a foreign operation in urgent need. That is, they associated solidarity primarily with trade union workers' solidarity or solidarity-in-struggle (category 3 in the Introduction). Over the course of its history, the EWC at Unilever has organized two protest actions. The first took place in 2003, after group management had informed the media about proposed factory closures during a press briefing held to report on its annual results, at which it announced a special dividend, but before talking with the EWC. Angered by this, the steering committee held its own press conference a day later at the company's head office at which it pilloried management, in particular over the moral questionability of simultaneously announcing large-scale redundancies and more money for shareholders. Workplace meetings were held simultaneously in a number of countries on the same issue.

> We prepared ourselves professionally. We had charts and agreed texts. It was on television, radio and made the front pages of the next day's newspapers. It caused quite a stir, and hurt them.

The action led to the media no longer being informed about such plans before the EWC. For a company highly dependent on the mass consumer market, public image is a particularly valuable and sensitive asset – a vulnerability that the steering committee was able to exploit.

The second protest action took place in 2007. The EWC chair, G., began his description with the following laconic observation: 'We achieved solidarity – once'. The occasion was the announcement of a dramatic plan under which twenty plants in Europe were to be closed, with the loss of 10,000 jobs. The EWC held an emergency meeting and agreed to undertake a protest action at the company's Rotterdam head office. Some 500 demonstrators attended from a large number – but by no means all – Unilever operations in Europe, most of whom were local employee representatives

and full-time union officials who marched around the headquarters building and handed a letter of protest to a representative of management. No
one attended from the company's Eastern European plants. Given the
difficulties entailed by organising such a central demonstration, with the
associated travel and in some cases accommodation costs, attendance was
largely confined to those with full or part facility time, or able to take two
days' leave. In organising the event, the EWC was strongly supported by
the two European Trade Union Federations in the sector, EMCEF and
EFFAT, together with a number of Southern European union confederations that covered the travel costs for some of those attending. This action
was also successful in terms of its public impact, and was widely reported
in the media.

One member of a local works council in Germany who attended the
event said.

> Twenty plants were to be closed. The action was agreed once it was clear we were
> not getting any further with words. We as representatives signalled to the employer
> that we were sticking together, and in this sense it represented progress. However,
> when it really came down to it, you couldn't actually say it was true solidarity. If
> someone has their back to the wall, then self-interest tends to take over and the
> common front can crumble. But it's possible to achieve something in the medium
> term. At national level we'd also never manage this if the group works council were
> to say 'We'll all stick up for each other until the end'. If you're under pressure, you'll
> make compromises with your management.

Subsequent assessments of this action diverged markedly. It was viewed
rather sceptically by the previous EWC chair, G., who was seen by his colleagues as a strategist with ambitious goals for the EWC. In his view, the
event only took place because of a very specific reason: a cut of 10,000 jobs.
'If I were to call for solidarity for an individual ice cream factory in France,
hardly anyone would come. And not much could be expected from the
national unions either. If I were to go to NGG[3] here in Germany and say
to them, "Let's go on strike for a day because a mustard factory is being

---

3   NGG (Gewerkschaft Nahrung-Genuss-Gaststätten): German trade union for food,
     drink, tobacco and hospitality.

shut in Dijon", they'd tell me that it had nothing to do with them. They're not especially European. It's a real obstacle'.

The English deputy chair of the EWC was also sceptical.

> You can express your anger with strikes and protests, but I'm not sure that it will change the decision. Looked at realistically, our protest in Rotterdam was just a few people when compared with the total workforce. However, we did put pressure on management because of the press and television reporting. But they didn't change the decision. On the other hand, the action certainly strengthened the bonds within the union groups.

In contrast, the Spanish representative was both more optimistic and more positive about taking action. '*They* saw that *we* will stick together when it's serious. What we achieved was fantastic, and it created real difficulties for Unilever. Although we have major problems with solidarity at Unilever Europe, other EWCs have even bigger ones'.

These relatively constrained forms of action on the part of the EWC contributed to the fact that it was taken more seriously by management. They showed, on the one hand, that the EWC was able to organize protests; and, on the other, that it did not derive its basic principle of action from such events.

The benchmark for pan-European protest has been set by the EWC at GM Europe (Opel), which has succeeded in getting up to 40,000 employees on the streets on days of action. All our respondents at Unilever stressed that they would not be able to organize on such a scale, and they noted how much they were impressed by the capacity of their GM/Opel colleagues in this particular respect.

Protest letters in the form of an open letter to the CEO of the group can be seen as a type of 'small format' protest. In November 2005, the EWC chair G., wrote such a letter to the then CEO about the proposed sale of Iglo, the frozen food business, of which the following is a (translated) extract.

> Dear Mr. Cescau, following the failed 'Path to Growth' [a multi-year large-scale rationalization programme running from the late-1990s instituted by the predecessor of the CEO, *authors' note*], a new beginning was to be established with 'One Unilever

[the current restructuring programme, instituted by the CEO to whom the letter is addressed, *authors' note*]. However, it is already clear that nothing fundamental has changed. Instead of markets, brands and consumers, we are still preoccupied with restructuring – that is, with ourselves. The 'shared services' decision [transfer of routine activities in finance and HR to Eastern Europe and India, *authors' note*] has triggered a shock in many countries. People are extremely frustrated and demotivated ... Why has the frozen foods business been put in question? Anyone who cannot make our well-known brand Iglo profitable will have failed across the board. Unilever must retain this business ... I am willing to discuss this in greater detail in person with you. Even better, this could be discussed at the next EWC plenary meeting.

The letter made clear that Herr G. closely followed the major strategic and economic decisions taken by management and was concerned to discuss issues with the head of the group on equal terms. He engaged with corporate policies, criticized, offered advice and sought to establish contact with the CEO, with whom he already had had a number of constructive personal discussions.

KRAFT FOODS

Both the content and level of information and consultation at the Kraft Foods EWC are very similar to those at Unilever. The 'hard' issues are also closures, disposals and relocations of operations, together with workforce reductions. For example, the EWC's actions were exemplified in its response to the closure of the company's plant in York (UK), on which the Norwegian EWC chair. B., reported as follows.

Two emergency meetings of the steering committee were held. We supported the colleagues in York, and gave them information. We played a role over the level of redundancy pay. Negotiations were conducted by local representatives themselves. During this time, there was a noticeable improvement in the work of the EWC, as we had close contact with the plant. We had also done the same in the previous year during the closure of the chocolate factory in Budapest. We learned a good deal about social compensation plans, redundancy, and outplacement support. We played an active role on this. As a rule, the company says this is a national matter. In contrast, we say that if production is going to Bulgaria, that's an international matter. I was kept informed by plant unions in both countries. We ensured that they worked closely together with their local managements, and when they couldn't make any more progress I contacted central management in Zurich and said: 'It can't be like this'. And the negotiating process was then restarted at national level. And as the steering committee, we sent a letter to the CEO, Irene Rosenfeld, in the USA. We put considerable pressure on the company to give people decent conditions.

As with Unilever, the Kraft Foods EWC also adopted a code of conduct for dealing with transfers of production. Additional output could only be taken on if the social position of employees had been properly dealt with at the plant that was relinquishing production. There was a protracted and vigorous debate within the EWC on this issue. The German EWC adviser noted:

> We did not want to set something down that was not realistic. The code does not demand the impossible. It simply states that we do not want to be subject to extortion and that by exchanging information we can ensure that the people affected are properly treated under national law and EU minimum standards. That is, don't say 'Let's have that production', but wait until proper provision has been made for the others, and hold off until then through not working overtime or refusing new shift arrangements.

One example of the successful application of the code was the case of the intended shutdown of a cheese factory in Spain, in which production was to be transferred to Belgium. The EWC and Spanish trade union opposed the closure, with the support of the regional and national government, and called for the plant to be sold rather than shut. A buyer was found, but set a condition that they should continue to produce a Kraft-branded product – that is, supply Kraft – for a transitional period of a year before entering the market independently. Management was not initially willing to accede to this, but was induced to do so by the Belgian works council, which stated that it would not accept any immediate increase in production and agreed to delay the transfer to help the Spanish workforce. The steering committee also insisted that the code of conduct should be formally complied with, and arranged for a meeting of the two works councils concerned to allow them to become acquainted, build mutual trust and discuss the details. Finally, the Belgian works council agreed to the delay – giving up a substantial amount of additional output for a year and the job security that this would have implied. Through the mediation of the steering committee, which played a crucial role, the Belgian representatives and workforce behaved with exemplary solidarity in line with the code of conduct. This instance was viewed by all our respondents as one of the most positive examples and tangible proof of concrete solidarity. It was also conceded that not all comparable instances had gone quite as smoothly.

The EWC concluded a European framework agreement with management on outsourcing that established that existing agreed and workplace provisions would be transferred to a new company. The EWC also sought to negotiate a framework agreement on social protection in the event of job losses due to restructuring. This also exhibited remarkable similarities to a comparable agreement at Unilever.

4.1.4 Relationships between EWC and management: the new spirit

UNILEVER

Group management initially adopted a sceptical, even hostile, stance towards the EWC. It had resisted the establishment of an EWC until shortly before agreement was reached in 1996. The usual practice in the company was to adapt the operation to any local legal requirements, at the same time extracting any business benefits that could be derived from this. The company had for some time adopted a transnational strategy and had been able to proceed with this largely undisturbed by local trade unions and works councils. There was concern that the Mediterranean model of polarized industrial relations would come to dominate the EWC, and management had had some experience of this at national level in France. However, once they realized that representatives from Northern Europe – the Germans, Dutch and, increasingly, the British – would be the key actors in the forum, they gradually shifted their position. In the first EWC study conducted by the present author (Kotthoff, 2006a: 61), an observation made by the EWC chair was cited.

The partnership approach of the 'Northern lights' prevailed. And management was surprised about the forum, that it was possible to work so well together. This was a complete surprise. They had expected a much more radical approach. The relationship between group management and the EWC has improved steadily. As they see that it's working, they gradually inch towards us. [*Interviewer: How did this come about?*]. Because the people who got involved were all from countries in which this approach was customary. For the moment, this has prevailed.

During the early phase of the EWC's existence, the chair succeeded in building a good relationship with the European HR director ('I had access at any time. If I called him, I could fly over for an appointment the next day') and also even had access to the group CEO. Another EWC member said: 'I think that the chair has the appropriate recognition from group management and that is a critical point for the effective operation [of the EWC]'.

This 'inching forward' has also speeded up over the years. What is noteworthy is the fact that the improvement has been continuous in nature.

Two factors favoured this positive movement. Firstly, from the mid-2000s, nearly all management positions had new incumbents, often much younger managers – mostly in their early-40s – who adopted a more open and conciliatory stance towards works councils, and were notable, as was reported, for their generally much lower levels of anxiety and tension. And secondly, in the wake of the concentration of the supply chain in Zurich, closer contact was forged between the steering committee and the locally-based CEO for Europe and European HR Director.

The managers in Switzerland are extraordinarily open to a particular group of us, but not in official forums, where they are not certain that discussion of long-term developments will remain confidential, because of the French members. That is a shame. (EWC chair)

Both the former and the new EWC chairs were very positive about the European HR Director (a Briton) as they were about his predecessor (also British), who has since become the global head of HR. 'Both are people who are really interested in constructive dialogue'. The former and current EWC chairs maintained ongoing contact with these two individuals. 'It's all based on a high degree of trust. I can call both at any time and ask a question, and I'll get a more or less honest answer. They might say, that's just between us, please don't use it, but this is just so you know. And – it works' (new EWC chair, H.) One positive development was that even the then European head (a South African) was included in this assessment. Although not the direct interlocutor on an everyday basis, 'he often is in discussions with us – he is someone who I can just call up'.

What is notable about these statements is that both the former and the EWC chairs are able to hold personal and confidential discussions with top managers without the need for interpreters, albeit not at the high level of linguistic accomplishment of managers, including those without an English mother-tongue background. This willingness of the German principals on the EWC to engage in language training, for whom competence in English is not a given in the way that it is for colleagues from the Netherlands and Scandinavian countries with their strong cultural orientation to foreign-language learning, has been an important aspect in explaining the EWC's level of transnational activity. However, despite the desire of both sides to draw closer together, a degree of caution, hesitancy and uncertainty has certainly remained – hardly surprising in view of the previous hostile stance of management towards European employee representation.

One of the main reasons offered by all the members of the steering group we interviewed as to why the current crop of managers was generally more open to engagement with the EWC than their predecessors was, along with the generational aspect, an entirely utilitarian consideration: they needed the EWC, they acted in their own enlightened self-interest as they recognized that, given the never-ending process of rationalization in the context of the new strategy of centralization, matters proceeded better with the EWC rather than in opposition to it. For example, the Dutch member of the feedback group noted: 'Restructuring would be very difficult, including for them. And they want us to offer our views. Yes – they need us'.

In addition to those factors promoting the relationship between the EWC and management, there were also a number of new constraints, and in particular the practice – now elevated to a philosophy – that managers should be replaced every three years, too short a time to develop genuine trust. Previously, it was customary for managers to hold their positions for ten years or more. During this period, the EWC chair G. was able to establish a close relationship with the European head of HR and, in particular, to the HR manager responsible for the European manufacturing operations. 'In my experience, we were able to develop a good relationship, although this took some time. It was different before; then they stayed for ten years or more. The company no longer wants to operate like this'.

The most emphatic about the change in management's perspectives was the British deputy chair, D: 'Most top managers nowadays have a social conscience. This can be a matter of cultivating an image, but if the image is wrong than they have lost twice over – once in terms of their credibility, and secondly their social standing. I think that this is a substantial issue. They have begun to look at the social side, even if it has taken a long time'.

He also testified to a wholly unexpected shift in the stance of the new national management in the UK.

> They now really try to consult us EWC members, but they do not know exactly how to go about it. They try very hard to comply with the EWC Directive through early inclusion of the trade unions, much more so than before. They explain their problems to us, and they tell the unions what the issues are much earlier. The old-style Unilever management is a thing of the past, the company is changing, changing its attitudes. It recognizes its obligations where the legal position has changed. Unilever will not act against the law. They are less antagonistic towards the unions than before. The manager (HR head of Unilever UK) is really an active participant in the national consultative forum. The company puts great stress on direct interaction with the people in the plants, as is usual in Germany and Holland.

Given the background of traditional industrial relations in the UK, this would appear to be a 180° turnaround.

The national-level and local works council members that we interviewed in Germany, the Netherlands and the UK all reported a constructive relationship with their current local managements. One German local works council member, who is not an EWC member, said:

> The managers here are all non-Germans. But we have a very good relationship. The plant manager includes us at every stage, and that's exemplary, really good. They operate the Works Constitution Act better than some German managers. I can always ask him what's in the pipeline, whether he knows what's coming up for

us – we have a good relationship. As a result, I can often find out here at the plant whether he knows a bit more about what the future direction might be. And I can send this up the line to the chair of the EWC to raise awareness of the issue, and any danger it might imply nationally and at European level. That is one option for including us in the EWC.

These positive assessments of local industrial relations are, admittedly, unsurprising given what we noted above: close and trust-based cooperation at this level is part of the Unilever tradition and a core aspect of the highly decentralized corporate structure that prevailed until the late-1990s.

In general, personnel management at Unilever, both at country level as well as group level, enjoys a fairly high standing. The new EWC chair, H., noted:

> HR management at Unilever has traditionally been more important than at other companies. I've noticed this again here in Hamburg (German Unilever head office) in the search for a new Labour Director for the D-A-C-H area (German. Austria, Switzerland), where our Dutch chair told me that he did not understand why German HR managers are all administrators rather then shapers. And here at Unilever, also in Germany, it was the tradition that HR was relatively influential.

KRAFT FOODS

As with Unilever, management at Kraft Foods was also initially unwelcoming to the EWC. However, there was one exception, which proved to be a stroke of good fortune: the then European head of HR was a Swede, familiar with participative arrangements from his home environment. Over time, a very strong and trusting relationship was forged between him and the Norwegian EWC chair, based on their common Scandinavian origin. This proved very propitious for the development of the EWC during its early years. Ms. B. describes the situation.

> The HR head was a Scandinavian, like me. He had a great deal of sympathy for employee representation based on dialogue. This helped convince management about the EWC, that it was necessary. He later said to me 'B. do you know that the reason why management initially rejected the EWC was not mainly because of the trade unions, but due to group management in the USA'. That is, the distrust was

so great that every tiny detail was checked by the lawyers. During the negotiations with us they did not utter one spontaneous word – everything was read off a sheet. I've actually seen copies – it literally said 'Good morning, thank you'. They just read it out, and we had to submit our questions in writing. If a new issue cropped up, they stopped the meeting, we had to leave the room, and the managers discussed amongst themselves what answer they should give us. They were so afraid! But then later, they decided to trust us.

More recently, the relationship has improved markedly as a result of the entire control of European production operations being centralized in Zurich, and the arrival of a new European head, a UK citizen, who also lived in Zurich. He was experienced by our interviewees as open and cooperative, and occasionally made time both for informal discussions with the EWC Chair as well participating in meetings of the steering committee. The usual contact for the EWC is the head of HR for all European production operations, who is also based in Zurich. He is a young American, who was also described as willing to act cooperatively and as approachable, but about whom some critical comments were made: 'He tries his best, but he does not really understand the German or Swedish style of employee representation through dialogue; he doesn't know what informing in a timely manner means. We have sometimes had problems with him. In some instances, his main concern is just with implementing a decision, not the decision-making process itself' (EWC Chair, B.).

In contrast, the relationship with the most senior European head of HR in London proved to be a difficult one, and the EWC had only sporadic contact with her. 'We don't like her. And I'd bet she doesn't like us. She doesn't understand what happens in the EWC. She only comes to our meetings if we ask especially, and then she is not interested. She talks down to us – a lot of fine words that avoid the real issue'.

The German EWC adviser categorized the basic stance of management towards the EWC over many years as legalistic:

They only do what they have to. They do not want to be pioneers; they are purely defensive. That was how it has been. However, more recently this changed. They have become positive since centralization in Zurich. They have noticed that having a European central representative body is advantageous for them within the new centralized structures. It makes things easier. In particular, they get direct feedback

from us from the individual countries, because their managers don't tell them everything. The EWC is a second channel of information to check whether what has been
decided actually takes place.

The overall impression is that management was increasingly including
the EWC in corporate processes. As a rule, it was informed – although
there are occasional differences over the appropriate time for this – and
it is consulted on HR issues. However, it has not been included, either in
the form of information or consultation, on major strategic decisions. For
example, it only found out about the Cadbury takeover at the same time
as the media. One reason cited for this was the need to keep the decision
confidential from the stock market. 'We are not called for in decisions about
such coups, but we were subsequently well informed about implementation.
They do not say to us, we have such and such plans, let's discuss it before
we make a final decision' (German steering committee member). Judged
from the perspective of German works council codetermination, both
German members of the steering committee considered that it was neither
real codetermination, nor the opposite, but rather something in between.

The German delegates on the steering committee noted the 'personal
esteem' in the context of the relationship between local and national management in Germany (mainly non-Germans):

> They value the opinions of others. That is real cooperation, *searching for commonali-
> ties*, getting a little closer; there is some common interest – namely, the development
> of the company as a whole in Europe. This only works if there is mutual esteem and
> one party doesn't block the other from the outset, which means they'll simply close
> up. This is the business of works councils, but some countries on the EWC haven't
> yet understood this in this way.

This was, in fact, a reference to the French representatives on the EWC
(not the steering committee). He continued:

> I have the feeling that management would now like to make more use of the EWC,
> including for major decisions. They regret that they still have to deal with issues on
> a national basis. For the Americans, the ideal would be for there to be just one works
> council – that would be the *non plus ultra* for them. I can talk with the EWC and

they manage that for all the countries, and then I'm done. But it would take some years before we get there.

However, the British representatives on the steering committee reported that local and national management in the UK – in contrast to British management at Unilever – did not view the EWC in positive terms: 'They don't recognize the EWC'. Nonetheless, local managers were beginning to be aware that top management was increasingly interested in the EWC. The French representative on the steering committee said on this:

> Initially, our national management did not think much of the EWC. But this has changed as they've realized that we have an impact on things. During the major restructuring projects that took place in recent years, they've seen these have consequences for the allocation of production between countries. Now that everything is decided in Zurich, they have more confidence in us and are aware that we really do work and can do a good job. They see the necessity for such an EWC.

The German representative on the steering committee interpreted management's motives in the following terms:

> Above all, management does not want any damage to the image [of the company], and they also want speedy decision-making. They have an interest in a large European unit. They've understood that if they do not behave reasonably with us, then they'll have problems in terms of time, and that costs money – an issue on which they are hypersensitive. This is also the point at which we can apply pressure and that also speeds up their willingness to cooperate. If we explain to them from the outset that we should do it together, then it's possible to construct a win-win situation, and I get them on board. In the case of our European framework agreement on rationalization, they noticed that it went really well. We laid things down on the EWC and all the countries then simply implemented it. It all ran incredibly quickly.

The steering committee meets once a month with management in Zurich, with the head of HR for production operations, and usually with managers of other European functions.

4.1.5 The steering committee from within: the protagonists in action

UNILEVER

As we have already noted, the steering committee is the focus and core of the EWC's activity. Our interviews suggested that the most important prerequisite for active and effective work on the part of the committee was the creation of emotional cohesion – a 'we-feeling' within the group – as well as the emergence of a common transnational perspective on social matters within the company.

The two key questions in this context are: have the main actors drawn closer together as people; and have they developed mutual trust? In addition, there are a number of further questions: what are authentically *European* questions and what are national questions, and what is the European responsibility and European loyalty of each member of the committee in terms of their demarcation from national responsibilities and loyalties? How does such a new view of things, and a sense of responsibility for a novel and larger whole, actually come about?

Our research established that the eight members of the Unilever EWC steering committee now look at issues through 'Europe-tinted glasses' and share a sense of responsibility for solving social problems in other countries. In short, they have developed a European consciousness. Intensive and principled engagement with problems at plants in other countries is now a key element in their day-to-day conduct as employees. This European perspective – that is, an understanding of interdependence between countries – has become a reality for these individuals.

This was by no means the case in the early years of the EWC. The UK representative noted:

> Like the EWC as a whole, the steering committee was initially a disparate group, dominated by self-interest. What's useful for me, how do I get information specifically for my plant? We behaved egotistically. Everyone was focused on their own operation and fought for extra production allocations. For us British, it was an especially difficult start. The UK representatives were not engaged in the issue, they didn't see what they could get from it. We didn't even really know each other.

In addition, there was a very serious North–South conflict at Unilever, both within the EWC as a whole and in the steering committee. The French representative on the steering committee was a committed and engaged CGT official with a militant understanding of employee representation. A good network existed between members from the Mediterranean countries. As soon as conflicts with management emerged, this group argued for immediate industrial action. All these members had personal experience in leading strikes and other actions at the workplace level. There had recently been a series of strikes, each lasting some weeks, at several French plants as well as other episodes that involved more destructive action and factory occupations. In the cases of two closures, plant managers were held captive, office equipment destroyed, and computers thrown out of the windows. This group then pressed the steering committee to 'show some bottle' and initiate similar actions in other countries – of which there was little prospect as the dominant forces on the EWC, primarily the Germans, Dutch and British, were not willing to support it.

As far as the work of the steering committee was concerned, a more important issue than such calls for industrial action was the fact that the French representative passed on confidential information to his trade union in France and to the press – often during meetings. This repeatedly led to serious disgruntlement on the part of management and the danger that the painstakingly created consultation process might collapse entirely. The EWC chair, G., was summoned to explain himself, but felt very exposed as a result of the action taken by his Southern colleagues and was extremely annoyed. Finally, this led to the adoption of a two-track approach for the steering committee: management stopped disclosing confidential information at the official meetings – which, in effect, meant that no information of significance was revealed. Important exchanges of information, on which the real work of the steering committee rests, were then diverted to another channel between management and representatives that embraced only countries in which a 'works council culture', that is a culture of confidential dialogue, had taken root. The feedback group is a product of this dual track structure.

The North–South difference is a major burden for the steering committee. In the usual course of events, such differences might have paralysed the EWC. To our astonishment, this did not happen at Unilever: in fact, the steering committee developed into an integrated and effective group with a highly-developed sense of collective identity. Our analysis below offers some explanation of why this was so.

On the differences between the countries, the former EWC chair, G., noted:

> The basic notion of dialogue is not accepted by the Southern Europeans; rather their position is – here we are, and there are you. I could call for a vote every time, but this is not good for unity. I have done this, but each time it hasn't worked. *There is a psychological firebreak running through Europe.* Our German type of codetermination is not accepted – one just has to be open about that. And this view is also in the minds of management from these countries.

On another occasion he continued on the same topic:

> We can only discuss future strategies to a limited degree as their Communist trade unions and parties immediately feel themselves obliged to pass the information along. This means that you're cautious on delicate issues. The British are very different. They have now moved much closer to our model. Managers have approached the unions in our plants and said let's discuss solutions together, and the British do it – including the unions – and we also act in a European way as the steering committee. This would be inconceivable for the French, the Italians, and the Spanish, completely unconceivable, at least for those that we have, who would go on strike tomorrow and not say 'let's discuss it'.

The British representative on the steering committee explained: 'The French have not endeared themselves by breaching confidentiality and giving information to the press on the very same day as the meeting. Management was very annoyed, and asked G. [the EWC chair] for an explanation. They threatened to pull out of the process of communication entirely'.

When the EWC chair, his deputy and the Dutch representative tried to negotiate a framework agreement on 'socially responsible restructuring and plant closures' with management, they were undercut by the Southern European cluster. 'This broke down because of the Southern Europeans. They set maximal demands: the concept of "restructuring" should not be included, as the EWC ought not to accept the fact of restructuring. They wanted nothing to change. And because we did not want to push this through against a minority, we initially dropped it'.

Four major factors have contributed to the fact that the steering committee has become an integrated group, despite the difficulties created by the North–South divide: individual continuity within the group; mutual understanding between those countries that have a works council culture (now including the UK); a strong stance on the part of this cluster towards the 'Communist friends' in the South on matters of substance, but matched by a respectful manner in dealings with them; and a favourable distribution of roles amongst the individual protagonists in the group.

The group has a high degree of individual continuity. It meets every month for one or two days of joint work. Although there are no truly close friendships within the group, there is a high degree of familiarity between members on which trust has been built. In particular, the numerous contacts that take place alongside the official agenda, such as during coffee breaks and after the meeting has finished, and during the shared dinner and drinks at the bar, where meetings involve an overnight stay, all offer scope for members to become better acquainted. The fact that the German EWC secretary speaks English, French and Spanish, and that there is no inhibition about talking very directly, contribute to creating the preconditions for a free exchange of views.

One of the two German members of the steering committee gave the following account of the social cohesiveness of the group.

> The eight representatives on the steering committee understand each other very well, have known each other for some years, and everyone knows how to get along with each other. In individual cases, this can be a problem, as we have a Communist friend from France who is in the ultra-left fraction – that's quite extreme. But he feels comfortable with us on the committee. He's also a decent individual. Despite these ideological differences, something has developed. But you cannot expect that everyone is always entirely open, and everyone behaves tactically on some issue or other (former EWC chair, G.).

> *Everything depends on personal relationships.* These have changed a good deal through our intensive work on the steering committee and in the feedback group. In the event of language problems, S. [the EWC secretary] plays a crucial role. We can sit down around a table in the evening without interpreters. This helps create a better personal

relationship, and we've come closer together as a group. The steering committee is a stable body, and the Southern Europeans are also part of this (new EWC chair, H.).

On the subject of developing a common perspective, one of the steering committee delegates noted:

> Previously, during meetings, people behaved as follows: does this concern my country? No, then I can do something else. This has changed based on our personal relationships with each other. For example, if something now were to happen in Poland, there is a statement in France on it, and vice versa. This was not always the case. Previously, if something was happening in France, the French member would make an announcement as would G., as the chair: the others would stay nice and quiet. Yes, it's very positive to report this, and it depends on having good personal relationships, and in turn that's due to the fact that, instead of meeting once a year, we now meet monthly and the feedback group more than this. It goes along the personal track, on the lines of: I like him, he's a good bloke, what he's doing can't be completely ridiculous. (Dutch delegate on the steering committee)

Personal familiarity creates trust. And this represents the bridge that spans the threatening abyss of opportunism. It is the prerequisite for cooperative and solidaristic conduct.

Both sides – North and South – have been more aware of the sensitivities of the other in recent years. The fact that the French 'couldn't keep their mouths shut' had meant that the previous EWC chair had often felt that he had been duped. One interviewee said that the new chair, who was no less concerned about this, had pursued a more proactive approach to the issue:

> Currently, management says that in the event of a restructuring 'We want to inform you officially, but you've got those French who can't keep quiet'. Then the new chair said: 'I can offer you a guarantee'. He then was provided with the information, and gave it to the committee, saying: 'I have given my word of honour, and then we will not talk about this'. There was then a long debate between ourselves and it turned out to be alright, nobody talked outside, but only because he had passed it on *beforehand*.

In particular, this approach had been proved to work because it had been discussed with the spokesperson for the Southern European cluster on the steering committee, the new deputy chair of the EWC, M. Our respondent continued, 'It was her idea that H. should commit himself in person and not with management, as the French representative did not feel any obligation towards management'. And H. himself said of the incident: 'They weren't always as respectful towards my predecessor. Perhaps I'm still wearing unearned laurels. I don't know whether it will work next time. It always depends on the case in hand'.

This incident also clearly shows that greater involvement on the part of the Southern European cluster in the leadership of the EWC, through transferring the office of deputy chair to Ms. M., bore fruit. And M. seemed able to perform this delicate balancing act. One observer commented: 'She plays a double role. On the one hand, she always says that the CGT is correct, and the workers are correct [that is, not white-collar staff, who have only weak union ties, *authors' note*], but she behaves very diplomatically in the feedback group, and does not divulge information. She tries to keep things confidential'.

Just as the Northern Europeans expect more flexibility from the Southern Europeans, and as Ms. M. is expected to exercise a double role in her area of activity, the Northern Europeans are also, for their part, prepared to take a back seat when needed. During a nine-week strike in a French plant, in which the French member of the steering committee was involved, and which included activities such as kidnapping the plant manager and damage to property, 'we [the North Europeans] tried to behave diplomatically – that is, not the Germans saying, "Hey, we don't want any of that", but rather we tried to skirt around it and the French were amazed when they realized there was some solidarity there' (German EWC member, who was not on the steering committee, describing the situation on the EWC plenary). This shows that the personal trust that had been created allowed both sides to move towards each other and cooperate, despite the major differences between them.

Ever since the 1970s, Unilever management has had, and continues to have, great concerns about militant trade union action in France and (previously) in Britain. One German EWC member commented: 'Following the events in Marseille [kidnapping of the manager, *authors' note*], management was thoroughly fed up with France. They seriously considered pulling out. I actually witnessed the discussion within management, along the lines: "We've had enough of France because it was managers who had been locked inside and threatened". But I suspect they won't really take this step because the French market is too important for them'.

Another EWC member, not a member of the steering committee, reported as follows:

> Cooperation in the plenary sessions has become much more constructive. Previously, there was quite a lot of mutual antagonism. That's now in the past. People understand each other better because they've worked together for many years and tried to do things jointly. The atmosphere's improved a lot. And management has also noticed and senses that this is helpful for their side – for example, if they want to restructure it might mean it costs them more, but they'll be able to do it with less emotional reaction.

One Dutch interviewee said, '*The "we-feeling" has grown*, and in some respects has become a friendship. Previously, countries sat in their own little grouplet. That's now broken down to some extent. If we're standing at the bar having a beer together, we're all good friends'.

Sociogram of the group

G., the German chair, was previously the leading individual in the EWC and its strategist. In this role, he demarcated the scope of the EWC – namely, the European dimension – and established channels of communication with management. He was described by colleagues as someone who, from the outset, was forceful in extracting a commitment form other members to concentrate on European issues. He introduced a certain degree of discipline and rigour into discussions, banned reports on local details and incidental matters (as he put it ironically 'Questions about why the toothpaste tube opens to the left'), and was often seen by some delegates as something of a strict disciplinarian. His priority was that the forum had to understand the company's overarching strategy and policy, and then draw the appropriate consequences for its own activities. He took full advantage of the leadership role that went with his office, setting ambitious goals for the EWC, and pursuing them with great rigour and zeal. He clearly, but diplomatically, signalled to the representatives from Southern Europe that their adversarial approach would not be greeted with universal acclaim.

This direct and determined stance did not always win him friends within the forum. Some delegates maintained a loyal, but distanced, relationship to him, as to an acknowledged, but sometimes solitary and headstrong 'boss'. He was not in any sense 'matey'. His strength lay less in socially integrating the group than in charting a course for 'Europe'. He constantly challenged the forum to take a wider perspective and develop a sensibility for the overall picture. During the final phase of his period of office, he grew increasingly disappointed with the fact that the persistence of the North–South cleavage had meant that he had only partly succeeded in his aim of concluding a number of important framework agreements. On the other hand, the success of the feedback group was down to him, and this ultimately proved to be the means for working around this difficulty.

When asked what were the main driving forces within the EWC, the current deputy chair, M., from Spain – and one of the founding members of the EWC – noted:

> It was how we worked internally, and in particular the chair, G., who always put forward very clear ideas. We had very vigorous debates and there were differences between countries. But our aims were always clear, and the guidelines also – we did not get caught up in unnecessary details, we didn't drift off the point, but we always moved forward, and we, as we said, we can thank the chair for that. Our differing mentalities and trade union cultures, North and South, led to some major discussions that consumed a lot of energy, but we learnt a great deal from this. Together we arrived at pretty clear positions towards Unilever.

The former British deputy chair, D., commented:

> At the start, the EWC was a disparate group. It was G. who brought it together, and got it functioning and working well. What was important was that the steering committee was initially small, with five members. The Germans and the Dutch took the lead, because they were familiar with how you do consultation, but they got a lot of opposition, also from representatives from the UK, because of their way of working.

Responding to the question as to who, in particular, was responsible for the EWC's progress, he said:

It was G., not him alone but largely. But some people thought he was operating his own system. He had a difficult job. [*Interviewer: 'Own system', do you mean German interests?*] No, no. He just wanted to keep to the main idea, he was very good at keeping to the essence of an argument, and leaving everything else to one side. He got us concentrating on the key things. And my English colleague, R., and me, we took care of the details and we never censored anyone if they started to talk about local details, and we both minuted it properly. G. only dealt with things that were important, and then sometimes stopped the debate if he didn't share someone else's views, and you felt overwhelmed by the chair. G. put pressure on management. He always asked for better information, with specific details on each business area, and the company did that too. Area for area. For the first time, we got a picture of how things really worked.

One of the Dutch members commented in similar terms:

> G. was the driving force. He could speak on equal terms with management and he also had a way about him that meant that management listened. He had worked with the head of HR over a long period, and the two could get along well. He was accepted by the other side. He was political in everything he did, thought strategically, and in his own way – to say manipulate would be going too far – but he always steered things well, and drew in the Southerners, despite all the frustrations he suffered. If we wanted something, then it happened, because he always had the majority behind him. But he'd always keep a bit of distance to the others. Sometimes he failed to take everyone with him, because they had the feeling, he's up there and getting on with it, we're just looking on. But he achieved a great deal, you have to say. The advantage with him was that he was very good at discussing with management, at the same level. He was acknowledged by the other side. He had access to the important people in the company.

D., the British deputy chair of the EWC, and a highly-skilled professional employee, played a different role in the group. As he said of himself, he was more of caring type and did not impose his views on others. He was fascinated by unravelling the mystery of corporate strategy and pursued understanding strategic business policy as a hobby. A Dutch representative vividly captured his role.

> D. could decipher what Unilever thought and what Unilever intended. He was an analyst, and was very good at it. But G. was the boss, and D. supported him in this role. And J. [a former long-serving Dutch representative on the steering committee]

was always arranging parties – he was the opposite of G. He was funny. You need someone like that in a group. Everyone had their role and their qualities. It was G., D. and J. who made the forum.

D. became an increasingly convinced adherent of the model of representation through dialogue, as practised in the Netherlands and Germany. He also became an advocate of this approach, which made a strong impression due to his status as a 'convert': a Briton as an ambassador for social partnership. His role in the group was to complement and support the chair, and he also contributed to the development of an overall European perspective in the group. He said himself:

> There continues to be a difficult balance between the Southern European team, which can quickly fly off the handle. They won't be told anything unless they can change it on the spot; they won't keep information back, to anyone. They just want to represent workers' interests solely and exclusively. They believe that they can protect everyone's jobs for all time, and they take no responsibility for the company. But this has changed slowly, as they're now willing to sign a document that contains the word 'rationalization' and to accept that the firm has to change. The Southerners still struggle with the wording, but they actually really prepare the background for such a document. Before they were anti everything. Now they're slowly starting to move.

The fact that group dynamics, individuals drawing closer to each other, time spent together – in short, building trust – have played a key role in the emergence of a common perspective was also evidenced by the fact that newcomers to the steering committee had not yet acquired this. D.'s successor as the British representative on the committee, who had been to only two meetings, had not spent time in company with the others and was not familiar with the processes, and did not, as a consequence, feel able to commit himself to the commonality of the EWC. He said about his role on the EWC: 'I think my role is keeping tonnage in the UK and keeping my factory in Warrington in longevity because that's what I'm elected to do: to safeguard my fellow employees here'. However, he left the door open to pulling back from this fixed position in that he supposed or hoped, but did not know, that there was more common European ground embodied in the EWC as he concluded with the expression '… but I really suppose that the EWC has a value'.

Ms. M., the Spanish representative on the steering committee, was an engaged and capable trade unionist with a Southern European approach, who had built a career in this milieu and sat on the national committee of her union. She had participated in the negotiations for the installation agreement and remembered that the Germans and the Dutch had been both very supportive and influential. She was accustomed to using a combative and stirring style of speech. Her role on the steering committee was mainly determined by the fact that she served as the official spokesperson for the Southern European cluster: that is, her task consisted of establishing the link between the steering committee and national representatives in the three Latin countries. Understandably, this was a difficult balancing act, as it concentrated all the North–South differences in one person. Conceivably, for the same reason, this role also offered scope for building links and reconciling these differing perspectives, and Ms. M. decided that this was her particular challenge. Although deeply embedded in the Southern European milieu, she also saw her role as that of a bridge-builder and, based on this, played a constructive and important role in the steering committee. In order to integrate the Southern Europeans more closely into the EWC, G., the tactician with a grasp of how to use power, also 'dealt adeptly' with this and helped consolidate Ms. M.'s status in the forum as a member of the feedback group and deputy chair of the EWC. This also serves to re-emphasize that one of the great strengths of the steering committee was that it did not avoid the issue of its internal 'firebreak', but rather accepted it and learnt to deal with it through lengthy discussions and exploring differences, and, as a result, was able to mitigate its impact. The cohesion of the group, which developed an internal culture of open debate and managing differences, was seen as having a higher priority than clinging to some notion of a 'one best way'. Members have developed respect for each other. For example, Ms. M. has nothing but praise for G.'s ability, as EWC chair, to act when needed to curtail certain discussions in order to construct an overall European perspective.

> Of course, the chair did not decide everything alone, but it's helpful, if there's a chair with clear ideas, and who doesn't allow the key issues to be lost sight of. We have come to decisions after long debates, and it's not easy to put together a German

character with a Spanish, French or Italian mentality – but these differences have in fact welded us together, and it was clear that we wanted a steering committee in which all trade union cultures were represented. And we have achieved that ... We have to make sure that our national concerns are raised, but we also have to retain a European view of things, we have to speak as Europeans. It would be a mistake simply to represent national interests.

Ms. M's ideal has been to link the advantages of both these cultures of representation.

> In France there was a restructuring. The employees kidnapped the boss for a day. This was naturally a shock for the Germans. The French were severely criticized, but themselves regarded the action as an achievement. One can ask, OK, kidnapping – maybe not such a great idea, but why do the Germans have to be so shocked? The French did actually achieve something. And one could then ask: why wouldn't the Germans use a tactic like that if it achieved something?

However, she also understood that the Germans would not embark on a strike quite as quickly. Following the protests in Rotterdam, she said:

> Of course, it would have been nice if each country could have gone on strike for an hour. But you have to understand if it's said that the law forbids that in Germany – you can't just go on strike for an hour. The French can put a plant out of action and demand an account from management, but that just won't work in Germany: that is, we have to stay as one, we can go so far and no further. [*Interviewer: Is the present situation on the EWC a mix of Northern and Southern culture, fifty-fifty?*]. It's difficult to answer that without oversimplifying. I would agree with the view that the Nordic culture puts more emphasis on dialogue and the Southern more on rebelliousness and insubordination. But there is no disrespect in the EWC and we've all learned from this, and we all back the need for dialogue. On the other hand, one can't get anything through dialogue alone – and in that sense we've made a contribution. It is important to bring these elements together, and that's enabled us to make some progress.

Whereas the EWC chair, G., sees the firebreak ultimately as a constraint, when looked at from the standpoint of the efficiency of representation, Ms. M. regards it as a factor that helps promote the activity of the EWC when considered from the standpoint of the need for a more syncretic approach.

The particular role of both the former and current Dutch representative on the steering committee consists in injecting the home-advantage of the company's parent country into the EWC. 'I am in the same office block in Rotterdam as the general manager for Europe and, if necessary, we'll go and have coffee together. He is very open. If something has to be resolved quickly at head office, then we'll do it – the Dutch'. The interviewee stated that he had such a coffee meeting on average once a month. The spatial and cultural proximity of the Dutch managers and representatives at the head office also rendered them somewhat suspicious from the perspective of the Southern Europeans. They feared that the Dutch representatives were too close to management.

The new German EWC chair, H., although representing a younger generation, is an experienced European with some ten years' membership of the EWC, five years on the steering committee, and two years as the EWC secretary to the former EWC chair where he dealt exclusively with European issues. Great hopes have been placed on him, with a feeling that he might represent a new phase of development for the EWC. The extent to which he is supported can be seen in the fact that he was elected with a large majority, despite being a case of a 'yet another German' and that another country should probably have taken on the role. Previously, he had been mainly responsible for negotiating the new EWC agreement and the framework agreement on social compensation plans. He took office with a clear set of objectives: building the profile of the feedback group; closer integration of the overall forum with the work of the EWC through changes in how plenary meetings were organized (with panel discussions); raising the strategic capability of the steering committee through including external advisers; and promoting the issue of 'training and employability' throughout the company. H. has also sought to increase the participation of German works council chairs in the work of the EWC, and he tried to encourage younger works council members to consider becoming EWC delegates.

KRAFT FOODS

The eight members of the steering committee meet monthly in Zurich. As there is no EWC office with employed staff, organizational work has been carried out by the Norwegian chair, Ms. B. At the time our research was conducted, a discussion was underway about the possibility of setting up an office as well as making further changes in how the committee should operate, such as establishing sub-groups for different areas of the company, greater use of external advisers, and moving to e-communication. Similar proposals had also been on the agenda at Unilever, some of which had been implemented – a situation that the delegates at Kraft Foods were aware of and which might have served as guidance.

There had been almost no turnover in the composition of the steering committee, although the body had grown by three members as a result of the accession of Central and Eastern European countries and the takeover of LU, the cakes and biscuits division of Danone. From the outset, there was a concern to achieve a high degree of continuity and the trade unions from Southern Europe were urged to relinquish their customary policy of rotating attendance. 'We thought it important that the people spent a good period of time on it, and we rejected the rotation principle. And B. [EWC chair] and M. [German interviewee] spoke with the people in the Southern European countries and said, "That's our principle"' (member of the steering committee).

This high level of individual continuity led to a correspondingly high degree of mutual social commitment and cohesion. Five of the eight members spoke English. For the others, a 'personal' interpreter was available during meetings. Between meetings, members maintained a lively interchange via e-mail and (for the English speakers) by phone. We took part in two meetings and noted that the committee was very cohesive. The EWC chair said:

> We now have good contact between the countries. At the start, it was difficult to work together, we didn't really know what to do and how to do it ... *We got to know and trust each other.* The most important thing was that we drew closer together. We held discussions on how we could work together using examples – for example, how we would deal with the case of production being moved from one country to another.

With some qualification, these statements also applied to the EWC as a whole. One major step forward was represented by a training event lasting several days that was held in Portugal. One particular reason for the high degree of cohesiveness within the steering committee was the fact that they could speak English with each other. The fundamental significance of this process of trust building is evident in the following comments.

> It's not primarily due to differing interests. These always exist. However, if it's possible to talk about these, then you can regulate interests. *It's the lack of familiarity that's responsible for the barriers* (German EWC member).

> Building trust is the alpha and omega. If you spend a lot of time together, then you warm to each other. If you send an e-mail, you'll know the person it's going to. That creates trust. We have built trust between each other. This is due to the frequency of our meetings. And since we spend the evenings together having dinner and a drink, you get to know each other better (French EWC member).

As with Unilever, the members of the steering committee have learned to take a broader view beyond their own local situation. 'When new members join, it's always the same. You have to get them to see that the EWC is not there to regulate the details of local problems in the event of a closure – that's for local representatives – but to discuss basic positions, what our strategies are. This calls for a different perspective' (German steering committee member).

One British deputy member of the steering committee noted, in similar vein: 'In England, we now appreciate what the issues are, those that come from the European side. It's interesting to see the problems that Kraft has in Europe and how they affect us. We need to get a feeling for the problems that touch on all employees across Europe'. Trust and solidarity are mainly evident in the openness that characterizes communication between members and the preparedness to view any changes and measures taken by management at an operation from the standpoint of the local colleagues.

> Solidarity could be greater, but it's already a good deal better than when we began. Previously, when transfers of production took place no one wanted to discuss it because they said – it's good for my plant, great, and they weren't bothered about the consequences for others. Now we're more open about things. The steering committee is more open. There's more trust (EWC chair, Ms. B.).

In terms of having a wider perspective, beyond members' local situation, one German delegate on the committee noted:

We should really see the EWC analogously to the company's European strategy. You have to be able to take off your national glasses. I am Kraft Foods Europe. Although I have a national responsibility, the business is a European one. It's also a matter of conscience. I get my legitimacy from Germany, but I can't cut out the European heart because that is the future. This can put you in a dilemma. Of course, I have to try and secure jobs in Germany, but only in a way that's sustainable for Europe as a whole. If the business is becoming more European, then I need to see how I can take my country with me, how I can integrate it, and make sure that, at some point, we become an integrated European whole that has the power to influence decision making by being at the same level as the company.

This respondent thought that the younger generation would develop such a perspective more quickly.

In response to our explicit question on solidarity, he responded: '*Solidarity is reflected in the issues that we deal with jointly as these are the basis on which solidarity grows*, it develops through this, and one has to look after it and nourish it. A European perspective has now prevailed within our steering committee'. Matters were not seen as having advanced as far in the EWC as a whole, as there was less scope for members to get to know each other on such close terms. 'On the steering committee, the situation is different, and there are fewer inhibitions in terms of phoning and e-mailing. The dynamic is good'. His vision for the future was that the EWC should acquire full codetermination rights, including on issues such as the allocation of production volumes.

The North–South difference is not as evident in the steering committee and EWC at Kraft Foods as it is at Unilever. Although the French members are swift to call for a strike in their own country – 'remorseless, inconceivable for us, totally crazy, it just doesn't seem to bother them' (German member of the steering committee) – they do not demand the same of the EWC.

Sociogram of the steering committee

The leading figures on the steering committee when our research was conducted were the Norwegian chair, Ms. B., the French delegate, Ms. I, the German standing advisor, Herr. M., and, until shortly before, the Austrian delegate Ms. C., who subsequently left. These four constituted the driving force responsible for the impressive developments observable at the EWC.

Ms. B., who had previous considerable experience in a range of union roles at national and Scandinavian level, was a very engaged chair with a high capacity for integrating members. Her main concern had been to ensure that all EWC members were included in the flow of information and that good contacts existed with them. She was both the leading figure in and soul of the steering committee. Not someone who set out to dominate, she radiated care and concern and who was tenacious in pursuing grievances.

B. was one of the founding members of the EWC. 'I could see clearly then that employees in the countries had to work together. That is not in the Norwegian interest but in the interest of all. It was quite obvious to me to work together as we do not get information if we are alone in one country'.

Ms. I., the French delegate on the steering committee, said: 'Trust in the steering committee has grown, mainly because of the good job that B. has done. She says, "We know this transfer is good for your plant, but we are also know that it's bad for plant X. And tomorrow, perhaps the same could happen to you, the tide can turn very quickly – any plant can be affected, even large ones that have always felt secure". Her influence has helped us achieve more cooperation and cohesion'. She continued:

> B. keeps members informed and makes sure that those who don't speak English get a translation. And she has always made clear what a European question is. Initially, people said to her: 'B., can you do something for me'. And B. said 'No, that's a local problem, not a European one – you have to resolve it yourself'. The steering committee has achieved its current role because B. has held it together. She is like an information bureau. She asks management good questions, and insists on an answer, as she is particularly persistent. She also plays such a major role, as people know that she is in contact with the company's top management, that she'll fight for them. She keeps the team together and this means that trust has grown and grown.

An English deputy member of the steering committee, who had only participated in two meetings to date, was very impressed by Ms. B. 'She is very good, she doesn't mince her words, she doesn't hold back from challenging management and putting them under pressure. She works very well with M. [the German EWC adviser] and gets a lot of advice from him.

She really coordinates everything very well. I would not want to do all the things that she does'.

The German members of the steering committee had a similar view:

> She is a boon, she understands the other countries, she is interested in international matters, she speaks good English, she does not think that the world can profit only from the Norwegian example, she brings people together, she takes the most pains, she maintains good contacts with everyone between meetings, she is the hub, she has taken care of everything in her quiet way over the years. The larger countries have never considered taking on her job. She is a stroke of luck. Such a job is very dependent on the individual – and we've been lucky in that.

That is the general view of Ms. B. within the committee.

The French delegate Ms. I., also with good English, was another driving force on the steering committee, and she and Ms. B. had become good friends – an alliance that also embraced Ms. C. from Austria – leading to a true concentration of 'women's power' within the institution. Ms. I. coordinated the eighteen French plants and was also the spokesperson for the Southern European cluster (France, Italy, Spain). She said: 'If a particular project is imposed in France, then I'll pass the information on to all the others and ask whether they have the same project. This takes time. I'll listen out for rumours and if I here anything, I let Ms. B. know right away'.

Ms. I. was a very proactive force on behalf of the EWC. Following the takeover of Cadbury, for example, she initiated contacts with representatives of Cadbury plants in France. A consistent and energetic representative, she does not entirely fit the cliché of a French trade union militant.

The German EWC adviser, Mr. M., also played a key role. He is a senior official of NGG and the official union adviser to the Kraft Foods EWC. His actual role and significance, however, extended far beyond this: in practice, he served as B.'s permanent academic and professional adviser and represented the strategic and analytical mind on the steering committee. He and B. formed an accomplished team, and were in almost daily contact by phone. B. noted: 'M. is very important for us: he negotiated the agreement with us. In particular, the company respects him. They often ask – "What does M. say about this?". He is a great support for me.

Although I do the job, he is active in discussions with me. He keeps us all together – he plays a very positive role'.

Other steering committee members also played a constructive role in cooperation with this core team, but local commitments meant they were unable to devote more time to European work. The two main desires for improvement in how the EWC should work expressed by our respondents were the establishment of an EWC office to support and relieve Ms. B., and local plant visits by steering committee members.

4.1.6 What is solidarity?

As noted above, our interviewees understood 'solidarity' *primarily* as solidarity-in-struggle: mass strikes and protest actions in support of plants in crisis in other countries – none of which took place at Unilever or Kraft Foods. All respondents agreed that the EWC could not organize large-scale protest actions and solidarity strikes on its own and needed the help of national and European trade unions. The German interviewees thought that their trade union would not participate in such activity.

The repeated strikes that took place at the French operations did not lead to protest and sympathy actions in other countries. Most representatives from Northern Europe regarded these strikes as too radical and as an inappropriate instrument. They waited until it had blown over and, at most, sent a diplomatically phrased note of concern. The French also had not expected to be supported by large-scale protest actions in other countries. One German interviewee at Kraft Foods stated: 'Conversely, the French wouldn't go on strike for us. In order to organize an action across Europe it would have to hurt all the operations, it would have to affect everyone in some form or another. And here there is no central trade union direction, there is a vacuum'.

As with Unilever, the benchmark and model was represented by GM Europe (Opel), where the EWC was seen as being able to manage these issues so well because everyone was suffering, and everyone was affected. In the case of Kraft Foods, headcount reductions were being pursued at a much slower pace, with ten redundancies at one plant and twenty at another. Our respondents noted that it was much harder to mobilize people under these circumstances.

Secondly, our respondents also associated solidarity with compliance with the code of conduct that the EWC had set itself a number of years before. This required that, in the event of transfers of production, the works council at the receiving plant ('winner') should delay the start up until the relinquishing plant ('loser') had successfully concluded negotiations on a social compensation plan. However, as already noted, this code was not always adhered to. When a Unilever ice cream factory was on strike in Italy, and management transferred production to a German plant during the action, the local German works council had not objected. The same happened when a Dutch margarine factory went on strike, and a German plant took on the output by working a Saturday shift. In this case, the EWC chair intervened and attempted to deflect the receiving works council – but without success. More recently, employees at a French tea factory went on strike and the output was transferred to Belgium. In this case too, the reproach made by the steering committee ('Why did you do that?') were of no avail. If two plants are in direct competition, it is unlikely that the code will be kept to. In contrast, one positive example at Kraft Foods was the transfer of cheese production from Spain to Belgium, where local Belgian employee representatives held back from accepting the new allocation until a satisfactory solution had been achieved in Spain.

The new English representative on the steering committee responded to the question as to whether there was solidarity between the countries as follows: 'In honesty, I sit there as a UK trade union rep. Solidarity is an ideal principle. With regard to internal competition, I don't think you can change that'.

The previous British deputy chair of the EWC was also sceptical. 'The problem is you are not elected by the group as a whole; you are elected locally. That would be a key barrier for solidarity'.

And a German interviewee noted. 'Solidarity? Yes, it exists – for example, joint declarations, things that are made public, where representatives from other countries want to criticise a bad situation in a country. But it has limits. If two plants are in direct competition, I've rarely seen it myself that one will give something up for the other. There are winners and losers'.

The majority of EWC members also subscribed to this 'realist', somewhat diminished notion of solidarity. They were sceptical as to whether solidarity understood as workforces making a major sacrifice ('sharing the pain') was attainable within a reasonable period. This was how solidarity was interpreted and no one was really surprised about people's actual behaviour.

There are two reasons at Unilever and Kraft Foods why less might be expected in practice in terms of 'solidarity as sacrifice' than called for in theory. The first is the frequency and regularity of plant closures, which led to a degree of desensitization on the part of employees. And secondly, management has been willing, under pressure, to buy itself out of problems in the event of closures by offering high, and in some cases very high, severance pay. This effectively served as a safety valve and took the pressure off solidarity. The mood then was: in the end it was not as bad as expected. The fact that pressure for more generous social plans often originated from the EWC – a major achievement in terms of its influence – lent this a certain paradoxical character: the better the social plans secured through the coordinating and bridging role of the EWC, the less bad the consequences of a closure were judged to be.

4.1.7 The EWC and local/national employee representatives

UNILEVER

The question of the relationship between the EWC and local works councils or company-level trade union representatives encompasses a diverse range of issues. In formal terms, the EWC consists of workplace representatives, often those that play leading roles in local representative bodies, enabling a close relationship to be established in terms of formal representation. However, since by no means all local representative bodies are directly represented by a member on the EWC, a distinction needs to be drawn between operations that have a member on the EWC, and hence a direct line to it, and those that do not. In those countries in which there is a national umbrella organization for local representatives, as is the case in Germany with central and group-level work councils, this difference is not serious, as a seamless cascade of links can be established through centralization within the umbrella organization, including to operations that lack direct representation on the EWC. However, a major structural difficulty exists in countries without such arrangements: the line of communication between the EWC and local workplaces is broken where there is no member on the EWC, and the EWC cannot transmit information directly to the grass-roots. The same applies for communication in the opposite direction. This situation prevails in the UK, in Eastern Europe, and to some extent in Southern Europe.

However, for some countries the EWC at Unilever has found ways of resolving this problem, most notably in the UK where a national Unilever representative structure has emerged that has also engaged the interest of management. For the Southern European countries, a start has been made in dealing with this issue through the appointment of a spokesperson for this country cluster (a role currently held by the Spanish deputy chair, Ms. M.). This individual not only speaks on behalf of this group but is also responsible for ensuring that information flows back to plants that have no direct representation on the EWC. The advanced stage of development of the umbrella body in the UK, and the engagement of Ms. M. in her role on behalf of the Southern European countries, has meant that the problem has been fairly contained in these two contexts in terms of formal and organizational links between the EWC and local employee representatives, with a mechanism in place to ensure that minutes, e-mails, newsletters etc. reach local operations. This is not guaranteed to the same degree in Eastern Europe.

A further non-organizational, but at the same time substantive, aspect of the relationship between European and local representation is the question of the extent to which local representatives are aware of and interested in the EWC and its specific field of activity. This leads on to a third aspect – namely the question of the substance of the representative relationship: whether and to what degree there is pressure for activity from below (for example, whether EWC members raise issues for discussion locally prior to meetings and take ideas or even proposals for formal voting 'with them to Europe' when they attend the EWC). That is, what is the form and intensity of practised democracy?

We asked EWC members in some detail about this issue in each of the case-study companies as well as a limited number of local representatives who were not members of the EWC. At Unilever, we interviewed local representatives at four plants: two British and two German.

A formal provision of information to local bodies took place in most countries. In Germany, this downward flow was especially intensive as both the EWC chair and chair of the group works council, G., regularly informed the latter body about upcoming EWC issues. In addition to meetings, he also held a weekly teleconference with works council chairs at the larger German plants, in which news from the EWC featured as a regular item. According to G., there was considerable interest in EWC issues, and this had grown in the recent past for a particular reason. 'They're interested because of the operational metrics I provide. They want to know: how's my plant doing, and what conclusions can I draw from the EWC information for the future of my plant. It's important for all of them that their plant is doing well'.

Their prime interest is to obtain useful information in order to enable their plant to remain competitive, with the main focus being the scope to conclude a local agreement with management to secure operations, based on the expectation that there will be a sufficiently early warning should the plant be at risk. One German works council chair expressed this in the following terms. 'If we obtain information from the EWC about general corporate strategy, it's possible to work out what that means in reality for us here. And you then have to make sure that your own plant is in good shape. You can see where the dangers might lie, what our strengths are, our weaknesses, and you can put two and two together'.

This focus on securing their own plant is not only characteristic of local works council chairs in Germany but also applies in other countries.

We observed an interest in the EWC in itself – that is, an interest in principle in greater Europeanization of employee representation – in the case of only one of the two German works council chairs interviewed for this study, and this was a function of the fact that this individual had had a close relationship with the EWC chair, who wanted to persuade him to put himself forward as a candidate for EWC membership. In this he was successful, as in subsequent interviews we discovered that he had become a member. As the representative of a relatively large plant, he also felt that he had a good chance of moving beyond the local level and becoming involved at national (group works council) and European level. In contrast, the other German works council chair, who was based in a small plant, had little interest in the EWC. He justified this initially with the argument that local matters predominated at the local level, and in particular by reference to the constant restructuring within the company ('restructuring mania'). Although this was certainly a plausible position, not only in this instance but more generally, it only touched on the surface of the issue and did not get to the core. This core issue was raised by this individual themselves at another stage in the interview:

> In principle, the EWC ought to be important for us, especially following the cen-tralization on Switzerland. You can't deny this. The idea is correct. But what I miss is some specific issue where I could say, here is an example of where it's had a posi-tive impact. [*Interviewer: How could this be improved?*]. Firstly, create the necessary closeness [between people], so that it's a tangible thing. I always have the difficulty that as long as I don't know people personally, then it all seems quite alien to me, and the issues are very remote. The EWC should visit plants and show its face – that would be interesting for me.

This local works councillor did not know that such plant visits were already taking place as the feedback group had not yet visited any German plants, probably because this was seen as less urgent than in other countries that were characterized by less scope for institutionalized participation.

The difference between this and the other German works council chair did not lie in any fundamentally divergent notion about representation or identity but principally in the fact that in one of the EWCs personal contact and communication had created a more direct presence for the EWC and in the other that had not taken place. Interest in an issue grows out of personal relationships, through familiarity and exchange. For one of the German works council chairs, the EWC had acquired an individual dimension that related directly to his own prospects through opening up a career perspective. For the other, who had never had any direct experi-ence of the world of the EWC, who had never met a non-German EWC

member and who was unaware of what EWC meetings were like, the EWC
was a remote and alien world.

The scope for drawing people into an issue through greater personal
familiarity is also influenced by structural considerations. One major factor
is the status and significance of a plant's works council within the overall
configuration of local operations in a country. In turn, the size of a plant
and its importance within the company's wider strategy also exercises an
influence, as do succession issues. For example, at a third German plant,
a generational change in the leadership of the works council was imminent. The current office-holder had been grooming a young works council
member for this role and he also wanted him to succeed to his membership
of the EWC so that the plant would continue to be directly represented, a
matter of some prestige amongst German works council chairs.

Contact between 'normal' local works council members and the
EWC, and their interest in it, also diverges to a considerable extent from
that of works council chairs, who are themselves members of the national
umbrella organization or, in the case of the Southern European countries, are the addressee for information in the cascading arrangements.
EWC members from all the countries reported that the interest of colleagues who were active only locally was minimal. 'They don't know much
about the EWC, the issue is a remote one. Their interest is low' (French
interviewee).

> The interest in the EWC on the part of colleagues on the works council is not much
> greater than in the workforce as a whole. Three or four (out of fifteen) are interested
> from time to time and ask me what news there is from the EWC. I report after each
> group works council meeting locally and also on matters from the EWC. I always
> say: Europe's where it's happening now, more and more. But I've had no success with
> this as there is a lot of discontent. They say 'What does Europe want to talk us in to'
> (German local works council member).

> There is some interest in a few cases, but not for the majority (British interviewee).

The significance of the EWC for local representatives depends to a great
degree on their local scope for action. This question is much more difficult
to answer than appears to be the case at first glance. On the one hand, it is

evident that decisions are being made less and less by local/national management and increasingly by central and European management. 'Zurich', as the byword for centralization at Unilever (and Kraft Foods), is clear proof of the correctness of this proposition.

On the other hand, local works councillors also advanced a proposition that, initially, appears hard to reconcile with this. The same works councillor who said, 'In principle, the EWC ought to be important for us, especially since the centralization on Switzerland – you can't deny this', also noted:

> Although Zurich puts its stamp on things, how we resolve matters internally is an issue for us here at the plant. Personnel management is often granted quite a good deal of scope. We also have some levers we can use locally. There are some opportunities to make use of codetermination, to refuse overtime, threaten the company that we'll refer issues to compulsory arbitration and so on.

This was also confirmed by other local interviewees, suggesting that HRM still enjoys some of the scope for local decision-making that prevailed under Unilever's former decentralized philosophy. It also corresponds with the observation made by the new EWC chair, H., that HR management continues to enjoy a high standing within the company. This undoubted substantial vestige of local autonomy on personnel issues should be seen in the context of the marked trend for local employee representatives to conclude plant-level pacts to retain operations (at least in Germany, the Netherlands, and the UK). For example, the same German works council chair explained:

> The workplace interest has the highest priority for our own local management and for us. We want to ensure that the plant keeps going. As the works council, we have chosen this path rather than the contrary position that blocks everything, as we know from experience that there are cases of sister plants in Germany that are no longer there. You can conclude from that that the path we've adopted is not the worst.

And the works council chair of another German plant said: 'As the works council, we've also made sure that the place is in good economic order – together with management'. For him too, the nexus between the works council and local management had the highest priority. The key issue was to ensure that the chair of the works council was taken seriously by management as a partner for discussion. 'There are works councillors that are not regarded as having passed the age of majority by management, and they don't get any information'.

We also asked EWC members and local representatives about *employees' interest* in the EWC and their inclusion in the process of European representation. The view in all countries was very sobering. One typical observation was as follows. 'There is no perceptible interest. They know that I am the EWC and that's it. That is, this just isn't a topic of interest for them. What they are interested in is whether the plant is secure, and that they get paid' (German works council chair). 'You sometimes wonder whether you should say something about the EWC at works meetings, but you then only refer to it in passing because you don't want to bore people' (another German EWC member).

All local works council chairs at Unilever in Germany also raised the issue of the EWC at works meetings. However, due to the only moderate interest shown, this usually took the form of a simple formal reference for the minutes.

In Germany and the UK, we also conducted interviews with ordinary Unilever employees on the topic of the EWC, and found the same situation in all cases. Interviewees knew nothing more about the EWC beyond the fact that it existed. They had nothing to say about what it did and what it represented. The whole issue was literally outside of their experience and did not generate any hopes, speculations or wishes about transnational representation. One typical response from an English manual employee was as follows:

> [*Interviewer: 'You have heard of the term "European Works Council"?'*]. Yeah.
> [*Interviewer: 'What do you know about them?'*]. Not a great deal. I just know that
> my best colleague [shop steward, *authors' note*] goes on it, and I think all the senior
> stewards feed into it. So, rather as far as I know, it is a more a roundabout of what's
> going on in Europe, where the tonnages are, I don't know. [*Interviewer: 'You know
> that because you are in a close relationship with your colleague?'*]. Yeah. [*Interviewer:
> 'Would you be interested in developing a better understanding?'*]. Yes.

Even this employee, who was a friend of the British EWC member and had considerable scope for obtaining information, knew nothing beyond this. The notion that there might be pressure for transnational representation from the grassroots would seem to be a rather idealized one.

4.1.8 Trade union federations and the EWC

UNILEVER

At Unilever, the relationship between the EWC and trade union federations was a delicate topic as management had rejected any role for trade unions at group level, vehemently opposed the introduction of an EWC, and has continued to refuse to allow external trade union representatives to attend EWC plenary meetings. National and European trade union federations are not involved in the EWC process. The Germans noted that they received barely any support from the NGG (German foodworkers' union) and IG BCE (mining, chemical and energy union), but have also not called for any. The Dutch and French said the same of their respective trade unions. There is no intensive and well-articulated structure for support and advice comparable with that enjoyed by German domestic works councils. Representatives from all the countries commented that their national trade unions are very underdeveloped as far as European cooperation is concerned. In particular, according to our respondents, in countries that did not have a dual system of representation, based on a separation between works councils and unions, but rather a monist system, with unions strongly rooted at plant- and company-level, national trade unions viewed the EWC very critically as unwanted competition. The statements made about the two European Trade Union Federations (ETUF) responsible for Unilever, EMCEF and EFFAT, were no less sobering: support had neither been provided nor requested.

One exception was the organization of the protest in Rotterdam in 2007. This was strongly backed both by a number of national trade unions as well as the two ETUFs, without whose help the event could not have taken place. However, this was a one-off occurrence that did not lead to any deepening of mutual relationships between the EWC and trade unions.

An entirely different question relates to the extent to which the conduct of actors on the EWC is motivated by trade union considerations. All members of the steering committee and nearly all members of the EWC were trade union members and active in their national organizations. This not only applied for the Southern European and British representatives, who were workplace officials for their organizations and had a strong trade union identity, but also for the Dutch and German representatives, who operated on a statutory basis and were formally independent of trade unions in these roles. The level of union density of manual employees in German and Dutch plants, primarily a result of the activity of works councils, was generally above 50 per cent and in some cases 80 per cent. Despite the diversity of ideological positions between countries, trade union identity constituted an important nexus linking the members of the EWC. Most of our interviewees wanted national and European trade unions to be more involved in the EWC's work. In particular, on the issue of 'solidarity' – understood to mean solidarity-in-struggle – their prime point of reference was trade unions.

As already noted, the openness of top management to contacts with trade unions has been a challenging area. However, some change did appear to be emerging from a quite unexpected quarter, namely the International Union of Foodworkers (IUF). In 2010, the first discussion took place between the new CEO, Paul Polman, and IUF officials. The occasion for this was a major conflict between Unilever and the Indian and Pakistani trade unions for tea plantation workers. The company has considerable influence over local political and administrative arrangements. In the past, it had broken up trade union meetings using the police, locked out 700 union activists, and pressured the workforce to join a company union for which it levied contributions. This led to a campaign by the IUF ('Liptons Tea') against Unilever, in which the company was forced to meet the federation.

After the first meeting, regular contacts were agreed between Unilever and the IUF. The chair of the EWC, H., also took part in the first meeting – a step criticized by some national trade unions in Europe, who made very negative comments, as they regarded the EWC as competition. When H. proposed establishing a World Works Council at this meeting, this was rejected by national union representatives.

This *rapprochement* at global level led to the EWC's taking the initiative to establish such contacts at European level: 'We said to Unilever that we did not understand that you are talking with the IUF at global level but not at the European trade union level, and we always thought that industrial relations in Europe were so much more progressive'. In response, Unilever stated that regular contacts with EFFAT and EMCEF should take place, and include the EWC. At the time of writing, the first meeting was imminent. However, some members of the steering committee warned that these meetings should not represent a parallel arrangement to the EWC.

Our interviewees also argued that one reason for the weak presence of the two relevant ETUFs was mutual competition: they had a 'spikey' relationship that had led to a fragmentation of union activity.

4.1.9 Summary

Both the EWCs that represent this pattern of solidarity represent working bodies with a capacity to engage with and influence management. Their main achievement consists in the fact that, after a protracted process, the steering committee has been able to secure recognition by central management as a discussion partner. There is an institutionalized procedure for dealing with transnational matters, in which the steering committee sees itself as a counterweight to management on issues of corporate policy and strategy and is able to articulate employee interests in a consistent fashion. Management, which was initially hostile to the EWC, has since acknowledged the value of a central instance for representing workforce interests at European level that actively seeks involvement with the company, not simply as a supplementary means for asserting its own production strategy in a top-down manner but primarily to coordinate and rationalize complex and diverse local consultation procedures. As such, the EWC offers an opportunity to accelerate consultation procedures in the company.

The steering committee is characterized by two main features: high internal organizational capacity *and* strong social integration. The individuals concerned have remained members over a substantial period and invested a good deal of time and personal engagement in their role. They meet frequently and regularly, and remain in touch between formal meetings. The main topics dealt with by the EWC are the large number of factory closures and disposals, transfers of production, and workforce reductions, often attributable to rationalization. The EWC cannot prevent closures and disposals of plants. Its main strategy has been to conclude well-resourced social compensation plans or, in the case of disposals, to ensure that previous terms and conditions can continue under the new owners. The EWC is both very assertive and effective on these issues, and, in view of the frequency of such events, the need for a European representative body is high.

Although the EWC is not the negotiating partner for social compensation plans, which are negotiated locally or nationally, it does coordinate the process, informing local employee representatives about the applicable standards and pressing management to communicate with local representatives where negotiations are held up. Its particular role lies in adeptly linking the stronger formal participation rights enjoyed by local representatives – as compared with its own – with its own scope for information and consultation at central level: that is, with its pan-European perspective and contact to central management. 'One can get a good deal achieved with the EWC if you tackle things properly'. The issue is for local and central representatives to play each other the ball, as it were, and link the two levels.

This represents an added-value, not only achieved as a result of the efforts of the steering committee members but also acknowledged by 'ordinary' EWC participants, who, as a rule, meet only once a year.

Both at Unilever and Kraft Foods, members of the steering committee have developed a common European perspective on how representation should be handled within the group, in which the focus is on transnational European issues. Where members do become involved in the resolution of problems in countries other than their own, they demonstrate a transnational co-responsibility. The critical element is developing an understanding of cross-border linkages within the company. Although the high degree of internationalization and centralization in both companies has meant that this has now become a necessity, the steering committee was initially much more particularist in orientation. The development of a common perspective was the result of time spent together and the successful constitution of the steering committee as a group with a capacity to take action.

The secret of success in such instances is the process of group formation. The absence of a single hegemonic force has been central to this as it meant that there was no typical home-country effect. Although no individual country dominated the others, it was nevertheless the case that the larger countries naturally had a greater weight within the body. The high level of resources enjoyed by the German contingent, together with their extensive experience in working within a consultative framework, meant that they tended to occupy the role of *primus inter pares*. At the same time, in both cases the chair developed a strong and legitimate leadership role, and enjoyed considerable personal authority.

In both instances, EWC chairs had been in office from the outset up until the time when our research was conducted (some 15 years). They were pioneers in Europeanising employee interest representation in their companies, always advocating a strategic perspective and making a decisive contribution to defining the specific competences of the EWC through convincing other members of the need to focus, firstly, on transnational questions and, secondly, pursuing results-oriented dialogue with central management. With a number of other key figures, these two chairs constituted the active core of the steering committee and represented a coalition of the 'doers'. In this context, personal characteristics and factors played a significant role. The protagonists were individuals who had invested a great deal of time and energy in the EWC, were convinced of the value of Europeanising interest representation in their companies, and who had found a positive way of working together that, in large part, rested on an interplay between different contributions and roles within a division of labour.

Over the years, awareness has emerged of a norm for what properly constitutes European representation. This does not mean that conduct always corresponds with this norm; rather, any sanctioning by the majority of steering committee members of members who breach solidarity, such as issuing a warning or setting out the consequences, serves as an indicator that help is needed. This has been an important step towards institution-alising the relationship.

The close interpersonal relationships that have been built over many years of group formation are the key to the emergence of solidaristic links. Individual familiarity, common experiences, and in particular the sharing of critical moments and conflicts are the basis for the growth of trust, and this, in turn, is the foundation on which solidarity can thrive. It is indisputable that the degree of Europeanization that has been achieved would not have been possible without cooperativeness, pro-social behaviour and mutual support – that is, without solidarity between the members of the steering committee. The significance of the emotional and affective constitution of the group can scarcely be overestimated.

What type of solidarity can be discerned in these two case studies? The prime form of solidarity in this instance is solidarity as a workplace citizen – that is, practically securing legal entitlements to information and consultation vis-à-vis central management. The protagonists are not pri-marily motivated by material interests but rather by a desire and demand for recognition as citizens with rights in law, not simply, as previously, at national level but also at the level at which the power of central management is located. The main impulse propelling the protagonists is their awareness and experience that the status of being such a citizen, enjoyed at national level for some decades, was being undermined by the centralization of decisions at European level, which therefore needed to be complemented by establishing a corresponding level of employee representation. The core issue is, therefore, achieving the appropriate correspondence of levels.

Securing this in the face of opposition and delay required the construc-tion of a capable and organized counter-pole to central management. For the EWC itself, this meant demanding and obtaining the status in reality that it was accorded in formal and legal terms. This necessitated exercising power, which in turn presupposed constituting a group capable of taking action, including the requisite group (and organizational) discipline. Both instances provide an impressive illustration of the extent to which the process of group constitution rests on the emergence of group solidarity and a sense of reciprocal obligation that can generate the required trust.

The ultimate aim of a capable representative body with rights to information and consultation at central European level is, of course, a more effective assertion of employee interests. Both these cases illustrate that this turns primarily on the interests of employees' own plants – and specifically, i) scope for obtaining better redundancy terms in a social compensation plan than could have been negotiated at national level alone, ii) securing an opportunity for catching up in inter-plant competition if a plant looks likely to fail to meet the required standard (scope for remedial action) and iii) more generally, being able to use the EWC to articulate the interests of an individual plant to central management. This represents the reciprocal solidarity of '*do ut des*' (enlightened self interest). And self-interested giving in this instance does not consist in any transfer of resources but rather in not actively seeking to gain a disproportionate advantage over another party on the issue of retaining operations. In contrast, compliance with a code of conduct, which requires relinquishing an advantage that one might have passively acquired as a result of management's strategy (such as moving output to one's own plant), is the exception rather than the rule in both these cases. All our respondents made it clear that if two or more plants are in direct competition for jobs, it is not possible to persuade one to make a sacrifice for the other, and any such move would culminate in the delegate concerned being voted out of office.

All this speaks for not overtaxing the concept of solidarity in such situations. A position in which the EWC has a say in determining the allocation of production between plants, comparable to that aspired to by the EWC at GM, would not be realistic in these two cases, at least for the foreseeable future. The main reason is that, as yet, actively playing plants off against one another has not reached the level of intensity found at GM, where employee representatives are actively egged on to engage in strategic mutual undercutting in an open struggle to obtain production commitments.

The context as far as activity is concerned is as follows. In both instances, perceived interdependence and the concomitant impulse to create an effective EWC depend on two structural conditions. The first is the high degree of centralization of the group's organization and management – that is, the establishment of a strong central power over individual plants, and in particular within the central office managing the supply chain. This advanced form of centralization of operational management has been the principal factor fostering a feeling of interdependence. The second is the high degree of corporate internationalization, with operations distributed across many European countries and without the formation of any evident centres, or deep roots in any one country. And since both companies are engaged in producing products for mass consumption, the distribution of employment, and hence seats on the EWC, broadly corresponds with countries' relative populations. EWC seats are assigned to the five large Western European countries in roughly equal measure, with a further fifteen smaller Western European and a growing number of Eastern European countries. This pattern of representation has prevented employee representatives from any one country becoming dominant within the EWC (home country effect) and also created the scope needed for the EWC to acquire its own autonomous influence.

However, in practice one of these five large countries, Germany, has acquired the role of the main guarantor of the EWC process, not because of the slight numerical advantage it enjoys in terms of seats but rather because of the more plentiful resources available to its members and the high level of professionalism of the national works council.

For workforces themselves, and even for the bulk of local employee representatives, the EWC remains an abstract and remote institution that acts far away from everyday life at work, and to which there are no living links. The members of the EWC, and in particular of the steering committee and its leading figures, are closely networked with workforces in their capacities as local and national representatives. However, their role as EWC members, and the world in which they exercise this role, remains an obscure one for most employees and local workforce representatives even in these two cases in which the EWC has been able to forge comparatively strong solidarity links.

4.2 EWC Integration with Codetermination at a German head office. Subsidiary solidarity

THE CASE OF FORD

4.2.1 Operational and industrial relations background

European bipolarity and 'walking out of Britain'

The Ford Motor Company is the icon of the car industry, whose name encapsulates the concept of standardized industrial manufacture and the integration of labour into this process ('Fordism'). This status is reflected, in turn, in the rich body of literature on the history of the company, and in particular for Europe, dealing with Ford's history in Britain, where the company was the largest industrial concern for over half a century.

The Ford Motor Company opened its first European production facility in England in 1911 in Trafford Park (Manchester), followed in 1931 by the opening of the Dagenham plant in Essex. The German plant, Ford-Werke, in Cologne was established in 1925. Although a plant had been opened in Bordeaux in 1916, the company has never been as successful in gaining a foothold in France as in the UK and Germany, the two countries in which the Ford's European history has been concentrated. This focus on just two large European countries, which has been very significant for the development of industrial relations, distinguishes Ford from the other case studies in this research. Only Sanofi exhibits a similar concentration on two countries, although the firm has not yet enjoyed such a long history.

When labour began to become scarce in Cologne during the 1960s, Ford opened a new plant in Belgium (Genk, in Limburg), close to the German border and in legal terms part of Ford-Werke. During the 1970s, greenfield plants were opened at Saarlouis (Germany) and Valencia. As far as the structure of industrial relations was concerned, this strengthened the German pillar and also added a new player, Spain, to the overall system. In the past decade, a large plant has been opened in Romania and a smaller facility in St. Petersburg. These countries and plants constitute the current European Ford world, which is still strongly marked by a long history of Anglo-German dominance, which Bordenave (2003) appositely characterized as 'bipolarity'.

Both these countries exhibited strong growth in the 1920s. The companies operated independently of each other, manufacturing their own range of vehicles for their domestic markets. Each operated entirely separately as far as product development, production organization and sales were concerned, but both were tightly controlled from Ford's headquarters in Dearborn (USA), which had to sign off on all major decisions. Up until the 1960s, this bipolarity proved very successful for the company.

The Ford Motor Company has traditionally represented a model of centralism, standardization, formalization, and a focus on adherence to rules. This was the essence of the approach of the founder, Henry Ford I, and has remained so. The structure is invariably characterized in the literature as a bureaucracy obsessed with control, pedantic in its insistence on management through internal rules, and leaving nothing to chance, with processes and mechanisms prescribed in detail, and a sprawling hierarchy with as many as seventeen levels. Overall, it is seen as capitalism's most perfectly functioning 'production machine', a paragon of organizational efficiency and a 'management shrine'. At the same time, stress is always placed on the fact that this 'machine' is not set in motion at the highest level by hired executives but by the Ford family, which retains more than 40 per cent of the (voting) equity in the company that, despite its size, is still paternalistic in many respects.

In Europe, Ford has not been able to apply its operating model entirely unaltered but has had to adapt to varied customer demands in its two largest markets, leading to an observable see-saw over time between centralization and looser control. In the view of some authors, after 1945 the relatively protected European market meant that a shift to decentralization became dominant, mainly in model development and sales.

In 1967, Dearborn inaugurated a radical change of course with the establishment of Ford of Europe, headquartered in Dagenham, which entailed a merger of the two previous poles and their integration into a global strategy. In anticipation of a common European market, development, design, the organization of production and sales were organized uniformly for the whole of Europe. Ford of Europe was the first Eurocompany in the car industry and, as such, was some years ahead of its time. For example, General Motors did not take this step until two decades later. Typical of Ford's focus on control was that despite this integration at European level, centralization took place in a very particular and circumscribed form: individual national companies were not subsidiaries of Ford of Europe but remained the property of the parent company, with Dearborn continuing to exercise direct control of European operations. Bordenave reports how Henry Ford II insisted on personally visiting all individual European plants. 'Ford's power over its European subsidiaries was very extensive, as it would be over Ford of Europe. Henry Ford II [CEO until 1979] often crossed the Atlantic in the company of his top managers, who would come along to supervise operations, visit plants and preside over important meetings ... With its bibles of procedures and instructions, the firm would acquire a reputation in control matters, often demonstrating a proclivity for efficiency achieved via the rigorous and centralising methods it had inherited from Henry Ford I. Ford of Europe was well and truly an extension of the Fordian values of integration and centralism' (Bordenave, 2003: 271).

Up until around 1990, Ford of Europe had considerable success with this approach and, at 11 per cent, had the highest return on sales of all European car manufacturers (Bodenave, 2003: 265). However, over the subsequent one-and-a-half decades the company's performance declined sharply, as did that of its parent company in the United States.

During the period of bipolarity, the British pole was larger and more important than the German. The establishment of Ford of Europe set a process in train that would reverse this, described by Bordenave as the 'shifting geography of Ford's production in Europe' and by Fetzer (2003) as 'walking out' in a massive emigration from the UK and strong expansion on the Continent, in particular through the opening of the two major plants at Saarlouis and Valencia that became the new 'productivity stars' in Ford's European world. Whilst the UK continued to be Ford's largest market (with 450,000 units sold in 2009, compared with 235,000 in Germany), the number of vehicles manufactured in the UK fell from 500,000 to 140,000 between 1960 and 2000, with a rise in Germany over the same

period from 200,000 to 1.2 million, and in Spain from zero to 400,000.
No Ford cars have been assembled in the UK since 2005 but only parts,
including engines both for Ford and for Jaguar (which was owned by Ford
between 1989 and 2008) and Land Rover (from 2000 to 2008). The UK,
once the Ford homeland in Europe, now imports Ford vehicles manufactured in Mainland Europe. As a consequence, in 1998 Ford of Europe's
management moved from London to Cologne, now the location of the
European headquarters.

Table 4: Workforce changes at Ford of Europe

	1980	2009
UK (4 plants)	30,000	7,000
Germany, of which:	22,000	25,000
Cologne	13,500	19,000
Saarlouis	7,500	6,500
Belgium (Genk)	7,500	5,600
Spain (Valencia)	8,000	6,500
Romania		9,000
Russian Federation		2,800
Total	67,500	56,400

Source: Ford of Europe, Communications and Public Affairs: December 2010.

Over the period in question, the British workforce fell by 77 per cent,
largely during the 1980s and 1990s. The reason for the unparalleled 'emigration' and the decline in Ford's UK operations was a direct function of
our own core interest – industrial relations. During the 1970s and 1980s, a
phase of intensive strike activity in Britain, Ford's UK plants were particularly affected, with knock-on effects on Mainland European operations.
Custom-and-practice provisions around the organization of production
also led to low productivity in comparison with non-UK plants. Bordenave

(2003: 86) notes that 'industrial relations greatly disrupted Ford's output', with the 'poor reliability of the British workforce' and a 'decline of the capacity to fulfil production plans without major disturbance'. Other factors also played a role in Ford's decision to shrink its UK footprint: these included scepticism about British policy towards the European Union and the issue of currency fluctuations. As a consequence, in the late-1990s, Ford of Europe moved its headquarters from London to Cologne, where its largely British management increasingly learnt to appreciate the German model of interest representation and developed a cooperative approach towards the works council.

The issue of plant closures at Ford of Europe has, therefore, been an exclusively British one until the very recent past. Up until 2012, no plant had been physically closed in Continental Europe, with one plant in Portugal sold (to GM Europe) and the plant in Bordeaux reduced in scale and transferred to a joint venture. The large plants on the Continent generally had stable employment levels. Relocations of vehicle assembly to Eastern Europe have also not been a major issue. The new plant in Romania manufactures a new model specifically developed for the Eastern European market as well as some Transit manufacture transferred from Turkey.

The main reason for inter-plant competition within a group, in particular in the car industry, is often cited as being the strategic use of parallel production in several countries, and concomitant regime competition and social dumping. This form of production allocation has not been used in Ford of Europe, a fact expressly highlighted by all of our respondents. Ford of Europe practices 'single sourcing': that is, a model is produced at only one plant (the Focus in Cologne, the Escort in Saarlouis, the Mondeo and Galaxy in Genk, the Transit and a special small car for the East European market in Craiova in Romania). Only the Valencia plant operates on the basis of parallel production for two models, the Fiesta and Focus, and therefore is subject to a substantial variability in terms of capacity usage. Ford has adopted a strategy of concentrating high production volumes in one plant – that is, few but large production facilities – and associated scope for a plant to specialize in one model (or two for lower volume models). When launching new models, the question of where it should be produced does naturally crop up, and with this competition between plants.

One central issue confronting employee representation at the company is the Ford production system, which is based on a rigorous application of lean production methods (and in particular teamwork), identification of best practices via benchmarking, and, based on this, the implementation of a globally uniform assembly system. As in most periods of its history, Ford is currently characterized by its sophisticated approach to fitting workers to the production system through selection, training and discipline.

Ford management was exemplary in showing how the success of benchmarking rested on establishing a convincing link between being 'efficient' and being 'social', rather than the converse of acting unsocially towards internal competitors and practising social dumping. This consisted in appealing to a type of sporting mentality, in which the company proclaimed its respect for distinctive local social practices and arrangements that were not only tolerated but actively cultivated.

Guest characterized the 'production model' that underpinned Ford's approach to human resource management as 'characterized by close integration with the business: thorough, tough, expertly handled and consistent practices, especially in industrial relations, and first-class systems to support "line" (i.e. production) goals and in particular to maintain continuity of production' (Guest, 1987: 508).

The key changes in company strategy at Ford of Europe in recent years were the divestment of parts manufacture in 1999 to Visteon and the placing of transmission manufacture into a joint venture with Getrag to form Getrag Ford Transmissions (GFT) in 2002/3.

History of industrial relations at Ford's two European 'poles'

The concept of 'Fordism' denotes a strategy both for production and for managing labour. This is the reason why the academic literature has not only devoted considerable attention to Ford's corporate and organizational strategy, but also to industrial relations at the company.

Between 1945 and the mid-1960s, management at Ford in Britain pursued the classic Fordist industrial relations paradigm. On the one hand, it paid above-average wages and, on the other, maintained tight control and discipline on the shopfloor, rejecting the then prevalent practice of workplace bargaining with shop stewards in favour of unilaterally setting employment standards and negotiating at company level with the trade union as a central negotiating partner: that is, managerial prerogatives and cooperation with central trade unions versus shopfloor bargaining. The company-level focus was emphasized by the fact that Ford remained outside nationally negotiated engineering agreements. This approach to company bargaining was not entirely unwelcome to British trade union organizations, inasmuch as they had an interest in preventing shop stewards from controlling pay bargaining. In the late-1960s, however, initially in Dagenham and then in other Ford plants, a body of militant shop stewards grew up, beginning a long phase of intense industrial conflict that often interrupted production, and which became the subject of several official reports commissioned by the UK Parliament and labour ministers.

This development culminated in Ford's 'walking out of the British workplace' (Bordenave). Tolliday (2002) suggested that this development in labour relations was not a direct result of the 'rigid' Ford system, but rather the outcome of contingent strategic action by leading figures both amongst shop stewards and management. Establishing Ford of Europe played a major part in this. Its aim – as already noted – was to standardize production, achieve economies of scale through single sourcing (one plant, one model), and set stringent efficiency comparisons through benchmarking in the context of incorporating Ford of Europe into the company's global strategy. Ford was the first, and most rigorous, advocate of benchmarking in the automotive industry. Benchmarking and the pursuit of best practice hit British trade unions particularly hard, as this deprived them of control over issues of working time management and skills, which were brought into line with best practice elsewhere (Fetzer, 2003: 400). This signified a major change in the objects of negotiation, and of conflict, away from customary local disputes over pay and conditions to conflicts over the adoption of working practices from other countries. This led to resistance to what British workforce representatives designated as the 'Cologne yardstick', which was also seen as a stick with which to beat the British labour force. Energy was no longer directed at resisting management but also, increasingly, aimed at the workforce and works council in Cologne, who were actively involved in the new modernization approach. Tempers reached a level such that in 1970 the British shop stewards and trade unions imposed a 'liaison ban' against their colleagues in Cologne, to which IG Metall shop stewards and works council members at Cologne responded with a protest demonstration at the plant against 'unfairness' in the distribution of investment between Cologne and Dagenham (Fetzer, 2003: 403). Such actions were repeated in the 1980s. In particular, when production of the Fiesta was stopped in Britain and transferred to the new 'yardstick Valencia', a greenfield plant, this was seen as an attack on the British workforce and representatives, who responded by calling for Ford to be nationalized and threatening to physically block imports of Ford vehicles from the Continent into the port of Southampton.

It was then clear that 'strike prone plants were in danger of losing production and employment' (Fetzer, 2003: 405). The British trade unions 'again and again pressed the company to use British production for British sales'. However, management made this decision dependent on the willingness of the trade unions to take steps against the large number of unofficial strikes.

As in Britain in the phase prior to 1970 – but not after – management also succeeded after 1945 in shaping industrial relations at Cologne to fit the Fordist strategy, which, admittedly, based on the different national context did not imply directly identical tactics. One particular feature of Cologne was that it was not IG Metall but rather the works council that negotiated on pay, and this was above the rates set out in the industry agreement. One consequence of this was that the level of union organization in Cologne was low, at 20 per cent, during the 1950s and 1960s. Within IG Metall, the Ford works councils were the strongest proponents of decentralized pay bargaining and their relationship to the trade union was a distanced one. What management had tried to achieve in Britain with the help of the trade unions, namely pacification of the shopfloor, found an institutional counterpart in Germany in the shape of the laws regulating works councils and collective bargaining. In the German case, the tactic was not to protect company-based central bargaining from shopfloor influence, but rather to minimize the influence of the external trade union. During the 1960s, IG Metall began a so-called 'Ford Action', under the leadership of the then executive committee member Hans Matthöfer and a group of social researchers in Frankfurt, to improve the trade union presence in what was in many respects a union-free automotive company, and this led to a notable rise in the level of union organization and a degree of rapprochement (cf. Wikipedia, 'Hans Matthöfer').

In the early-1970s, the Ford works council, under its left-wing chair Gunter Tolusch, experienced a period of militancy, with several unofficial strikes intended to thwart the repatriation of the high profits earned by the company to the USA. In the mid-1980s, Wilfried Kuckelkorn was elected chair of the works council. He became strongly associated with participation and involvement on the part of the works council in Ford of Europe's new benchmarking and lean production strategy, earning him the reputation of one of the early inventors of the term 'co-manager'. In this instance, Tolliday's hypothesis of the contingent actions of individual agents is probably appropriate, as Kuckelkorn became a central figure in the development of industrial relations at Ford of Europe for the next two decades, and also the founder of the EWC and its guiding spirit over the first ten years of its existence.

The old tension between the Ford works council and the trade union re-emerged with particular vehemence during IG Metall's 1984 strike for a 35-hour week, in which neither the Ford workforce nor the works council were active participants. The works council agreed with management that those employees who wanted to strike had to take the time as holiday. During the most intensive phase of the strike, Ford workers were given time-off (Fetzer, 2003: 411). At that time, the works council had just signed a productivity pact, in the form of a workplace agreement in which they agreed to minimize any obstacle to efficiency, quality and profitability as a condition for future investment.

As the current IG Metall coordinator for Ford confirmed, this has remained the essence of the script for the relationship between the works council and trade union at the Ford plant in Cologne (which also embraces the Saarlouis plant). And de facto, collectively-agreed pay is still negotiated by the central works council and then formally signed by IG Metall.

> As far as collective bargaining issues are concerned, the chair of the central works council conducts the negotiations, and that's all arranged with IG Metall. The collective agreement is worked out in detail at local level, and then put before IG Metall, and we sign it. This is the outcome of a particular history in which the direct involvement of the trade union was shut out.

There is now a more relaxed and cooperative relationship in which these 'special relationships' are accepted as a legalized historical routine that no longer provokes any animosities.

The immediate prelude to the creation of the EWC was constituted by the company's 'walking out of Britain', the unparalleled experience of the absence of solidarity on the part of employee representatives on both sides, together with a growing appreciation of the German industrial relations model on the part of the majority-British Ford of Europe management. Employee representatives from both 'poles' had had intensive, but intensively hostile and spectacularly unsolidaristic, experiences with each other that more closely resembled an inter-plant war than inter-plant competition. Having glimpsed over the precipice, Kuckelkorn set about establishing reconciliation and rapprochement. A then member of the central works council at Cologne, currently a member of the EWC, said: 'He began to build good contacts mainly in England. He travelled there himself to get personally acquainted, built relationships that meant people could call each other and have someone to talk to. By the late-1980s the path was clear to European cooperation on the employee side'. However, most of the younger German actors we encountered in our research were unaware of this dramatic prior history. Only the positive side remains as a crystallization of handed-down knowledge. One said: 'European cooperation began here before the EWC. Good contacts have always [!] been cultivated via the works councils of the European plants and a common understanding has been achieved so that one works not against each other but with each other'. Talk of 'we also had contacts to the others before the EWC' is now a standard response at Ford, implying that the establishment of the EWC did not presage any fundamental change.

From this prior history of the EWC the following are relevant for the next steps in our analysis:

1. Relationships between employee representatives at plant-level have been enduringly shaped by the two main countries, the UK and Germany. This confinement to just two dominant actors, that is the dyadic structure, was particularly conducive to the emergence of rivalry.

2. Following the establishment of Ford of Europe, European-level management continued in the tradition of the US parent company of pursuing an active strategy of company-specific industrial relations. In the UK, this meant integrating the trade union into pay setting and industrial relations to contain the influence of the shop stewards, who were seen as less reliable. In Germany, it meant setting great store by the works council and building close cooperation with it, even on pay setting, while containing the influence of external trade union organization.

3. Based on the extremely divergent experiences with industrial relations in the British and Continental parts of the company, and despite a highly centralized approach to labour relations and HRM, management had no interest in centralising or standardising industrial relations in Europe. Rather, its main strategy was to regulate industrial relations locally and nationally with the aim of enlisting plant-specific social and cultural characteristics to boost productivity. One noteworthy fact is that central European management itself sought direct contact with local employee representatives and did not leave this entirely to local management.

4. Ford's typical strategy of inter-plant competition over efficiency and productivity (benchmarking) was not primarily used as a means to practise social dumping but rather to drive continuous improvement. In this respect, of all the European car manufacturers, Ford most closely resembles Toyota.

4.2.2 *Structure and development of the EWC*

With just nineteen members, the Ford EWC is the smallest in our sample. It consists only of members from production operations, with a consequent concentration on just six countries, of which only four are in Western Europe. The UK has five delegates, as does Germany; there are three from Belgium, three from Spain, two from Romania, and one from France, as well as a delegate with guest-observer status from Russia. Aside from the British delegates, the composition of the EWC, which meets twice a year, has generally been highly stable. The formal designation is also noteworthy: 'European Ford Works Council'. It is the only example in our case studies in which the term 'works council' is used, rather than 'forum'.

The composition of the EWC does not accord with the current national distribution of the workforce, with the UK doubly overrepresented and Germany correspondingly underrepresented. The composition can be read as a sign of respect for the former importance of the UK within the company, and no one has as yet called for it to be amended. However, one of the Spanish delegates did criticize this discrepancy in our interview.

The EWC is chaired by D., the chair of the German central works council, who is located at the Cologne headquarters and who is also deputy chair of the company's supervisory board. Between 1996 and 2002, his predecessor in all these office was Wilfried Kuckelkorn. The EWC role is an auxiliary task for him, and accounts for a small proportion of his working time. Up until now, the deputy chair of the EWC has always been a British delegate.

Over a long period, the steering committee had just four members, two permanent (Germany and the UK), and two rotating (from Belgium, Spain and Romania) and met three or four times a year. The structure was changed shortly before our research was conducted, with an expansion to seven permanent members, but with a reduction in the frequency of meetings to two each year. This is the lowest frequency for steering committee meetings in our study, and is also an indicator of the fact that the steering committee cannot operate as a working body in the sense that we have used this term in our other case studies. The EWC chair noted, 'We do not undertake the operational business [of the EWC]'. The steering committee does not represent an operationally active group, and individual members are not in ongoing contact between the small number of meetings.

Routine management of EWC work is conducted by the EWC secretary, G., who is one of three academically-qualified advisers employed by the central works council in Cologne and responsible for Europe. He speaks the languages of all the countries represented on the EWC, including Romania. He also maintains contact with EWC members between meetings. He is the professional 'Mister Europe', whose role is so central for the EWC that most of our interviewees identified the EWC with this individual.

When the EWC was established in 1996, a major role was played by Kuckelkorn, a convinced European and also a member of the European Parliament between 1994 and 2004. Based on his MEP status, he was able to draw on valuable resources that eased the process of forming the EWC, such as contacts with the European Commission administration in Brussels, a professional interpretation service, and, in particular, a full-time EWC assistant. In this respect, the EWC was 'spoilt' from the outside, according to some of our interviewees. This can probably be attributed to the fact that it is still difficult to get EWC members to learn English, given the presence of helpful professionals who relieve them of this necessity. For example, the Ford EWC is one of the cases in our research with a low level of competence in English on the part of non-native speakers. Only the Belgians represent an exception. This neglect of efforts to communicate in a common language, however, serves to hamper the development of informal bilateral contacts and group cohesiveness on the body.

One specific feature of the Ford EWC is the strong formal participation of national unions. So far, four full-time officials (from Germany, the UK, Belgium and Spain) have participated as 'experts' in nearly every EWC meeting. This represents an unusually close linkage between national union organizations and the EWC. The reason for this is also unusual, as it was management who thought it desirable for the competent negotiating party for the company in the UK to be present at the EWC. In order to facilitate this, the three Continental trade unions also had to be included. This indicates the extent to which the prior industrial history of a company is so closely interwoven with how the EWC operates.

4.2.3 *Activities and representative efficiency of the EWC*

During the course of our research at Ford, we soon encountered the somewhat confusing finding that, at first glance, the EWC has deliberately, and inexplicably, constrained its field of activity. Whereas other EWCs complain that management defines as few issues as possible as being subject to European representation and as many as possible as local, in the case of Ford it is the principal figures on the EWC who pursue this approach. In fact, it is their declared aim to deal with as few issues as possible at European level. As a consequence, and when compared with other EWCs, the EWC at Ford has markedly narrowed down its daily operations and radius of action. On the other hand, in one field of activity not provided for under the EWC Directive, the EWC has an unusually strong presence and effectiveness – that of negotiating European Framework Agreements, where it is probably the most successful of all existing EWCs. It concluded the first European Framework Agreement in 1999, and since then around a dozen further agreements that regulate a number of central issues. The most important of these have been:

- Framework agreement on the divestment and separation of Visteon in 1999, in which the EWC succeeded in obtaining a number of concessions for the protection of those employees in component plants who transferred to the new company. In practice, and for the most part, these employees retained their status as Ford employees. One part of the agreement required the establishment of a committee to oversee the implementation of the agreement. This was the first framework agreement concluded by an EWC, and as such was a pioneering achievement.
- In 2002 a framework agreement was concluded on the separation of the transmission division into the Getrag Ford Transmissions joint venture, which broadly applied the Visteon arrangements.
- A framework agreement that, based on the previous two agreements, set out social standards to be applied in future divestments or separations.

- In 2005 and 2008, two framework agreements were concluded on restructuring the development division that established development volumes for the European development centre in Cologne and had a major impact on the future status of Ford of Europe within the global group.

These agreements undoubtedly represent major successes for the EWC. However, our interviewees noted that they were possibly principally because *management* wanted a single binding European solution, given the scale of the Visteon separation, and for reasons of cost and efficiency. The Visteon separation affected some 22,000 employees in Europe and 52,000 in the USA. The EWC succeeded in agreeing a common strategy in the form of a 'Declaration of Mutual Solidarity' within a fairly short time, and initially intended to negotiate jointly with the American UAW trade union, but this was rejected by management. The UAW then went ahead and obtained a favourable deal for the US workforce, which spurred on the EWC in its negotiations for the European area. The Visteon agreement was a breakthrough in terms of the recognition of the EWC as a negotiating partner for pan-European agreements. This was also formally acknowledged for future European negotiations in a 'Memorandum of Understanding' (2000), albeit with the definition of 'European' being expressly dependent on management agreement.

In view of the massive breakdown of solidarity experienced by British and German employee representatives only a few years previously, the fact that such a 'Declaration of Mutual Solidarity' became possible calls for some explanation from the standpoint of our concern with solidarity. We are unable to offer any quick answer to this, given that, as will be seen, the EWC does not currently exhibit strong or emphatic feelings of solidarity. However, it appears that the object of negotiation – Visteon – had certain features that facilitated such a common approach on purely rational and instrumental grounds, and without the need for any specific emotional foundation. The most important aspect was that the event had not generated inter-plant competition; no plant stood to gain from the separation and all only stood to lose from it (with the exception of Belgium, where there was no parts manufacture). In particular, there was neither competition in the area of benchmarking and best practices on labour issues nor over the allocation of models and production volumes. One further feature was that, given the large number of employees affected, the situation was evidently both urgent and serious. A third factor was that it was advantageous for national trade unions to be present at the EWC table, and even for contacts to exist with the UAW. What had originally been intended for quite different reasons – limiting shopfloor bargaining in the British plants – now turned out to facilitate European cooperation on the Visteon question. The fourth, and most important, factor for the success of the negotiations was, admittedly, management's considerable interest in a uniform European regulation of this mega-issue. A strong case can be made for the fact that the events at Visteon helped crystallize the role of the EWC, and that this was subsequently given formal consecration and remains valid today. This states that the EWC is there to deal with rare events and developments with especially serious negative consequences that affect all to an equal extent. However, it is not there to resolve competition between plants through applying an overarching strategy to guide decisions on model allocation. In response to our question 'Are these issues that come up every few years?', the EWC secretary G. said: 'Every few decades!'.

During the course of the prior history of the EWC, only two issues have fallen into this category: a mass transfer of jobs, which would have led to a serious deterioration in working conditions without an agreement (Visteon, Getrag); and the extremely important issue of securing of Ford of Europe as a development centre with its own scope and potential for innovation – that is, a prospect of future development that could be deployed in all the European locations. All the framework agreements concluded so far have been associated with these issues. A third 'once-in-a-decade' issue is also now beginning to emerge: that of alternative fuels and forms of propulsion, and the consequences of electric vehicles for employment levels. All national delegates and plants are aware that fundamentally new propulsion systems would not only render the company's own internal combustion engine manufacture obsolete (for example, if electric motors were built by Bosch), but also a range of associated functions. The issues this raises are by no means amenable to immediate decision, but the EWC has decided to prepare itself through organising information forums, drawing on internationally acknowledged experts on the impacts of these new technologies. What has been critical for the EWC in moving into this area has been the fact that there is agreement about the future significance of this issue within the forum and that solidarity action, as seen in the case of Visteon, would be probable should analogous events take place. 'Everyone on the EWC is fully aware that this affects us all because it would have enormous job implications' (EWC secretary).

The motto of the EWC can be reduced to the following proposition: engagement only on rare issues with major consequences, but then 'getting it right'. Interestingly, factory closures, product allocation and model transfers do not feature on this list.

The EWC secretary G. referred to the reason as to why the EWC has restricted its scope:

> Our experience was that employee representation is very different in each country, is very attached to its own traditions and has its strengths. This already means that the European scope is very limited from the outset. As yet, countries have been able to sort themselves out in critical phases, but subject to an overarching European axiom: no one takes anything away from anyone else.

A German EWC member noted:

> Most of these issues are dealt with by the plants themselves. We [that is, in Cologne, *authors' note*] also let them do this autonomously. We have a clear aim: no discussion of national topics within the EWC. We always point out if someone says something would be a topic for the EWC, then we say, 'Folks, that's really a national topic, you have to deal with it locally, we're not going to interfere because that would be fatal'. In Cologne, we wouldn't let another plant discuss our local issues. We have a clear limit. Leave national matters where they are, that's our credo. No one wants to be told what to do by anyone else on the forum.

And as with the EWC secretary G. ('No one takes anything away from anyone else'), this respondent also followed this immediately with a general, and initially indecipherable reference to another credo: 'No cheating!' Agreement on this second credo indicates that, in addition to the emphasis on autonomy and local representative strength, and alongside the notable self-denying ordinance adopted by the EWC, there is a common understanding within the institution of a European norm of solidarity. Deciphering what this means will require some further effort. However, before turning to that, we offer some further evidence for the EWC's self-imposed limitations.

Plant closures have not been an issue for the EWC, although several plants had been closed in Britain since the establishment of the EWC. One interviewee commented on this: 'Plant closures are not an issue. The reason is that all those plants that have so far been closed have been in England, and the English colleagues have not raised this issue up to the European level. They didn't want to fight'.

Similarly, model and production allocations are also not an EWC matter. Although, as our respondents repeatedly emphasized, the pressure exerted by this issue, that is inter-plant competition, is much less than at GM Europe due to the single sourcing strategy and plant specialization into particular model classes (small-medium-large), from time to time it can happen that when models are allocated, a similar situation of competition can arise at Ford, albeit in a more attenuated form than at GME. However, this problem is dealt with at Ford exclusively at local level, so that potential conflicts between plants are not fought out openly. The key term is 'local plant security agreement' or 'investment security agreement'. This 'agreement' is the main means of regulating interests at Ford of Europe. At Cologne, the works council concluded the first plant security agreements in 1994 and 1997, and the works council at Valencia the most recent. At the time this research was conducted, the works council in Genk had been negotiating on such an agreement. As yet, the plant in Romania has not been subject to any such uncertainties. Only the shop stewards in the UK have refused to conclude such an agreement. The object of these agreements is usually to regulate in detail processes for improving work organization, but also concessions on social measures and facilities. For example, the Spanish local representatives agreed to relinquish the works canteen. However, concessions on pay appear to be taboo.

The term 'local agreement' is not entirely appropriate as Ford is unusual in that central European-level management can become directly involved in local negotiations. As such, these agreements could more properly be denoted 'central individual agreements'. Local employee representatives not only sit opposite local management, which might not have powers to negotiate on the issue in question, but will also have direct contact with European management. One respondent described the course of events in the following terms:

> Local managers negotiate, but advised and controlled by European management in Cologne. Local managers will then say on particular points: negotiations are interrupted, as they have to go the phone and call up Cologne and ask them what they think. And the head of Europe will either give the thumbs up or thumbs down, and then they can carry on locally. It's very typical that someone from Ford of Europe will travel to Spain, Belgium or to Saarlouis and sit in on the negotiations. I know that even the head of Europe themselves has been to Spain.

This also calls to mind the reports of Henry Ford II's personal contacts and visits to individual plants and countries. One conclusion that can be drawn from this is that centralism does not always mean the same thing. Usually, it implies a hermetic separation between the highest levels of decision-making and the lowest levels of execution, with a cascading of control through a chain of command in which only adjacent links are in contact with each other. However, in this case, in parallel to this, and complementing it, there are shortcuts that skip the space between upper and lower levels, despite what the centralism textbook might prescribe. The basic assumption of the EWC Directive, namely that employee representatives in foreign subsidiaries do not have contact to the central decision-makers in the company's home country and need the EWC to span this gap, does not, therefore, entirely apply in this case. At Ford, when needed, the head of Europe will personally engage with local employee representatives.

One full-time official from IG Metall reported critically on the negotiations for a plant security agreement in Belgium.

> They are assembling the two large vehicles there, S-Max and Galaxy. One of those is supposed to be built in the USA as from now and the issue is to secure the future of the plant with a new model or with an allocation of another major model. There are local negotiations about this, but it's not an agenda item at the EWC, and there has been no discussion about it. You don't get involved in it. No consideration is given as to whether we could develop a European strategy to support the plant.

However, EWC members thought the current approach was the right one. They said that local representatives were strong enough and confident enough to take care of themselves.

The logic behind the functioning of this form of locally practised, but transnationally communicated, interest representation within the group is the deeply-anchored free market credo subscribed to by employee representatives at Continental European plants (but not the British). These are convinced that ultimately it is sales, the market, that secures a plant and is the basis for allocating output, and that good interest representation consists in supporting management in its efforts to succeed on this market. One EWC member confirmed: 'Management decides where an engine will be produced on economic criteria. If they want to go to Romania, for example, our task would be to make it clear, on the national side, that we can produce this engine in Cologne at reasonable cost. This is then not an EWC matter, it's national: how can we present this so that we are able to compete against a low-wage country'. This interviewee added that, for its part, management conducted itself cooperatively in relation to the EWC.

There is agreement on the EWC about non-interference on local matters together with the rule that EWC members report on current local negotiations in their countries and the outcomes of these at EWC meetings. This rule was adhered to in an exemplary way by the Belgian EWC members during their recent negotiations, as our interviewees from other countries reported with satisfaction. However, the rule was breached by the Spanish EWC members in 2009, who had still not yet reported on the substance of these negotiations, generating serious disgruntlement within the forum and contributing to the isolation of the Spanish delegates. 'The chair of the Spanish plant representation made an agreement with management without telling us anything about what had been negotiated. We were all annoyed with him' (German interviewee).

One instance of serious competition between plants occurred in the past between a British factory and the transmission manufacturing plant in Cologne. This competition was defused by local employee representatives bilaterally in a remarkable demonstration of solidarity, in which the Cologne side took on the main share of solidaristic behaviour. In order to retain the British plant, during the allocation of two new transmission models Cologne gave up an opportunity to obtain a large volume of production. One respondent described what took place:

> We agreed with the English side that one of the transmissions should go to the transmission plant in England and one to Cologne, although we in Cologne knew that the British transmission plant was less economically efficient than we were. Without us, the plant in England would have ended up being closed. It was a major piece of solidarity here to say that both operations had to be retained. It then turned out that the English plant could not operate competitively and in the intervening period we had plenty of opportunity to say 'That's enough now, we'll play the national card and sort things out with management so the English plant gets closed', it would have been possible, but we didn't do that.

This occurrence did not become an issue for the EWC, indicating that a solidarity norm had emerged in the bilateral transnational relationship between local representative bodies that one of our interviewees denoted as a 'our second credo'. This states that no one should cheat on anyone else, and not exploit opportunities to someone else's disadvantage. Resolving competition issues was not addressed as a central field of activity by this EWC: rather, not taking advantage was seen as a behavioural norm, or better, a virtue, imputed to local workforce representatives. This maxim, which was not strategically agreed but understood as a bilateral predisposition, should be seen in the context of the history of Anglo-German conflict and efforts to overcome it.

The topic of health and safety is also not dealt with on the EWC. The German delegates did attempt this once when they submitted a draft for a European Framework Agreement. 'We worked up a text and sent it around. Everyone said "Great", but there was no concrete response. At the next meeting, we asked – "What about it?" Everyone said, yes, very important. We sent the text around again, again no response. Then we said, okay, that's understandable, everyone's got their own agreement on this, and they're all good'. The reason why there was no feeling that action needed to be taken on this issue was that Ford had equally high standards at all its European plants, so that any further engagement with this issue by the EWC would have been superfluous.

Within the EWC, D., the chair, exercises a particular role by virtue of his position as a central and influential actor within the German system of codetermination at the European headquarters in Cologne. He has direct access to and good contacts with European management, including not only the head of HRM but also other board members. If colleagues from other countries ask him, he will also deploy these advantages on their behalf. This can involve digging out information specific to their plant or putting pressure from above on local management in other countries in support of local works councils. As such, he acts as an *advocate* for the others. Although he is accorded this designation based on his role as EWC chair, as far as his impact is concerned, it rests on his influence as chair of the German central works council and deputy chair of the company's supervisory board. This type of activity is not official, and circumvents the EWC forum. D. himself denotes it as informal, as a form of personal assistance offered discreetly and without fanfare. Other local employee representatives participate in this way in German codetermination.

A German EWC member characterized this advocate role in the following terms: 'G. (EWC secretary) gets a call along the lines of "We've got a problem, could D. (EWC chair, central works council chair, deputy chair of the supervisory board) have a word with Mr. Fleming (European head). And then D. will say to management: listen guys, there's a problem, solve it or who knows how it will all end'.

D. himself notes that he helps a good deal through 'informal channels'. When asked, what does 'informally helping' mean, he answered:

> I'll say, if a forge is to be closed in England and the responsible manager is in Cologne, then, of course, I'll talk with him. [*Interviewer: Do you make use of the options available to you as chair of the central works council locally?*]. Yes, yes, but not formally at the works council level, that's clear. But of course we do that, no question. We also do that with the colleagues in Romania. That was about the pay system. They came to me and asked whether we could help. And then the chair of the trade union came from there to Cologne and we organized a joint meeting with management here.

A Spanish EWC member reported on a case where D. had intervened with central management on their behalf. And a Belgian member related: 'Clearly, the Germans have got the good contacts. Cologne is the mother plant for Europe. Although I can call up Cologne from here in Genk if I want a contact with a manager, I can't do that discreetly, as informally as the Germans. [*Interviewer: Do you do call D. and ask him to drop by the boss?*]. Yes, that happens when necessary. First, I'll call G. (EWC secretary) and he'll discuss it with D., and then he'll approach the boss'.

Another member answered the question as to the added-value the EWC offered in view of the extent to which it had restricted its scope. 'Now a plant can say to its manager that if we don't get this sorted out, then we'll go to the chair of the EWC. It's a little bit of security for the local works council to say, there's a European office in Cologne that can support us if we're at a loss here. Otherwise, the plants look after most things themselves'. The influence of the 'European office' in these cases is evidently based on the fact that it is located at the head office in Germany.

The full-time IG Metall official had the following impression of Ford. 'The Germans don't really need the EWC as they have access to management. The EWC is a platform for those that don't have this direct access. The chair, D., approaches European management for them on a case-by-case basis'.

What was interesting was the EWC Secretary, G., who was always the first of port-of-call for this route for interest representation, and even for the role of advocate:

> Yes, D. is an advocate, like his predecessor, but that was even more the case before. It's become a little rarer, because European management has learnt that it's possible to speak directly with representatives locally, and not everything has to run through the chair. The centre-periphery relationship isn't as marked. Countries also have direct access to European management. But if it's a matter of getting information, finding something out fast on an important issue that affects the local plant, then D. is the person who get's a quick call and finds it out, or contacts the supervisory board. Colleagues know that, and they make use of it.

According to this statement, the role of advocate had shifted from direct intervention to being more of a retriever of background information.

The 'advocate' role as a mode of activity in interest representation is a fairly common phenomenon in EWCs in which the company has a German corporate head office. 'Advocate for the diaspora' is a particular type of EWC identified in an earlier EWC study (Kotthoff, 2006a). In contrast to most EWCs of this type, at Ford 'advocacy' is, however, not the only mode of achieving representative effectiveness at European level. The two other levels are the capacity to conclude European framework agreements and direct communication between local employee representatives and European management. This is not about advocacy on behalf of the poor neglected brothers and sisters, adrift in the periphery, but rather an occasional service offered in friendship for self-confident and strong-minded local interest representatives who, as a rule, are well able to look after themselves.

Protest action against management as a form of EWC activity has not yet been undertaken by the Ford EWC, a further point of contrast to GM Europe with which it is often compared. Our respondents at Ford also – proudly – noted this distinction. They say that they are entirely capable of undertaking protest as a last resort, but, in contrast to the GM Europe EWC, prefer the path of cooperation. One Spanish delegate said: 'There are other options for exercising pressure, such as bringing in D., the EWC chair. He sometimes intervenes on national matters if asked. We have asked him to do this as our Spanish plant manager is nervous about management in Germany and also of the EWC chair. And he's been active on our behalf'.

At Ford, there is an unstated consensus not to press the pace of transnational interest representation too hard, but to engage in the process cautiously and limited to what it necessary. 'Necessary' is deemed protection against serious unforeseen events, such as workforce cuts, that affect everyone to the same degree and where there are no winners, only losers. A political strategy that extends beyond this, such as Europeanising employee representation with ambitious joint goals, has not been developed. However, two of our respondents – the EWC secretary and the German trade union representative on the EWC – considered that in the future the EWC will have to take a more strategic approach if it wants to succeed. One said, 'Initially, we missed out on giving the EWC a common strategy, a task, something that was the common point of intersection of what we want to achieve. No analysis has been done, but we talked around it for a couple of years. And then the big issue of Visteon arrived. And the train set off in this direction. And we're still heading along that track now ...

The critical point is that we do not have the bond of a common strategy because we do not have many European issues with major ramifications'. And the other said: 'The EWC does not have a strategy. It decided to take the pragmatic course: to achieve as much as possible with as little effort as possible. It thinks that what the Opel EWC does is too big and consumes too much effort – always developing a new common strategy'.

4.2.4 Relationship between the EWC and management

The industrial relations tradition at both Ford's German plants has customarily been a cooperative one, with management and works council working closely together. Similar developments were also reported as characterizing the situation in Belgium and Spain. This constituted the main difference to Opel, with its traditionally more adversarial industrial relations. One consequence of the relocation of Ford's corporate headquarters from Britain to Cologne was, therefore, that the German culture of codetermination acquired a greater weight within the overall configuration of European industrial relations at the company. Management hoped that this path of social partnership would also diffuse through to England. Although it did not set out to obstruct the establishment of the EWC, it stressed that it wanted its remit to be confined to a small number of issues and that most matters should continue to be regulated at plant level. The most salient fact about the relationship between the EWC and European management was that, up to the point at which this research was conducted, there had been no disagreement over this between the two parties. Whereas Ford represents a model of standardization and uniformity in almost all other matters, in the field of industrial relations it has adopted the opposite track of individual plant-based arrangements – but located in a framework of centralized monitoring. The principle has been to implement the highly centralized Ford production system with as little conflict and disturbance as possible through flexibly adapting it to the specific social and cultural features of each plant.

Contact between the EWC and central management takes place in the main through the chair of the EWC. His function as occasional advocate

for the others is accepted. Indeed, far from running counter to the dominant paradigm of the plant-based management of industrial relations, this
complements it. By contrast, what does require some explanation is the
fact that management agreed to recognize the EWC as a negotiating partner for voluntary European Framework Agreements. This was provided
by the EWC chair D. himself: 'During the Visteon issue, the nightmare
scenario for management was that countries would drift off individually.
They quickly noticed that they'd be overwhelmed if five or six countries
started negotiating and that was the decisive moment when they said,
"Okay we'd rather sort it out with the EWC: and then they can make sure
it's put into practice at national level"'.

One EWC member characterized industrial relations in the following terms:

> The long-standing European head F. was always open for works councils, *in all coun-*
> *tries*. The new head of Europe, O., is similar, although he does not have a production
> background. That is the culture at Ford, that's how it has grown. They've always said
> 'We pay higher wages than the trade union has negotiated'. Cooperation was always
> good. We have never had to walk around brandishing the statute book.

4.2.5 *The EWC and the steering committee: the protagonists in action*

Given the much smaller gap in the number of members and frequency of
meetings between the EWC and steering committee, drawing a distinction
between these two bodies is not as important at Ford when compared with
the other case study companies in this research. The EWC has a somewhat
higher frequency of meetings than at other companies and the steering
committee a much lower frequency. EWC meetings were described by
our respondents as formal rituals, an opinion we also arrived at following
our participant observation of these sessions. Each country reports on
the employment situation at its operations, followed by a presentation of
the general topic, and finally proposals are collected for the presentation
at the next meeting. It is rare that a meeting has to deal with a pressing
matter requiring decision. The frequency of meetings was only stepped up

during the periods in which the European Framework Agreements were being negotiated.

One Belgian member said:

> My problem is that the issues on the agenda are not the ones I'm interested in. I always make a clear distinction between the official part and the unofficial part. What takes place during the official part, okay. But when we have a meal in the evening, then quite different things come up, and people say things that don't crop up in the official session, where you're not really confident to express your feelings and what you really think about something because you don't want to stir anything up.

Another non-German member added:

> What's important is the informal session on the fringes of the meeting. I might get a little hint from T. (EWC chair) and from G. (EWC secretary): don't forget this or that or think about this or that. You can't do this during the official meeting. But when you're having dinner or standing at the bar then that's how we talk about things [*Interviewer: Is it important to have a good link into the works council in Cologne?*] Yes, that's more important than the meetings. [*Interviewer: Do other countries participate in German codetermination?*] Yes of course. Cologne is the mother plant for Europe.

There is no strong group cohesion. In fact, the bonds between members are weak, both in the EWC as a whole and on the steering committee. One delegate from Belgium noted: 'The people are isolated, there is little contact between countries'. A Spanish member reported in similar terms: 'I would say that cohesion is not great. It's a bit better on the steering committee, you're pleased to see each other and you listen to what the other has got to say about their country, but you don't really get to know each other more closely. There are no friendships'.

This is surprising in view of the limited number of members and the relatively low level of turnover, especially on the steering committee. The main reason for this lack of 'we-feeling' is a context in which the main focus of representation continues to be at national level, leading to a low intensity of contact, major language barriers, and the absence of a European strategy. The EWC has not become an ongoing active working group. Country groupings keep to themselves during breaks in meetings, and there is little bilateral exchange. People attempt to have informal individual discussions with the Germans, D. and G. The more relaxed atmosphere in the evenings during dinner and at the bar is mainly attributable to the polyglot EWC secretary G., whose highly developed communication skills mean he can circulate among all those attending. He noted: 'The country groups stick together. Language is a barrier. And we do not have the advantage that many of them speak English. In principle, it's only the Belgians, and a few Germans who can speak some English, and a Romanian'.

In contrast to the EWC at the other case study companies, there is no requirement at Ford for members to learn English. The chair, D., says that everyone should be able to use their mother tongue as employee representatives' knowledge of foreign languages will never be perfect, given the lack of time for language lessons, and people would be less confident in speaking. 'Nobody here has to kill themselves with broken English'. This insistence on speaking in mother tongues is seen by most as a privilege. This, in all probability, has its origin in the fact that the original EWC founder, Wilfried Kuckelkorn, had been 'spoilt' in his role as an MEP by having access to professional interpreters. However, paradoxically, this has not proved beneficial for forging internal cohesion.

Most contacts during and on the fringes of the meetings, especially during the long interludes between meetings, centre on the secretary G. He described his task in the following terms:

> They ring me up, I'm the interface, they want to have information, often related to very specific areas – for example, there are three transmission plants and someone will want to know how much the other produces and I'll find that out. I'll call the other two in their countries and ask what they make. It's that type of thing. Mostly it's where there's been some complaint and often, of course, in connection with our European framework agreements. It could also be that something is not being complied with. Then they want to know from me whether how they see things corresponded with what we agreed. They'll say, my national manager has never understood it, can you go to the head of Europe in Cologne and say that he needs to speak with our national managers so that he gets it. And then I tend to be the go-between. [*Interviewer: And what happens then?*] It depends what it is and, it depends on the level. Either I can resolve things here with colleagues at my level [European HR management, *authors' note*]. It might be that that doesn't work. And then I have to go a bit higher, and then D. (EWC chair) will do it himself. But overall there aren't that many questions, we're not overburdened. Someone isn't calling up every day.

The EWC has a clearly recognisable sociogram: there is a cooperative 'three-country constellation', that includes, together with the two key German actors, D. and G., the Belgian and the Romanian representatives on the steering committee, with the British playing a special role and the Spanish the outsiders. The issue on which opinion is divided is that of local plant security agreements. The Germans, who more or less invented this instrument, commend it to the others, albeit with an obligation to keep each other informed.

A highly trusting relationship emerged between Kuckelkorn, his successor D., and the full-time British trade union representative R. and his successor O. This found expression in the fact that both UK officials supported the strategy of plant security agreements, and with this a more cooperative and participative model of representation. However, not only did they not succeed in prevailing with this view domestically but ran into strong resistance as it was seen as interference in local matters. O., the full-time official, was very concerned to prevent the closure of two British plants and keen to strike a deal with management based on a commitment to keep the plant open in return for relinquishing some established terms and conditions, in particular the 'short Friday' (lunchtime finish). The workforce and shop stewards were not willing to agree to this. The plant was eventually closed. One German interviewee noted: 'O. failed there, even as a powerful full-time official he couldn't push it through'. In another case of a threatened closure, although the workforce at the plant at risk was prepared to make concessions, employees at other British plants were not willing to accede to management wishes that this should also apply in their operations. 'The other plants said they wouldn't given anything up to save that bloody little factory. Instead they negotiated a pay rise of 5.4 per cent. This hurt Ford, but management said: "Okay, take the money, we'll sort things out with you another way"'. On the concessions, this invariably involved hard-won 'custom-and-practice', but not serious incursions into pay. From the standpoint of our respondents from elsewhere, these mostly seemed to be minor issues and obsolete practices, and they failed to understand why they were defended so adamantly.

The other five British delegates, who were shop stewards, were also classified as rooted in this milieu and characteristic way of thinking by our respondents from other countries. They were seen as uninterested both in the EWC and in colleagues from other countries, and viewed as inactive. One said: 'I just can't understand it, it's a riddle to me. The English mentality at Ford is still like it was in the 1970s. They don't want to fight for their plant – they just want to see the cash. *It's always the same: the company says, we're going to close it, the union says we'll go on strike, the company turns up with a sack load of money, the people leave, and the demonstration is cancelled*'.

Another interviewee commented, 'Now we have another new generation of English [representatives] who just don't understand, don't grasp that the EWC is a useful instrument. I'm sure that the next plant to close will be in England. And the English will take the money yet again, and nothing will happen'.

As we have already noted, the English bloc on the EWC is – for now outdated historical reasons – so large that it is not possible to make any progress without it. One of our interviewees took a very pessimistic view of the future: 'If they are not more proactive, it will be pretty hard to achieve anything'. This particular constellation is one of the weak points of the EWC.

While the speakers for the three cooperating countries on the EWC were disappointed about the British delegates' passivity, their feeling towards the Spanish delegation was more one of irritation and annoyance. This was dominated for a long period by their spokesperson and steering committee representative, P. Two years previously, he had concluded a plant retention agreement with management without informing the EWC. This breached a fundamental rule of solidarity in the EWC – namely transparency – and he was subsequently isolated within the forum. One motive for his conduct according to some other members, was his personal desire for power. A Belgian interviewee noted:

> P. is the head of the Spanish employee representative body. It did not suit him to play second fiddle to Germany, that this was the power centre – it injured his pride. He saw himself as a competitor to Kuckelkorn and then to D. He always listened very carefully to what happened in Germany and said: 'Okay, I can do that myself. I don't need the EWC for that'. And then he made an agreement with management without telling us anything about what he had negotiated. We still don't know. We were all annoyed with P. He then stopped coming to quite a few meetings. The

Germans tried to get him back on board and got IG Metall involved, using neutral ground to try and get talks going with each other. None of it worked. Then we said: 'Okay, run your plant into ground'.

After P. had recently left office, there were fresh hopes that the Spaniards would begin to participate more and act with greater loyalty to the group. The role of the Spanish delegates on the EWC is a clear illustration of the significance of individuals as an explanatory factor.

The relationship between the cooperative triumvirate of the Germans, Belgians and Romanians is characterized by the fact that they are open with each other, keep each other informed, and engage in discussion. They have created mutual trust. Despite that, they rely more on the strength of their own local representatives than on the EWC. In 2003, the Belgians encountered a difficult situation as production volumes were transferred to Turkey and the third shift cancelled. The Belgian spokesperson on the steering committee said that he had expected more solidarity. 'We got the EWC involved, but the only thing I found was an ear, in to which I could speak, and a shoulder, on which I could have a good cry. I understand that, it's not a reproach but, of course, everyone was thinking about their own jobs. I couldn't mobilize colleagues in my plant to strike for other plants'. A German delegate perceived the Belgian colleagues in the following terms. 'They also said to themselves, hmm, will we get the support in the EWC? They definitely don't rely on it. They look after themselves and that's always worked out well'.

Also in the Belgian case, it was not clear at first glance how transnational interest representation has functioned at Ford of Europe. The matter was not officially raised as an issue on the EWC, although the Belgians had introduced it. On the other hand, one of our interviewees noted, 'Saving Genk was also down to D. (EWC chair), as he had pulled strings in the background. And it was also important that the colleagues in Belgium had taken serious strike action, but a lot was done behind the scenes in Cologne. The Belgians had then got another van to replace the Transit'. This again shows the significance of the advocate role of the 'doyen' within the German codetermination arrangements, who strained to ensure that no one left with empty hands and expected that others would also respect this principle.

The EWC representative for the second German plant in Saarlouis did not have high expectations of the EWC, and was rather restrained in terms of involvement. A colleague said, 'He's got everything sorted in Saarlouis. He doesn't need the others. And when he does need something, then it's the chair of German central works council'.

4.2.6 Differences between the EWCs at Ford and General Motors

In recent years the EWC at GM Europe has had a high profile both in the media and research literature and established itself as a benchmark: it was a comparator to which our interviewees at Ford made repeated reference. In particular, they were concerned to distinguish themselves, in a critical sense, from the GM/Opel EWC because the 'way things worked at Ford', as they put it, were quite different. Their core proposition was: Ford of Europe has traditionally had co-operative industrial relations, and GM Europe confrontational. Therefore the EWC operates differently.

D., the EWC chair, criticized the – now famous – 'pain-sharing' axiom adopted by the GM/Opel EWC (equal distribution of losses across all sites) as a short-sighted view of solidarity:

> We've also had difficult restructuring exercises and overcapacity. At the same time, we were lucky that we were able to agree with management that certain things should be concentrated in certain countries, and not that each county would build a Fiesta and its own engine. That was the decision that distinguished us from the Opel strategy. They just had the slogan – equal pain for all. But what that means is that if all three plants are doing badly then you're going to put all three in a difficult position.

And similarly, with a glance at Opel, he explained:

> A plant closure was never a European issue for us. That is the difference to Opel, where, if something is about to be taken away, some say, 'Ah, outcry, European issue'. We're extremely rigid about this demarcation and we say very clearly, yes we have to know, and information exchange is important, we try to help each other informally as much as possible, that's very clear, but we do not have European negotiations on such issues.

Another German interviewee at Ford saw the distinction in the following terms:

> The basic principle for our management is to adjust capacity to demand, but not to take a tough stance on this and do it in dialogue with the trade unions. GM management do it exactly the other way around. Those people in the USA didn't even realise they owned Opel and it was only when Magna wanted to buy it that they caught on at the last minute.

At Opel, works councillors were held to complain about their own management, and the relationship was perceived to be a difficult one, with no trust. Management were seen as attempting to play plants off against each other. The perspective on how the EWC behaved was:

> Always put everything into the public domain, make a commotion, and protest, protest! In contrast we operate with the slogan: think what's best for the company. That's what we Germans have always set out as the first principle. The principle of share the pain at the Opel EWC is very bad for the company because it pulls the rug from under your feet as every plant then becomes unprofitable. I can tell you already, in a few years Opel will be finished.

In particular, our respondents at Ford distinguished themselves from the way in which the GM/Opel EWC organized its public relations. One German delegate said, 'It's a basic principle of both management and ourselves in the works councils that we act but we don't talk too much about it. So, for example, on plant retention and on the Visteon issue we've often discussed this principle with management along the lines of – we don't need to go to the press and make a big statement. It's better if we keep it to ourselves'.

Our full-time official from IG Metall, who has dealt with managements at both companies, said: 'At Opel they're quite different types than at Ford. I know them both. Opel management is very confrontational, it wants to block every negotiation at European level. You have to see the way that the Opel EWC behaves as a necessary form of defence'.

At this point in the other case studies we also analysed the role of trade union organizations within the EWC process. This is not necessary in this case as, in contrast to the other case studies, the trade unions are already sitting at the EWC table, and, as such, have been included in our treatment of the ongoing work of the EWC.

The same considerations apply to the issue of a separate treatment of the concept of solidarity. It was clear, in contrast to most of respondents at our other case studies, that the concept of solidarity at Ford is not primarily solidarity-in-struggle (protest actions, strikes on behalf of other plants). The demand for solidarity is focused in this case on a requirement for openness in terms of the mutual provision of information and informal pragmatic 'neighbourly' assistance, but without any major overarching political or social-ethical aspirations. *This represents a modest, pragmatic and concrete understanding of solidarity in concordance with the principle of subsidiarity.*

At Ford, the main priority for the EWC has not been to elaborate a set of common strategic aims as a political actor or to work closely together to form the sort of solidaristic group needed to achieve such an objective. Rather, the core of industrial relations in the company is seen as lying in the autonomy and strength of local plant representatives. Joint European action constitutes a back-up mechanism for emergencies in which all plants are equally and catastrophically affected by the same threat. Responding to such an emergency should not be confused with the defensive strategy adopted at the GM/Opel EWC. The Ford EWC has been able to work on the assumption that, in the event of an emergency, management will conduct itself in a cooperative manner and will not preclude the option of solving the problem through a European Framework Agreement. This more modest notion of solidarity is evidenced in a more reticent understanding of the role of the EWC. The surprising persistence of a strong role for local and national representative bodies in one of the most internationalized and centralized companies can be explained by three factors.

A. By the decision to supplement the principle of 'local autonomy' with the additional axiom of 'contact to central management'. Direct contact between European management and employee representatives at individual plants is unusual and not an element usually noted in the literature. However, at Ford it is central in any understanding of the particular way in which transnational interest representation operates. Central management's interest in local employee representation can be seen as being anchored in Ford's preference for large plants and its predilection for cultivating local socio-cultural embeddedness as a factor that can boost productivity.

B. The existence of strong local interest representation not only in the company's European homeland but also in other countries.

C. The advocacy role of the chair of the central works council at the company's German headquarters. Other plants benefit, when needed, from the scope offered by the German codetermination system. At Ford, this advocacy role is not intended as a form of charity for a group of 'have nots' – see (B) above – but as a form of diplomatic intercession on behalf of 'medium-sized powers' that are fully competent in terms of interest representation. The relationship between those directly involved in company-level codetermination in Cologne and local representatives elsewhere represents a consortium between a primary power and a number of independent medium-sized powers that have chosen to form a loose and expedient alliance.

Given the profound industrial changes in the automotive industry, such as excess capacity and the resultant need for mergers together with paradigm shifts in technology and transport policy, doubts have been expressed by some actors as to whether this model of transnational interest representation will be up to the challenges of the future, with warnings that the EWC might need to adopt a more transnational and strategic stance.

4.2.7 Summary

Concluding European Framework Agreements, one function of EWCs that extends some way beyond the scope provided by the EWC Directive, is often viewed as one of the most demanding indicators of the representative effectiveness of an EWC. Measured against this yardstick, the Ford EWC is not only the most effective of the case studies included in the present research, but also in a wider comparison. Not only did it conclude the first such agreement, but it has also negotiated the largest number of such agreements to date, and without exception has always addressed 'hard' issues connected with employment security and retention. On the other hand, the Ford EWC is also notable for the self-denying ordinance it has adopted to restrict both the range and level of its activities. It defines its remit very narrowly. Those problems that lie at the core of EWC activity at Unilever and Kraft Foods, such as plant closures, transfers of production, workforce reductions, rationalization and plant security, are explicitly treated by the Ford EWC as local problems that lie outside of its scope and on which there is no joint approach. Such issues simply do not appear on the agenda of the EWC, which does not view itself as a strategic political body representing common positions to central management. This restricted remit also means that the EWC has relatively little to do. It is not a working body engaged in ongoing activity, and has the lowest frequency of meetings of all our case studies.

There is agreement between management and employee representatives on this more limited definition of what constitutes a 'European' matter. This can be summed up as: deal with as many issues related to interest representation as possible at local level and as few as possible at European level. This represents a case of a *subsidiary* understanding of the Europeanization of interest representation.

The continuing significance of local representation can only be understood in the context of management's strategy. Although extremely centralized in terms of organization and management, the company cultivates a very high degree of local independence for individual plants in the field of HRM and industrial relations, recognising that particular local sociocultural features can serve as a productive factor within Ford's characteristic pursuit of continuous improvement. All Ford's Mainland European operations have strong local representative bodies that are willing to cooperate with local managements. Locally negotiated plant security agreements in which the EWC is not involved – even as a coordinator – have been the main instrument for regulating local interests over a long period. In addition, central management also seeks to maintain contact with local representatives during such negotiations.

Central management in Cologne, largely made up of British executives, regards the German culture of codetermination as a benefit and promotes cooperative relationships in other countries. This micro-corporatist approach to industrial relations marks a major difference to GM Europe, where the EWC operates against a background of a culture characterized by conflict and a lack of trust.

Productivity-based competition between plants is supported by local employee representatives and seen positively and self-confidently as a spur, as long as it is not pursued using unfair means. It is circumscribed by a set of normative provisions.

The basic structure of the EWC corresponds with the home-country model. Its organization is closely tied to that of the central works council at the German headquarters in Cologne. The post of EWC chair is held in personal union by the chair of the German central works council, who, if needed, will assume the role of advocate to central management on behalf of the others. One notable feature is the presence, at the request of management, of senior national trade union representatives from all four Northern and Southern European countries at EWC meetings. Although these officials normally take a back seat, they play an important role in negotiations over European Framework Agreements.

Group solidarity (solidarity type 2) in the forum is relatively weak, due to the low level of activity, and this also affects the constitution of the group and group discipline. The British delegation does not actively participate and has withdrawn from the philosophy of micro-corporatism that dominates within the group. The spokesperson for the Spanish delegation behaved in a spectacularly unsolidaristic manner and has not responded to the normative pressure from other members. Relationships within the EWC are not structured like home affairs but more as foreign policy. At first glance, there is also no 'solidarity-in-struggle' (solidarity type 3), as protest actions against management are not a central issue for the EWC. Below the visible level of everyday operations, there is, however, an underlying trade union solidarity that only evidences itself in rare situations, as with the threats that prompted the first framework agreements. And it is also manifested in the relationship between the British and German delegates, which, based on their prior experiences in which solidarity broke down, has been marked by efforts at mutual concern and respect, despite difficulties in appreciating each others' perspective.

At a national level, all plants have had experience with strikes and protest actions, so that there is always a slumbering potential for this form of solidarity in the background that can be drawn on should one of the issues defined as European be involved. The predominant form of solidarity is a utilitarian one – enlightened self-interest (solidarity type 1) – as evident in the two most significant fields in which the EWC is effective: defensive alliance in the event of a massive systemic threat to all, and the role of advocate exercised by the chair of the German works council.

Compared with the first pattern of solidarity 'EWC as a working group in dialogue with management', the Ford EWC has a low degree of solidarity that fits with its limited sphere of competence and codetermination. Should the forum widen its scope to embrace more strategic codetermination, the most important prerequisite for this would be to invigorate group solidarity.

4.3 Protest solidarity: The advance of the Southern European model of representation in the EWC of a German company. 'Protest solidarity' vs 'Participation solidarity'

CASE STUDY: BURGER-MILLER[4]

4.3.1 Business and organizational structure

Burger is a long-established German manufacturing company with a rich industrial heritage. It has some 40,000 employees, and produces a high-quality technical product range with a largely skilled workforce. For many years, it was not a highly internationalized business, and had only two small

---

4   This case study has been anonymized at the request of the chair of the EWC.

production facilities outside Germany. This changed dramatically in 2004 when a new CEO inaugurated a new – and for observers surprising – strategy of product diversification through internationalization. Burger bought the British firm Miller, a highly internationalized business with some 25,000 employees, whose main activities were in manufacturing simple products produced in a low-tech context with a less skilled workforce, including a high proportion of agency staff. Miller was an interesting target for Burger as, for historic reasons, it had access to distribution channels and manufactured basic products that were especially well suited to emerging markets. As well as its main plants in the UK, Miller had a number of large production operations abroad, including a plant in Germany.

The new company, Burger-Miller, employs some 70,000 staff in three divisions:

A. The previous Burger business, with 37,000 employees
B. The previous Miller business, with 20,000 employees
C. A new business division, created out of a number of additional small acquisitions, into which were placed two of the Miller plants and a small sub-assembly facility formerly owned by Burger that produces low-tech products that complement those made by Miller. This division has 12,000 employees.

The new company's CEO is the chair of the former Burger management board. The head of division A is, as might be expected, also German. The head of division B is English, and the head of Division C is American. The composition of central management clearly reflects the drive to internationalize the businesses. Other management levels in the Divisions B. and C. were also not staffed with German nationals following the acquisition. Instead of 'Germanising' these posts, Burger adopted a strategy of internationalising management. Even within the former 'core' Burger division (A), lower and middle management was increasingly 'diluted' by non-Germans. The CEO's strategy, seen by some interviewees as tilting to a shareholder value approach driven by financial considerations, is that of accelerated globalization, in which the group is being opened up and transformed with scant regard for sentiment or tradition. Although the company's German roots are often invoked, many Burger employees have found it difficult to come to terms with change on this scale. Whereas up until very recently the company's operations were entirely German, almost half the production in the new group now occurs outside Germany. What once was a focused high-tech manufacturer has been catapulted into a conglomerate with a large share of low-skilled workers in its foreign operations.

Economically, the first five years following the acquisition were characterized by rapid growth and the integration of Miller into Burger. In 2009, the company's position deteriorated seriously on the European and US market, in part due to the financial crisis. Since then, policy has shifted to cost cutting, rationalization and workforce reductions. By contrast, the company is growing in Asia, and in particular in China.

Internationalization has culminated in a divided organizational culture and approach to personnel management – a situation that has had a decisive impact on employee representation, and in particular for the EWC. On the one hand, Division A continues to be characterized by relatively skilled employment and a continuation of established industrial relations with the workforce subject to high levels of agreed provisions and close cooperation between management, the works council, and the relevant branch-level trade union. In contrast, outside Germany the organizational culture and HR approach was characterized by all our respondents as that of a 'bad employer', with industrial relations that were extremely strained in some areas. Local and regional management was viewed as uninterested and inexperienced at operating with works council structures and as hostile to trade unions. The gap between working conditions and industrial relations in Germany and in other operations was much greater than in the other case studies in this research.

Management's strategy was very evidently directed at preventing any movement, however gradual, on the part of the international parts of the business towards German codetermination arrangements. A firebreak had been carved out between the employment and social standards that prevail in Burger in Germany and those at Miller operations elsewhere. Labour costs are an especially important factor for Divisions B and C due to their product mix, in which cost competitiveness is crucial and production more variable, with an associated strategy of lower pay in these divisions and the use of agency staff to cover sales and production fluctuations.

The only identifiable connection between the two organizational cultures is the role of the Labour Director (*Arbeitsdirektor*), a statutory corporate position that is filled by appointment by the trade unions at Burger and who serves as a type of industrial relations director. This individual is deeply embedded in the German part of the group and its culture, but is also responsible for international operations. In practice, however, internationalization has also led to a decline in the influence and significance of the Labour Director. One of our German respondents noted, 'It doesn't matter to me under which Labour Director I work here as his role has been reduced so much through the most recent restructuring that they no longer matter. Their influence is negligible. This means that in the future we'll have to talk less with the Labour Director and more with real management board members'.

There is little competition between manufacturing plants in different divisions, and the fact that Division A is almost entirely located in Germany means that there is no inter-plant competition within this division. The position is different in the case of some technical and organizational operations, where inter-site competition emerged when a technical centre was relocated from the UK to Germany, and a logistical centre was moved back from Italy also to Germany. Both these instances became important issues for the EWC. The most significant organizational and strategic concerns for the EWC at the time of writing were the large-scale workforce reductions being implemented as a consequence of cost-reduction and rationalization programmes. In all, 1,100 employees were scheduled to be 'released' during 2009 in Division B (Miller) and Division C. The existence of an employment security agreement with the German industry union meant that Miller employees in Germany were largely spared in this.

4.3.2 Structure and development of the EWC

The EWC has thirty-one members: eight from Germany, five from the UK; four from Italy; three from France; two each from Spain and the Czech Republic; and one member each from a further seven countries.

The five-person steering committee includes representation from Germany, the UK, Italy, France, and Spain. The EWC chair is W., from Germany: he is also the long-standing chair of the local works council of a Burger plant, and has full facility time. Although he is a member of the Burger central works council, he does not chair this body, creating a situation unusual for Germany in which the role of EWC chair is not occupied simultaneously by the chair or deputy chair of the central works council but rather by someone who, although well networked, is not one of the principal figures within the German codetermination system.

Herr W. is a convinced European who sees the internationalization of employee representation in the group as a necessity to match the internationalization of management. As a consequence, a large proportion of his time (more than two thirds of his time allowance) is spent on his European role.

The steering committee meets every two months, with more meetings if needed, and in recent years has convened at least eight times a year. Four of the five members speak English, so that only one interpreter is needed for the one member. They are in frequent contact by e-mail and phone between meetings. The EWC chair has a full-time assistant in his works council office at the local Burger plant, and both are supported by a works council secretary, enabling this local works council to function additionally as the EWC office. The assistant participates in all meetings and discussions, so that, in practice, he should be viewed as an additional member of the steering committee.

There is a high level of individual turnover within the EWC as a whole, with 30 per cent of the members changing at the most recent election in 2008. The British contingent, in particular, is highly unstable in composition. Of the five British delegates, who only joined the body shortly after the takeover, none is still a member. In contrast, the steering committee is a more stable unit. Three of the five individuals have sat on it since the takeover in 2004 (including the chair) and two since 2008.

The installation agreement for the EWC – along with that at Sanofi – ranks as the most generous of all of those in our study. It grants the EWC a high level of resources and scope: two regular EWC meetings each year; a three-day training event every two years; the establishment of working parties; the right of the steering committee to carry out paid plant visits; and a right to call on expert advice. The reason for this generosity on the part of central management lies in its desire to win over the employee side at both Burger and Miller for the acquisition.

The EWC's provision with resources would suggest that information and consultation operate relatively unproblematically and at a high standard, and that the EWC's representative effectiveness would gain from its being linked with the established practice of German codetermination at Burger. However, this is not as fully realized as might be expected. The formally generous working conditions and resources for the EWC are, in practice, only extended to the steering committee. In contrast, if ordinary EWC delegates call for similar provisions in their own countries, there are often difficulties with local management. We heard reports of cases in the UK, France and other countries outside Germany where EWC members did not receive e-mails because they were not granted access to a PC and in which EWC members were prevented by local management from participating in an EWC meeting. Surmounting such 'blockades' required the intervention of the EWC chair and secretary, who were able to exert pressure on local management via group-level managers at the company's headquarters. The gulf between formal institutionalization and reality is even wider on the issue of the actual significance of the EWC as a consultative body. Although the EWC has a real impact, this rests on other than its provision with resources. The EWC chair, Herr W., noted: 'Looking at the resources, we can say that we have come a fairly long way, but aside from that ...'

One astonishing observation in the case of the EWC at Burger-Miller is that, as a latecomer that was not founded until 2004, it has achieved a high level of institutionalization within a short period of time. It was established at a propitious moment. The rapid internationalization of the company through large-scale acquisitions meant that there was unanimity on the part of all those involved about the need to set up an EWC. The members of the SNB (Special Negotiating Body), which negotiated the installation agreement, were engaged and in some instances enthusiastic, supporters of the EWC project. There were a mood of exhilaration and a sense of a new era, 'a consensus, even a high degree of solidarity' (SNB member). Central management was initially welcoming.

This meant that within the EWC as a whole, a feeling soon developed of a common European group identity, despite the high level of individual turnover. 'A common understanding emerged. In some cases friendships developed. There was a common cause in that we wanted to be a joint platform in relation to management. One cannot say that the French work against the English or the like, that's not how it is' (EWC chair). This astonishing early mutual openness was also facilitated by the fact that there were few worries about mutual competition due to the company's organization. And during the growth phase, the topics raised for the EWC were generally unproblematic and allowed members to grow closer together. One respondent summed this initial phase up appositely as follows: 'It was a period of forging solidarity that had not yet encountered a challenge.'

One precondition for success in institutionalizing the EWC was the fact that W., as EWC chair, had an ambition to make the European track of interest representation into an important and significant pillar of overall interest representation within the group alongside the German system of codetermination. From a German standpoint, such a development would be 'natural' and it would have been reasonable to integrate and attach European employee representation to the strong tradition of German codetermination, as happened at Ford. In terms of the structure of its industrial relations, and as with the EWCs at Daimler, BMW and other flagships of German codetermination, the company would have 'properly' been predestined for the EWC type that we have denoted 'Advocate for the Diaspora' (Kotthoff 2006; cf. the case study of BMW in Whittall, 2000). However, one of the key features of this case, and of this research as whole, is that this home-country model did not come about.

According to a number of our respondents, and in particular non-Germans, the German industry union, which had some influence in Burger and which had played a significant role in establishing the EWC, subsequently lost interest. This change appears to have led to some distance between the German and European sides of employee representation within the company.

A German interviewee analysed the position within the company in the following terms.

> The EWC is not seen as relevant within the company by the union or German works council members, and is just an offshoot as far as they are concerned. It might have some significance for the non-Germans, they say, but we've got our own network to management. The EWC and German codetermination are two parallel worlds that have nothing to do with each other – something that management has noticed and which has meant that the EWC has not had any chance of developing into a serious discussion partner for management.

The first big test for the EWC came with the transfer of the technical centre from the UK to Germany, which led to a cut of 130 jobs at the UK operation and a gain of the same in Germany. The EWC did not pass this test. It was informed too late and consultation was far from comprehensive. It was not able to make any difference to the decision and also was unable to influence the social provisions for the workforce. Of more long-term significance than this instance in itself was the impression on the part of the bulk of the non-German delegates on the EWC that the German trade union was not willing to lift a finger on behalf of their British colleagues and, in fact, was thought to have been secretly pleased by the additional jobs in Germany. 'This discredited the German representatives of the EWC for a long period. There was a good deal of tension and mistrust, and a creeping feeling of impotence' (German interviewee).

Distrust of 'the Germans' has become a characteristic feature of the EWC. The social constitution of the forum has been the product of a certain, if generally submerged, anti-German feeling. This suspicion, however, does not extend to the 'German Europeans' at the head of the EWC, that is Herr W. and his assistant, although both are affected by it. For example, the German EWC secretary, perceived by the non-German interviewees as a valued and highly trustworthy individual, said that he also suffered personally from this anti-German syndrome. 'I regard myself as a communicative person and I approach the others in very open and unguarded way, but had to learn that we Germans are seen in quite different terms, in a more negative way. This is connected with the fact that the company is a German one – that is they don't mean me personally but it still gives me a hard time'.

In view of the passivity of some German EWC delegates, and based on the critical stance of delegates towards 'the Germans', delegates from some other countries have drawn closer together and, as a consequence, have acquired a good deal of scope to shape the institution and determine its direction. One non-German delegate summed up the mood in the following terms. 'The key thing is that the Germans don't dominate'.

One factor that has proved disruptive in the relationship between the Germans and other members is the gulf in the level of social provision between the Burger workforce in Germany and Miller operations in other countries. The Germans on the EWC noted that employees in the Miller plant in Germany also did not enjoy the same level of terms and conditions of Burger employees, although they were not as poorly positioned in this respect as Miller staff in other countries.

> There is solidarity amongst the non-Germans against the Germans, and they say 'The Germans have got everything that we'd also like to have'. But many Germans don't have that as well (German interviewee).

Making such comparisons, and the resultant envy, was seen as misplaced and inappropriate by the chair of the German central works council. In his view, EWC delegates from other countries were not comparing the conditions in their operations with those at local competitors – that is, other low-paying plants, with even poorer pay and conditions, but with a high-profile and prestigious German undertaking. 'As far as they are concerned, Burger is a "mighty fortress" because it is a German company. They are comparing us with DAX-listed companies, and that's like comparing apples and pears' (member of the German group works council).

This shows that the merging of so many different worlds, such as those of secure and well-paid Burger employees and less well-remunerated workers at Miller plants in other European countries, can overtax the scope and boundaries of employee representation. The EWC operates in an environment of low-pay and poor working conditions, whereas the central works council and industry union at the corporate centre are part of a world of good – German – employment conditions in a major German firm.

The chair of the central works council confirmed this distanced relationship between employee representatives from these two worlds that co-exist within Burger-Miller. 'I'm always very reticent as far as the EWC is concerned, because I think that this is quite a different body'. He considered that the expectations that the non-German majority on the EWC has of the central works council and industry union – that they would support an adversarial strategy based on protest actions and strikes – were a 'projection'.

> There is a lot of projection there. They only see the good conditions of our codetermination system. These are pre-judgements. They are excessive expectations, based on the idea that German works council and unions are powerful. This completely fails to grasp that our hands are tied because of the law. It would be inconceivable if we, as the central works council, seized the management board and locked them in. That's standard operating procedure in France. It's all too easy always just to expect things from us Germans.

The power of the trade union at Burger rests on a level of trade union membership of over 70 per cent, compared with the very low level of union organization in other countries. This alone is sufficient to deter the German union from taking risks on their behalf.

As such, this represents a similar divergence between industrial relations cultures to that encountered at Unilever. The main difference between the two EWCs consists in the fact that, in the case of Unilever, these differences were the subject of open discussion and did not lead to the assertion of a 'Southern' model of representation. At Unilever, the EWC had the structural scope and power to work effectively and exercise influence, a circumstance bolstered by the fact that over time it succeeded in winning recognition from central management. In contrast, at Burger-Miller, these conditions were absent, and representation became separated into two parallel worlds.

4.3.3 Scope and effectiveness of the EWC

Information and consultation

If we were to adopt the same yardstick for judging the effectiveness of the EWC at Burger-Miller that we used at Unilever and Kraft foods, namely as a body which aims at achieving a degree of transnational impact as a consultation partner for management, then it would not score very highly. In this case, the view of one of a non-German steering committee member would apply. 'Although there is a ritualized form of communication and of culture, the difficult topics are only dealt with superficially, if at all. There is a large number of meetings compared with other EWC, but it's difficult to put your finger on the output'.

Nonetheless, the EWC does have a social impact, even quite a strong one, albeit achieved through a different path to transnational solidarity. This effect is not the product, or at least not primarily the product, of consultation between the steering committee and central management but rather the outcome of decentralized transnational networking by local and national employee representatives. The impetus for action comes from below, from the power and force of an authentic and unmediated trade union movement. Its modus operandi is resistance, and its aim is to construct grassroots-based countervailing power. It consists more in saying 'no' than in codetermination and as such is a form of activity that more closely resembles the culture of representation characteristic of France rather than that of Germany or Sweden. Despite the fact that the company is the only German case in our study, the dominant model in terms of the culture of the EWC is the Southern European or French model.

Our initial concern in this section is to consider in more detail what the EWC has achieved, or not achieved, in the field of information and consultation. The major issues considered at the meetings of the steering committee and the plenary sessions of the EWC have been the relocation of the technical centre and of a logistics operation, and the imminent transfer of some IT functions to Asia.

One constant in these measures has been the fact that the EWC was informed at a very late stage, and in most cases only immediately before the measures were implemented, with no 'genuine' consultation in any of these instances. The national managers responsible insisted that this was a purely national matter and that the EWC should not be involved. This dispute about what is 'national' and what 'European' has run through the entire course and practice of the EWC. Large numbers of meetings have been held, the steering committee has issued an official statement for the EWC in almost every case and called for consultation and changes in the measures proposed, and, in particular, has sought to involve central management in the person of the Labour Director to put pressure on national divisional management. However, all this has had little effect. All our respondents were unanimous in saying the success was meagre. We now illustrate this with two examples.

The most significant issue before the EWC was the transfer of the technical centre. This occupied several meetings of the steering committee. Management offered the British workers affected a transfer to Germany but, as might be expected, this option was taken up by very few. The issue in negotiations at national level in the UK turned on achieving a redundancy scheme offering decent levels of severance pay, offers of training, and assistance in job search etc. The EWC sought to influence national negotiations through its contacts with HR. However, this was not successful. The EWC chair themselves said, 'We were not able to reach a satisfactory outcome. The British are still angry. The whole issue has put a very serious strain on the EWC'.

A more recent instance, dating from 2009, was the move of a logistics operation from the Netherlands to Germany. Only highly qualified staff and middle management were offered a social compensation plan by central management but not less qualified staff. There was no active works council at this location and the level of trade union organization was low. In view of management's hard stance, the workforce attempted to establish a works council on their own initiative on an ad hoc basis to negotiate better terms. This was not recognized by management. In response, the workforce went to court but lost the case as a works council had to be established before a conflict in order to have any rights of intervention. Although the chair of the EWC was able to induce the Labour Director to visit the location, he was unable to smooth over the situation.

If one tries to draw a balance, it's difficult to document what actually has been achieved. It's rather modest, not really very much (Dutch member of the steering committee).

The matters dealt with by the EWC float on top of a sea of problems that have gone untouched. 'In 2009 alone more than 1,000 people were made redundant in Europe, of which we perhaps dealt with 50. Everything else was dealt with exclusively locally – or not at all. The EWC had no influence on this, there was no consultation' (North European interviewee). The EWC was not even informed about the sale of a Miller operation in France. Top management of the two strongly internationalized divisions (B and C), individuals with no experience of working with German codetermination, have not recognized the EWC as a partner for dialogue and have ignored its rights to information and consultation.

The meagre success of consultation has meant that the EWC chair has been pressed in particular by delegates from Southern Europe to be more open to protest actions, strikes, and demonstrations – an approach that he has found hard to accept as a works council member with a commitment to industrial peace. He noted: 'It has been considered whether we should engage in joint action with the European-level union confederation. On the other hand why would they want to be involved in such large-scale actions? We've got an economic crisis. The pressure to save is not coming from the company'.

The pressure on the Germans on the steering committee and in the body as a whole to switch to a more activist approach has gone up with each successive event. Matters came to a head in the spring of 2010. Under pressure from the French and Italian EWC delegates, for the first time the steering committee undertook an action, although at a fairly low level. During a meeting with management on the issue of relocating operations, all members of the steering committee left the room, leaving management on their own. Internally this action had a liberating effect. The non-German members were quite euphoric afterwards and said that this represented a decisive shift in course and that the EWC was now on the right path. The German side within the steering committee confirmed this new burst of energy in the group, but was more cautious in its assessment, thinking it might simply have been a flash in the pan. In the eyes of the non-German members this action was not simply an accompaniment to their expressing an opinion to management within the context of a cooperative approach focused on consultation, but represented a switch in the EWC's approach to a different mode of interest representation.

Direct local networking and trade union grass-roots activity

This form of transnational effectiveness has a number of facets. One of these is that the French, Italian and Spanish representatives have increasingly translated their own domestic pattern of trade union 'actionism' into the EWC and steering committee. One of our interviewees expressed this as follows. 'The EWC is now showing more determination'. There is a greater readiness to engage in spontaneous actions and shows of resistance. Aside from the action undertaken in connection with the decision to transfer the technical centre, a further action was taken in connection with a French campaign against precarious work. Central management realized that it had to adapt to a style that it had wanted to avoid – namely, the approach that its national managements in Southern Europe were well acquainted with.

A further aspect consisted in the fact that some members of the steering committee shifted their engagement into the business committees that focus on networking local employee representatives at plant level in their respective divisions. The main goal here was to move towards direct face-to-face contact in sub-groups, with the aim that these should gradually be able to become independent of the central structure of the EWC. Some EWC members were also seeking to regionalize activities and devoted the bulk of their efforts to building networks of EWC delegates and local employee representatives into a Southern country cluster.

What these initiatives have in common is that, underground and in the grass roots of the company but within the formal structure of the EWC and drawing on its organizational resources, some of the key figures on the EWC are pursuing a strategy of building transnationally networked local nodes for resistance, and, as a consequence, setting in train a dynamic that differs from the classical Central and Northern European model of works council activity.

This is a list, a static picture of the way in which the EWC has operated. In the section on the steering committee (4.3.5) we present the protagonists in action – moving pictures, as it were – in a form that offers more insight into their actions, motives and contexts. However, before that we need to devote some attention to the way in which management behaves in relation to the EWC.

4.3.4 Relationship between the EWC and management

This relationship has two sides. On the one hand, the CEO, who works closely with the works council and trade union in Germany, has sought to make a good impression at European level, not least in relation to the European Commission with which he has a number of contacts on trade and competition issues. This approach is reflected principally in the fact that the Labour Director, who originates from a trade union milieu, is not only available at any time as the first port-of-call for the central works council but also for the chair of the EWC. This stance is also reflected in the generous EWC installation agreement. In contrast, local and national managers outside Germany, and in particular the heads of non-German business divisions, have little sympathy and understanding for the EWC, and in some cases are unfamiliar with its role. The stance of management outside Germany, with its ignorance of the EWC, is clearly and deliberately not subject to sanctions from central management. The chair of the EWC noted:

> It is not possible to transfer the German codetermination model to Europe as management says, 'In Germany we've had that forced onto us by the union but we're not willing to transfer that to Europe'. So I can call for it as much as I like. In Germany, colleagues are protected [from redundancy] through the option of changing their terms and conditions, but in France they just dismiss people. Why do you take such differing approaches? I think that if there wasn't an EWC, this wouldn't bother management.

Most non-German representatives on the steering committee take a more critical view of top management than the EWC chair, primarily because of the division into good German conditions negotiated for social compensation plans and poor ones for everyone else. For example, a Southern European delegate noted. 'The EWC is not really an important institution for management. We're just a stone on the path that they need to tread around'. Another Southern European delegate said, 'You ask whether management takes us seriously. No, they don't ...' She complained that the divisional heads did not come to the annual meeting. 'The Labour Director comes. But he's just from HR'. This is another illustration of the lack of influence of the Labour Director and his department within the new Burger-Miller company.

German works council members noted that the social order of the company had changed and that the form of employee participation was now seen as a necessary evil and only practised where strongly legally protected, namely in Germany, and evaded elsewhere, an approach seen as a 'strategy of divide and rule'. One German EWC member said, 'Admittedly, from the standpoint of most employees in other countries, one could drop the first part of the name Burger-Miller'. In terms of the change in the corporate culture, management noted that it would lose orders if it improved industrial relations in other countries, given the competitive pressures in their area of the market.

4.3.5 *The steering committee: the protagonists in action*

In addition to the five elected members of the steering committee, the EWC assistant should also be included as a protagonist in the process as he plays an important role in the inner life of these groups, so that in practice the operational heart of the EWC comprises six individuals. The sociogram of this group is relatively transparent. At the heart are the two Germans: the EWC chair and their assistant. They constitute the organizational core, the EWC office. They have a similar view of the EWC, based on the German works council's model, which is why they regret the division between the EWC and the central works council. They prefer the model of consultation and consensus, built on the power of dialogue and the effect of an open door to top management. Their wish is that over the long term the

EWC should benefit from codetermination at Burger, in part based on the fact that the German EWC chair is now a member of the company's supervisory board, which was previously not the case.

A second cluster comprises the French, Italian and Spanish representatives. In particular, the first two of these support a policy that leans towards the trade union grassroots and establishing a countervailing power within the organization through transnational networks of local representatives, and both are very active in this field. One particular feature of these three consists in the fact that when they said 'we' they did not only, and sometimes not primarily, refer to the steering committee but to those 'ordinary' EWC members who shared their views, but who were not members of the steering committee, and also to national employee representatives, that is their clientele, whose representatives – and spearhead – they consider themselves to be within the steering committee. Based on their work with grassroots networking, they have a more marked identity as delegates. They think from below.

The EWC assistant said, not only in relation to the steering committee, but to the entire body:

> The French and Italians bring a lot of dynamism into the body, spontaneously, they press for action, they are more provocative in what they call for. Not only the French representative of the steering committee, but also the other French EWC members. One of these is even general secretary of a French trade union and operates like one. They introduce a lot of initiatives, and one can't really say that about the German EWC members. The Germans see what the French and Italians do in some respects as a disturbance. They say they've got no stamina, these are temporary initiatives, and that it all blows over quickly.

When our research was conducted, the British delegation on the EWC had not yet really established itself and participated only irregularly in meetings. There was a high turnover of individuals and the most recent representative simply stopped attending, but without informing the others. The UK, the second largest country after Germany in terms of the significance of the business and its employment numbers, had not yet really properly arrived on the EWC and steering committee.

Up until 2008, the steering committee formally operated along the lines of a works council. There were frequent meetings on current issues, as noted above, on which the committee issued a statement, and where the German chair sought in both formal and informal discussions with the Labour Director, 'to get something' for the workers affected. This was the German way. Although the Southern European representatives repeatedly pressed for action, they were unable to prevail on this within the steering committee and also not in the body as a whole, in part because they were not supported by the Eastern European delegates. The change came at the plenary meeting in early-2009 against the background of the company crisis and the closure of the logistics location in Italy, which formed the backdrop to the protest action. The Italian member of the steering committee reported as follows.

> At the annual meeting in early 2009 there was a great deal of frustration about the fact that the issue of mass workforce reductions in Europe was not being officially dealt with. And the French and we Italians said: we need to take some action. We are usually the driving force on the EWC and have started the most initiatives. We wanted to travel to Germany and demonstrate: then the other countries said, we are not strong enough. And then our German chair said: there are other forms of action that all can participate in. Ultimately this was a compromise, a lower level of escalation than we wanted. We decided to disrupt the official meeting with management at which there was to be a discussion about workforce reductions in Italy. This strengthened our internal cohesion because *we showed our colours. We showed management that the EWC has become more determined.*

This action was experienced as a major solidarity event. A French delegate commented: 'We showed the Italian colleagues that we were with them in their struggle. This was not conceivable beforehand, we did not have this solidarity, now it looks as if things have progressed'.

The Spanish representative on the steering committee, who had played a major role in pushing the 'French line' in the committee, commented on this action in the following terms:

> It was the first time that we really had a group identity. All the members were evidently concerned about what was taking place in Italy. It was the first time that I had the feeling of being part of a team. We had the support from all, including from the

Germans on the forum. We showed management that we were sticking together,
that we were a real team. They now know that we will stick together. Now that the
crisis has affected everyone, we're showing solidarity.

And the French steering committee member said: 'Yes we are happy because
we've been working hard from the start to build a network and to get to
know each other properly and now it's much better, now we are really
friends. We are now thinking in the same way. This is a good way to tackle
these issues'. He then made a remark that could serve as a motto for this
path to transnational solidarity: '*This is how we do it in Southern Europe*'.
He continued: 'The Northern and Southern way is not the same approach.
Previously we just listened to management, and now we take action. And it
was funny because for us French this is quite normal, but the other countries did not want that reaction because it's not their way of doing things.
Just walking out of the room, for the Germans that's just not right'.

Other delegates also talked about the positive movement towards
a common European consciousness. One Nordic delegate commented,
'There is now a European consciousness. I often hear in discussions that
someone says we must think that we are all Europeans. That is, it's growing. The way in which discussions are held is gradually changing. There's
more reference to a European identity'.

This feeling of solidarity also affected German and Nordic EWC
members. One of them, also a member of the works council at the German
Miller plant, said: 'This strengthened our feeling of togetherness: we – the
European employees of Burger-Miller'. And he added a – for us surprising
– comment. 'More such actions need to be taken'. He also noted, critically,
in relation to the signs of a change in the atmosphere in the climate of
codetermination at the German Miller operation, 'The issue of industrial
relations needs to be re-calibrated if we no longer have a dialogue in which
we are treated as equals. As a trade union we need to think whether we are
prepared to live with this or whether we should resist. Overall there is a
high willingness to engage in strike action. There is unease in many corners.
In principle, there are rumblings of discontent the whole time'.

The specific background for this untypical criticism from that part of
the company that we designated above as 'good German' is the statement

made by the CEO in the context of the German debate on the introduction of a minimum wage: that, in future, the hourly rate for newly-hired German staff on the lowest grade at the German Miller plant should not exceed €9.10. The interviewee saw this as an attempt to import the division in the European part of the company into the German part, and hence as a breach of tradition. He commented: 'That really set something off amongst the people here. And management has not understood that, simply because things have remained quiet. But that's a clearly false interpretation'.

Even if this unusually severe language for the German part of the company could be seen as a statement uttered in the heat of a possible pay dispute, and there is no imminent prospect of harmonising conditions in the First World of the company with those of the Second, this reactions shows that the 'French way' is resonating in the First.

4.3.6 Summary

The EWC at Burger-Miller was first established in 2004, following the acquisition of Miller. It had an auspicious start: both the installation agreement and the level of resources were generous. Based on these favourable initial conditions, the EWC swiftly developed into an active and well-organized forum. Although the level of turnover in the EWC as a whole is high, the composition of the steering committee has been relatively stable. In addition, it meets frequently and has ongoing and intensive communication between meetings. Four of the five members of the steering committee speak English, considerably easing communication. The steering committee is a working body, as with Unilever and Kraft Foods. However, it is not (yet) a body that exercises a significant impact on management decisions through processes of institutionalized participation. The reason for this is that although HRM supported the establishment of the EWC, in practice the key decision makers in the business divisions have withdrawn from dialogue and cooperation. As a consequence, the EWC has a low representative effectiveness.

Burger, a long established company, experienced a very rapid process of internationalization following its acquisition of Miller. As a consequence, the original German core of the company now only accounts for half of the turnover. This has led to a bifurcation into the 'good German' part, with good terms and conditions of employment and strong interest representation, and a 'bad' non-German part, which does not enjoy the same degree of employment protection and whose employees are now subject to the rigid HR policies and practices of divisional managers who are no longer embedded in the German culture of codetermination. The outcome has been two parallel co-existing worlds within one company. The Miller world, with its poor conditions, is the sphere in which the EWC operates. This means that whereas one might expect a company with deep roots in the German tradition to exercise a strong home-country effect, this has not, in fact, come about – in contrast to Ford, where a German home-country effect has become deeply anchored in a non-German company. One major reason for this at Burger-Miller is that the German central works council and the industry union do not identify with the firm's rapid internationalization and concentrate on retaining the status quo in terms of their terms and conditions. As long as the company was still enjoying rapid growth, these issues were not especially evident. The situation changed abruptly as a result of the 2009 financial and economic crisis.

One feature of this EWC is that it initially embarked on its work with a strong sense of European élan. From the outset, there was an underlying idealism within the EWC, anchored in a remarkable openness to ideas of trade union internationalism. 'Solidarity' in this case is an integral part of internal communication and also encapsulates how members perceive themselves. On this basis, an astonishingly high level of internal cohesion has emerged over the short period during which the EWC has existed.

The central experience in this was the relocation of two operations from other Western European countries to Germany. Since then, and despite the solidaristic and European way in which the German EWC chair and his assistant have conducted themselves (the EWC office), distrust of 'the' Germans has become a constant in the EWC. This also created space for a move towards a more adversarial approach to representation, led by a coalition of Southern European delegates, and putting the more cooperative line favoured by the German EWC office under pressure. Whenever central management refused such cooperation, the call for protest and building a countervailing power gained ground and has been expressed in a number of actions. The Southern European members of the steering committee have become engaged in building union networks between locations and constructing grass-roots trade union power. Ironically, a form of employee representation rooted in Southern European adversarial and militant traditions appears to have taken root in the only German company in our study.

Solidarity evidently plays a major role in both the self-perception and activities of the steering committee. The primary form of solidarity guiding the committee is trade union solidarity-in-struggle. Group solidarity, which is a prerequisite for this, has developed well both during the initial phase of the EWC's existence, when there was a strong feeling of embarking on a new era, as well during the subsequent disputes over the correct representative strategy.

This EWC is marked by a tension between solidarity-in-struggle and the solidarity of industrial citizenship: that is, between trade union grass-roots action and dialogue and cooperative participation, with the German delegates supporting the latter. Interestingly, this company, of all those considered in this study, is least characterized by the presence of solidarity motivated by utilitarian self-interest. Rather than material interests, the issues have been fairness, equal treatment and recognition of rights to union membership and organization. Against a background of a high proportion of a generally lower-skilled workforce and workers on precarious employment conditions, the call to acknowledge the rights of employees as workplace citizens has become a clear and insistent demand.

One notable fact in this case is the absence of the home-country effect that might have been expected given the background of the company. The EWC is neither an appendix to nor an extension of the works council at the corporate centre. However, it is the industrial relations arrangements in the homeland that have led to this EWC structure, not out of any inclination to provide for it but through a lack of concern that has led to a degree of detachment. In effect, this represents a 'negative' home-country effect.

What will be critical for the future is how the CEO and other senior managers might respond to this new experience of an EWC that is developing into a protest movement and a possible source of disruption. Although at the time of writing there were few signs of this, the German tradition of 'conflictual partnership' that is strongly embedded at Burger means that the possibility of a learning process and a return to this aspect of its historic path should not be ruled out.

4.4 The EWC as information analyst. Solidarity as a gesture of sympathy

CASE STUDY: SANOFI

4.4.1 The company

The French company Sanofi-Aventis, currently the largest European pharmaceutical company, was created in 2004 through the hostile acquisition of Aventis by the smaller Sanofi-Synthelabo. Both of these component parts had themselves emerged from earlier mergers that had taken place just a few years previously. Sanofi-Synthelabo was the product of the merger between Sanofi (a division of the oil group Elf Aquitaine) with Synthelabo (a division of l'Oreal); and Aventis was the outcome of the merger of the then largest German pharmaceutical company, Hoechst, with the French pharmaceutical group Rhône-Poulenc. The current largest shareholders in Sanofi-Aventis are the French oil group Total (the fourth largest in the world), which acquired Elf Aquitaine in 2000, and l'Oreal, the largest cosmetics company in the world.

The hostile takeover, which took place with the heavyweight support of the then French economics minister Nicolas Sarkozy 'in the interests of France' and as a result of clever tactical manoeuvring by the then head of Sanofi-Synthelabo, Jean-François Dehecq, a friend of Sarkozy's, was a political gesture that stirred strong patriotic emotions on both sides of the Rhine. Those involved on the German side felt that they had been caught off guard, with the German press opining that 'Germany is impotent' (Die ZEIT, 5 August 2004). German employee representatives – both the works council and trade union – were opposed to the merger.

The preceding merger between Hoechst and Rhône-Poulenc had been relatively well balanced in national terms, as the chair of the management board was the previous chair of Hoechst, Jürgen Dormann. However, in the merger between Sanofi and Aventis the Germans were relegated to the back row. Although, in order to calm tempers, Dehecq made a gesture of reconciliation, with ten of the eighteen top positions in the new group reserved for Aventis managers, of which six were German, after a short time only two Germans remained and they had to make do with relatively minor roles. German influence in top management is now practically non-existent. As a consequence the name Aventis, a designation that at least had some resonance for those originating from Hoechst, was removed from the company's title. Since 2010 the company has been known simply as 'Sanofi'.

Following this large-scale merger in 2004, Sanofi then embarked on a number of smaller acquisitions, but in 2010 landed a big fish in the shape of the American bio-tech company Genzyme, bought for €20 billion. Sanofi has been commercially successful in recent years. Sanofi (without Genzyme) employs 55,000 people in Europe (105,000 globally), of which 25,000 are in France (45 per cent) and 10,000 (18 per cent) in Germany, which is by far the largest operation outside France.

Table 5: Sanofi operations in Europe

	France	Germany	Italy	Spain	Hungary	Poland	UK	Total
Production	19	1	5	0	3	1	3	32
R&D	9	1	1	2	1	0	1	15
Marketing, sales & distribution	5	2	1	3	1	1	2	15
	33	4	7	5	5	2	6	62

The structure of the company is characterized by a high proportion of employment in research activities (globally 17,000 staff = 16 per cent) and in sales (qualified pharmaceutical representatives and product advisers). In contrast, there is lower proportion of staff in direct manufacturing activities when compared with other industrial companies. The skill level of the workforce is also comparatively high.

The most significant organizational changes following the merger in 2004 affected the marketing and sales areas, which were placed on a more globalized basis and divided into country clusters. However, Europe is not dealt with as a single sales region; rather France constitutes a single organizational unit that also includes – perhaps curiously – Canada. Although there is a European marketing director, who also chairs the EWC, they are not responsible for the home country, France. This suggests that Sanofi is not a classical Eurocompany but retains a strong orientation to its national home base in France, from which it is managed in a centralized and very hierarchical fashion.

The complex history of the company is evidenced in its highly diverse structure in France, where there are a large number (thirty-three) of small operations. Prior to the merger with Synthelabo, Sanofi was a medium-sized firm that had grown over several years through acquiring a large number of small pharmaceutical companies spread across the entire country, each of which produced products for a wide range of medical conditions. As a consequence, these operations have never been, and are currently not, in direct competition with each other. The acquisition of the Frankfurt-Hoechst site injected a very large-scale chemical operation with a very different industrial history into what was previously an SME. Within the Sanofi group, this German location continues to have a number of unique features that, as we shall see, are also reflected in the structure of the EWC. It is by far the largest production operation within the group (with 8,000 employees in production, compared with the next largest's mere 500) and is also very homogeneously structured as the sole manufacturer of Lantus, the insulin medication, which is Sanofi's largest revenue earner in the pharmaceuticals area, accounting for 16 per cent of total turnover. This product is also the largest single pharmaceutical product by revenue in Germany, and Frankfurt-Hoechst is the largest production facility for manufacturing insulin in the world. In acquiring what was once Hoechst, Sanofi got hold one of the largest blockbusters in the history of pharmaceuticals.

In terms of the organization of production, for reasons of production security there are two facilities for each of the main products to ensure continuity of output should one plant drop out. However, this has not led to strategic competition between sites. For example, the backup facility for Lantus is also located in the Hoechst industrial park. Competition between production operations is, therefore, relatively insignificant. In contrast, there is vigorous transnational exchange in the fields of marketing, sales, research and administration. A large proportion of employees has a direct working contact to the headquarters in Paris and has worked there for shorter or longer periods. As such the level of internationalization, measured in terms of contact to the French head office, is high.

Sanofi has grown strongly in Eastern Europe (Hungary, Poland, Czech Republic) through acquiring existing companies mainly involved in the production of generics. Its generic business (the third largest in the world), now sells in Western Europe under the name of 'Zentiva', the Czech manufacturer that it acquired, in order to highlight the Eastern European contribution to this segment. There have been no major transfers of production from west to east as a result, with this issue, therefore, not a particularly salient one for the EWC. In general, the overall economic situation of the group has been characterized by expansion and growth.

Compared with the other companies in our research, Sanofi is much more strongly marked by the influence of a dominant personality, the former general manager and figurehead of Sanofi, Jean-François Dehecq. He was at the head of Sanofi during its development as a medium-sized company over a period of some forty years, and was its effective founder. He merged Sanofi with Synthelabo, and, with the help of his excellent political connections, was able to turn it into the Europe's largest pharmaceutical group through the 2004 merger. This old school *patron* retired from day-to-day management in 2008. His successor, Christopher Viehbacher, has a financial background and before moving to Sanofi had a twenty-year career at GlaxoSmithKline. This change, with a top manager with an Anglo-Saxon corporate background, has marked a new phase in the history of Sanofi, which has had an impact both on corporate culture and industrial relations at the company.

In social terms Sanofi is a conglomerate that comprises four pillars, the cultures of which have not yet been integrated, and is dominated by the culture of the main parent company Sanofi-Synthelabo. This has led,

in particular on the part of German management, to disappointment at
a high rate of turnover. One German manager cited in the German business press noted: 'German expertise was not wanted. In Aventis we had a
flat hierarchy and a large degree of freedom. Following the merger every
decision has been made centrally, almost feudalistically, in Paris' (*brand
eins*, 09/2007).

Sanofi is confronted by the same challenges facing other large international pharmaceutical companies.

- Innovation in cost intensive research, on which previous successes
  rested, is no longer sufficient and the pipeline for products ready
  to bring to market is too thin. The company is aiming to reduce
  its own research in favour of acquiring small highly innovative
  companies with a correspondingly high share price, particularly
  in genetic engineering. The rundown of research capacity is one
  of the two major issues in the company. Sanofi is currently closing several research sites. Alongside this, the business in generic
  products is being strongly expanded, in particular with the view
  to developing country markets.
- Reducing the equally high-cost distribution system that operates
  through pharmaceutical sales specialists. In the context of cost
  savings being undertaken in health systems, doctors are now prescribed lists of cheaper medications, reducing the effectiveness
  of specialist sales representatives who have now been redirected
  more to dispensing chemists and hospitals, of which there are far
  fewer than doctors in general practice. The consequence is a general
  reduction in the use of pharmaceutical sales specialists, previously
  the guarantee of sales success and who accounted for a large proportion of overall employment.

Industrial relations have taken on a particular significance since the merger
in 2004. Dehecq was very adept at overcoming German resistance to the
merger through his strategy of making friendly approaches to both the
workforce and German employee representatives involved in corporate governance and codetermination. As well as giving noteworthy presentations

to the workforce in Frankfurt, he also wooed the EWC, and especially its German members. In addition, Dehecq granted the German works council a seat as observers on the management board, although this was not required by law. His charm offensive and political skill proved highly effective. From the standpoint of the German works councils, the merger has proved a successful experience. They are more positive than the reported comments expressed by some managers. The guarantee of no compulsory redundancies at the German operations has been kept to, and the number of employees has actually slightly increased. Contact with central management in Paris has been at exactly the same level that they were accustomed to within German codetermination arrangements. To our great surprise, our interviewees in the Hoechst site did not exhibit anything approaching a psychology of defeat or grief for the dismantling of the old Hoechst AG: rather, there was a positive and optimistic mood. There is no longer any trace of resistance to the merger on the part of employee representatives.

4.4.2 Structure and development of the EWC

Each of the two companies that came together in the 2004 merger already had an EWC. For Dehecq it was very important that steps were taken during the early stages of the merger to prepare for the constitution of the new EWC. This new EWC was welcomed from the outset, was established without any friction, and was founded on an emerging mutual respect and scope that initially prompted a degree of euphoria. The EWC agreement was seen as extremely progressive. For example, it included a section that defined consultation in a way that was very close to codetermination, in that the views of employee representatives had to be taken into account in decision-making. The agreement also provided for a three-day training event every two years. In contrast to the EWCs at Unilever and Kraft Foods, this was welcomed by management. This is also probably the reason why Sanofi was commended by the academics and trade unionists that we consulted in preparing our selection of the best case studies for this research.

The EWC has thirty-six members from fourteen countries: twelve from France; seven from Germany; three from Italy; three from the UK;

all other countries have either one or two members. In line with the French model, the EWC chair is a manager, with responsibility in this instance for European marketing. The deputy chair, a speaker for the employee side, and also 'First Secretary' of the EWC is French, Ms. Z. As 'First Secretary', she has two deputies, one French representative and one German The EWC has two plenary meetings a year, which are always held at the company's head office in Paris. All seven German delegates have been on the EWC since it was established in 2004, and five of them were previously on the Aventis EWC. The same applies for those delegates who joined from the Sanofi-Synthelabo EWC.

The steering committee has nine members: four from France (two French secretaries and two further members, each of the four representing a different trade union); two from Germany (the German deputy secretary and another delegate); and one member each from Italy, Spain, and the UK. The committee meets frequently, with sessions held every month in Paris apart from during holiday periods so that, on average, there are ten meetings a year.

The distribution of seats both in the plenary body and in the committee has a clearly bipolar structure that closely resembles that of the Ford Europe EWC. Two countries, in this case France and Germany, have an absolute majority, with France the dominant force.

The French activists on the EWC (secretaries, steering committee members) are senior trade union representatives (*délégués syndicaux*), who are responsible for workplace collective bargaining, rather than members of other workplace participation forums, such as the *comité d'entreprise* and *délégués du personnel*.

The composition of both the committee and the EWC as a whole has been generally stable since its inception in 2004, primarily because the French delegates do not practise the rotation of members between different unions that is customary in other companies, as the overall French contingent is large enough to allow all five trade unions represented in the company to have a permanent seat.

The agreement also lays down that the full steering committee can undertake three trips, each lasting for several days, to local plants in countries in which the company operates, an option which it usually fully exploits. The EWC First Secretary, the chair of the employee side, Z. has full facility time for this function, with the other members of the steering committee having about 15–20 per cent of their working time released for this part of their activity – a fairly high proportion. All these factors taken together mean that the EWC functions in a favourable environment and this might lead one to expect it to be a very effective body. However, this is not the case. Both its effectiveness as a representative body as well as its transnational European orientation, and most significantly its solidarity, are lower than the other case study companies considered here.

For its members, the development of the EWC is divided into two distinct phases: the period when Dehecq was CEO; and the subsequent phase under the new CEO. The first was seen as a positive era, in which the EWC flourished; the latter, in contrast, is viewed as a period of stagnation, with a decline in the quality of industrial relations. In none of the other comparative firms has the personality of the top manager had such a critical role in delegates' perception of the EWC. At the time of writing, the EWC was effectively paralyzed. Nearly all those whom we interviewed spoke of dashed expectations.

4.4.3 Scope and representative effectiveness of the EWC

The management of the business, meetings and negotiating routines of the EWC have been strongly shaped by the French pattern of trade unionism, a culture in which delegates from other countries, especially those from Northern Europe, have felt rather unfamiliar, leading to both confusion and internal friction. This turned on a number of very deeply inscribed behavioural scripts. The most conflictual areas are as follows.

Ideological statements. The first is the practice of reading out almost identical resolutions or opinions on the same topic by the representatives of the five unions represented on the EWC, both at internal meetings of employee representatives as well as at meetings with management. This practice clearly was intended by representatives to secure their legitimacy in relation to their own union organization. Both the German and British delegates had difficulties with this practice as it took up a good deal of time, was not directed towards achieving results, and, in particular, hampered constructive dialogue with management. 'We Germans wanted more discussions with the employer and more genuine internal exchange, but instead we got these very politically motivated resolutions, one after the other. We said we've to get away from these resolutions and move towards constructive dialogue that moves things on' (German respondent). This ritual seems to have abated somewhat in internal meetings after several complaints from colleagues, but not, however, in meetings with management where it still dominates.

Written documentation. The management of business in the EWC is strongly influenced by the fact that detailed written minutes are taken of all meetings and discussions, and these are then made available for correction and authorization by all the French trade union groupings within the EWC and returned with changes and additions. This practice of writing and rewriting, which is seen as both ineffective and pedantic by delegates from several other countries, occupies a substantial proportion of the work of the EWC secretaries – so much so that as far as these delegates are concerned the minutes that are finally produced with such an investment of effort are seen as largely irrelevant and insignificant ('waste of time', 'waste of paper').

Consultancy. In France, the practice of consultation for employee representatives differs from that seen in elsewhere in Europe. Large consultancy firms exist, whose sole task consists in providing economic advice for workplace employee representatives and, in particular, for EWCs. Each EWC has a budget line, which can be considerable, for this purpose. They are brought in to analyse the accounts, and in particular to undertake any special studies in the event of proposed measures such as mergers, takeovers etc. They produce voluminous reports, presumably of a high professional standard, the utility of which, however, was not always entirely clear to many delegates from other countries as, instead of being regarded as a means to an end by the French delegates, they appeared to be seen as valuable in themselves, at least as far as our respondents from other countries supposed. For many of these delegates, the production of such obligatory 'doorstops' conveyed an impression that there was an obsession with moving mountains of paper and engaging in unproductive EWC routines, and this type of consultancy was seen as an extremely sterile exercise.

These observations illustrate that simply the everyday operating routine of workplace employee representation in one country can lead to considerable confusion and frictional losses if transferred to the EWC through that country's dominance.

High level of activity. The activists (secretaries, members of the steering committee) spend a large proportion of their working time on EWC activity. They are also in regular contact with each other between meetings and there is a lively exchange of e-mails and audio conferences. The language problem is of less significance than in many other EWCs: the lingua franca of the body is French. Of the five non-French delegates on the steering committee, two come from other Romance-language countries and speak French fluently, as does one of the German members, so that of the nine members only the German and the British representative need an interpreter. Most of the small talk around the formal meetings with non-Francophone members takes place in English, as a surprisingly high proportion of 'ordinary' members, including the French, have sufficient English for this, probably as a function of the level of education of the workforce in general and their professional role.

This high level of activity stands in remarkable contrast to the meagre effectiveness of the EWC. In response to our question as to what it had achieved so far, we obtained very tentative or negative responses from our interviewees.

In recent years, several small research, sales and also production operations had been closed or experienced reductions in personnel. This topic had been intensively discussed in the EWC, with the EWC sending messages of solidarity and the steering committee making use of its right to visit several of the operations affected. For the EWC members involved, these visits were significant as, for them, the aim was 'solidarity' in a very specific sense. One German participant reported, 'If a plant is at risk than the steering committee will hold a meeting there. We only go to show solidarity, we declare ourselves to be in solidarity and we want it to be documented that we've held the meeting there. We attempt to draw attention to these operations through such gestures so that they get a little bit better known in public'. A Spanish respondent described the situation in similar terms. 'Cases of closure are intensively discussed within the forum. We try to demonstrate a common European solidarity'.

As we have noticed in other case studies, the visit of the steering committee is a major event for the local operation. However, in contrast to the other cases, these visits do not involve any action. The steering committee does not coordinate or intervene in negotiations on a social compensation plan at local level, nor does it seek to transfer headquarters influence to a local operation. That is, the delegation cannot exert pressure on local management by virtue of it headquarters influence. In practice, it arrives with empty hands and must, therefore, restrict itself to symbolic activity.

In this case solidarity is something that is 'declared', 'demonstrated', and 'documented'. Since it does not culminate in any concrete activity, it consists only in gestures. It is not intended to provide specific assistance and it also is not seen as representing any form of protest action to support those affected, which, given the dominant French trade union culture in the EWC, is somewhat surprising. Rather, sympathy and solidarity are staged, as it were. Nonetheless, the effect is astonishing. One German member of the steering committee said that people at the plants that were visited were 'very moved'. Another said: 'They nearly fell over backwards. We might have helped them, although I did not have the impression that we did very much. But that didn't matter, we supported them, we helped them with words'.

The opinions of the German delegates towards such a politics of grand gestures can be seen in this revealing remark. 'It's *only* for solidarity'. And one of the French interviewees remarked, somewhat sarcastically, 'The trips have a very touristic flavour, purely representative'. As noted above, the entire steering committee – nine individuals – undertake these visits.

One topic that had a considerable importance in internal discussions in the EWC, for which it has no institutional competence, was that of pay and living standards at national level. In response to our question as to what important issues the EWC dealt with, one of the German interviewees commented as follows. 'There are very few issues that are specifically related to the EWC. But we've spent a good deal of time talking about wages in individual countries, different levels of purchasing power, pensions, and employee shares'. By 'issues' he meant specific company-related demands that either were, or could become, the object of dialogue and negotiation with their own management. There were none of these.

One French EWC delegate confirmed that discussion primarily turned on matters that had no immediate practical relevance for the EWC: 'There is a lot of discussion about pay developments, how one can reduce the differences and how one could get some convergence between pay levels'.

Another German delegate set out a telling impression of the significance of issues dealt with by the steering committee: 'On the steering committee we discuss small issues that are not that significant [*Interviewer: Do you talk about factory closures?*] Yes, of course there is always something that comes up. But big issues? I would say that one big issue is always the level of pay in different countries'.

The significant issue of restructuring in the pharmaceutical sales force had been a topic that had led to considerable discussion. The French EWC chair (First Secretary) mentioned at one point her own personal record of achievement.

> I'm proud that we've engaged with the problem of the decline of the profession of pharmaceutical sales agent as our French trade unions did not want to accept that anything was changing. The EWC did a good job on this and we were able to form a committee and obtain a report from consultants. I insisted on this as the secretary.

The report – and with it the committee – proved to be fruitless, however, as it had no practical consequences and did not culminate in any demands being formulated for discussion with management. The EWC did not succeed in elaborating positions that were sufficiently developed to enable consultation to take place on the two key issues for representation: cutbacks in research and reducing the number of specialized pharmaceutical field sales staff.

The more energetic approach of EWCs in the other case studies (Unilever and Kraft Foods) when confronted with identical challenges of plant closures and headcount reductions primarily consisted in improving the conditions in social compensation plans through coordinating and acting as an intermediary between local negotiations. The inactivity of the

Sanofi EWC on this central question might have been linked to the fact that employees in the pharmaceutical branch had been 'spoilt' by conditions that were evidently well above those in the food industry, and that companies in this sector voluntarily made higher severance pay offers when they had to 'release' staff. This would imply that the need for representation on the part of the EWC might, perhaps, be lower.

As we have already noted, the EWC was welcomed by the former CEO, Jean-François Dehecq, and had an auspicious start based on a good EWC agreement. In the context of this elevated mood, the steering committee set itself an initial project of negotiating a framework agreement with management on health and safety. However, this was prevented by the two most important French trade unions in cooperation with EMCEF, as they regarded EWCs' having a negotiating mandate as representing competition with the trade unions and were rigorous in rejecting it. Those French EWC members who were initially in favour of this were then put in their place. This internal trade union conflict led to a lasting slowdown in the pace of development within the EWC and ultimately also contributed to its paralysis.

Both French and German respondents said that the EWC did not offer any added value for them. In their countries, the scope for information and consultation obtainable through national representative institutions was seen as much more significant and fruitful than the EWC. However, they did feel that the EWC had an important function for smaller countries. By 'smaller' they meant those countries that lack strong national structures of employee representation at workplace level, primarily the UK and in Eastern Europe. In fact, the UK is represented on the EWC through a national representative body encompassing all Sanofi plants (Sanofi UK Forum). This meets four times a year with management and has internal meetings ahead of this: good cooperation has been built between the two sides and its work was judged to be very positive by our British respondents.

In addition to the fields of activity already noted, the main concern of the EWC, drawing on the help of consultants, is to analyse management reports and announcements. One French delegate said:, 'The issue is to work out the strategy and find out what is happening in a country'.

Following detailed preparations based on these analyses, managers are confronted with very specific questions at the plenary meetings in order to tease out more information. This takes place on the basis of the deeply-held assumption that management will always stonewall and not provide information voluntarily – in fact will attempt to cover up things up – so *that developing an interrogatory style to extract particles of information is seen as the prime activity of the EWC.* One French member of the steering committee described the procedure in detail as follows:

> In our case, within national bodies the procedure is that we receive a three-year strategy from management. Using the opinion obtained from an external adviser, who we know well, we are then in a position to confront management in the forum and say: 'If you do that then I will say to you what will happen and if you do that what will happen'. And so we can enable things to be changed, slow down very grave developments and exercise quite a fundamental influence over their decisions.

This language reveals the psychology of the game: management is 'confronted' as in an interrogation. Another French respondent noted, 'We demand explanations from management'. These are then parried move for move: if you do this, then I'll do that. The discussion has more in common with duelling, with visors lowered, than with open debate. This national model has been transposed one-for-one to the EWC, with the only difference being that delegates from other countries expressed serious reservations about the conclusions drawn by the French respondent, who said: 'So we can change things'. On the contrary, they have the impression that nothing has changed. The fact that the EWC changed nothing in reality was the main complaint of most of the non-French delegates.

This represents a mode of interest representation that is extremely fixated on the written word and on a belief in the value of knowledge and research. It might be seen as productive were it to lead on to action. However, it was precisely this that was felt to be missing by the north European delegates. One German member described his experience of the course of a plenary meeting in the following terms. 'If you're sitting there and none of the managers really say anything, you begin to think, my God, does this have to be like this, is that what I'm going to waste three days on?' This respondent expressed some understanding for management's stonewalling as it could not rely on information being kept confidential. 'I can understand this as management has often fallen flat on its face because the meeting was hardly finished and everything was already in the newspapers. There is a high degree of mistrust'.

In a previous study (Kotthoff, 2006a), this type of EWC in a French company was designated as 'Information analyst' engaged in 'sparring with management'. During the course of this earlier study one German respondent from a French electrical engineering company noted, 'Questions are put very sharply in France, the boss is put under pressure and the blows go backwards and forwards but there's no cooperation ... we Germans say [in opposition to this, *authors' note*]: we want to get somewhere, we want to achieve something, let's do it that way'. We were astounded to find these very same characteristics in another French company. Since the designation 'information analyst' is also very apposite for Sanofi, it has been used once again as the heading for this case study.

The EWC is preoccupied with these rituals of information analysis and of managing trade union competition. The gap between these routines and practical action is bridged by the notion of 'solidarity', understood as symbolic activity that takes the form of gestures of sympathy, albeit certainly with some emotional impact. The Northern European delegates saw this as a form of behaviour that had no impact or practical outcome. They did not understand 'what it was about'. What it was evidently not about was dialogue, results focused consultation, and cooperation.

The low level of added value of the EWC for the French and German delegates and their praise for their own more promising national options for interest representation has meant that there is no shared perspective on representation, nor any real European consciousness, within this EWC.

Overall – as the following quotations illustrate – the view of our respondents was predominantly negative.

> On balance, the EWC does not offer us a great deal because there is no great emphasis or value placed on Europe as each local operation has its own works council. The other countries gain from this, in particular the small ones that do not have their own arrangements. For France, there is not much in it. (French delegate)

The EWC does not help the French and the Germans a great deal as they can help themselves. The incentive for us Germans is that we can use it as a wider network because we sometimes hear things in Paris that we haven't yet heard here. We can use this to impress our local managers. (German delegate 1)

What comes out of it? Little. Apart from our initial agreement: that went quite well. (German delegate 2)

We don't actually really need the EWC. But despite that we are very solidaristic because we know that there are others who do need it. I always say that we should engage in the EWC because nobody has such a good set of arrangements as we Germans. (German delegate 3)

The EWC functioned much better when we were still Aventis. (British delegate)

No convincing development, no, nothing – peanuts. (French delegate)

This is how it is – we're not satisfied because it doesn't really work as we'd like it to but we will stick with it. Because if we weren't there it would be even worse. (French delegate)

On balance you couldn't say that we've achieved a great deal. (Spanish delegate)

On a scale from 1 to 10 most of our interviewees placed the EWC only at two or three.

So why do people stick with it? Why is there such a high level of activity? Why does the steering committee meet so often if it achieves so little? At first glance there is no more satisfying answer to these questions than – routine. This was set in motion by the former 'patron', who was the sponsor and true soul of the EWC.

4.4.4 Relationship between EWC and central management

Relationships with central management are the most delicate aspect of this EWC. In the perception of our respondents, a change had taken place over time. As already noted above, the former CEO, the *patron* and progenitor of the merger, was seen by all as an impressive and indeed charismatic individual, who embraced the EWC with open arms and never shied away from contact with employee representatives. Indeed, he had a degree of reverence for the EWC. The stories told about him are so identical in content that it is appropriate to talk about an emerging myth: for example, that during the EWC plenary meetings he stayed in the room from the first to the last minute, patiently responded to all the delegates' questions, was approachable after the meetings to discuss any local concerns, and conveyed the feeling to all that they were safely in his charge. Some said he actually enjoyed the EWC; it was his baby. Meetings with him were interesting and discussions very open, which was somewhat atypical for French EWC meetings. Instead of duelling and an antagonistic drilling away for information, all ultimately in vain, there was a relaxed and amicable discussion. The Germans said he was more German than the Germans. Whether he was truly open, or simply pretending to be, whether the good mutual contact between them led to nothing more than conjuring up a good atmosphere or had real substance is hard to establish. Those who we spoke to were enthusiastic about the mood. And during that period there was a concrete project in the shape of the proposed European Framework Agreement.

A German member noted: 'The *patron* greatly supported the EWC. He treated you with respect. He thought that everything was very good and that you could achieve something with this instrument, the EWC. For him, being openly European was a political issue. I had a personal track directly to him as I had been the deputy chair to the EWC at Sanofi-Synthelabo'.

The break with this came in 2008 with the arrival of the new CEO. All our respondents stated that he had little interest in the EWC, and he would only attend plenary meetings for an hour or two before lunch and then disappear, and that afterwards the managers who were there did not say anything concrete because they were worried they might say too much. This disregard for the EWC was also expressed in the fact that responsibility for managing the everyday business of the EWC was placed at a much lower level of the corporate hierarchy than previously. A mid-level personnel manager (head of department), who was not even responsible for a European level function and who was not seen as having any real influence on management, became the official contact point for the EWC and attended the monthly meetings of the steering committee. The chair of the EWC is now the head of marketing for the European region. She has little knowledge about European employee representation but does try to comply at least formally by attending steering committee meetings occasionally for a short period.

The French EWC First Secretary noted: 'The new people are much less interested in social dialogue, and that's made it really difficult. Everything was very good with the former *patron*, and we got a very good agreement with him'.

> With the new CEO there was a turn for the worse, before it was positive. There is no longer the enthusiasm for the EWC amongst management that there was before. We're now a little bit caught between two stools. Management does not give much time for the EWC, it's placed lower down in the hierarchy and the important people do not attend (Spanish delegate).

A French member of the steering committee: 'With the old *patron* we had a truly warm relationship. Things are different with the new one. There's been a major change, even one could say a breach. There's no longer exchange, and there's a degree of hardening of positions. The restructuring within the research area took place without real reference to us. There is little interest in the views of the EWC or the trade unions in France'.

One French EWC delegate, a member of the CGT, noted:

> The new CEO treats the EWC in a demeaning way. During meetings the telephone rings after ten minutes, he has to go out, and does not reappear. This is an affront, you can only get angry. Social rights are losing ground here in the company. Personally I would be in favour of simply standing up and saying no. This is a fact, one needs to begin by testing the limits in order to be able to have a discussion. This desire to test out our relative power is growing into a passion. Our management is too fond of string pulling and if the string breaks then the result would have to be – action!

A third French interviewee also took a militant line during the interview: 'Since the new CEO took office the EWC is less respected. Things are going downhill. With the old *patron* social dialogue was seen as very important. We just can't get used to the new arrangement, we need to be much tougher. I'd like to organize a large-scale demonstration in all countries. The company is making high profits and is dismissing people: a scandal!'

It would be reasonable to suppose that in such a strongly French company, French employees on the EWC would enjoy a home advantage in their relationships with central management, such as privileged access. One French delegate said on this: 'No, at the level of the EWC this is definitely not the case. I'll tell you as a French person, perhaps the others will tell you something different'. In fact the others said exactly the same. A British delegate said, for example: 'During the epoch of the *patron*, our French colleagues were very much in control of the meetings. Now there is a different working relationship with the new CEO. They can't control him. He says to the French "We're European, not French"'.

Because of the way in which the merger took place, German EWC delegates also had a privileged relationship with the former CEO. They had access to him at any time and nurtured the style of communication with him that they were accustomed to within Germany. They have managed to achieve the miracle of continuing this special relationship with the new CEO.

A German delegate noted:

> We've also managed to get close to the new CEO. As works councillors with strong rights we're used to this, we wouldn't allow this to be diminished, and if that happened we'd simply arrange a meeting with him. However, the British, for example, would not do that. Nor would delegates from Eastern Europe. They would never ever personally speak to a member of top management. They do not have the same expectations as us. We say: 'We're not going to the monkey, we want the organ grinder', we want to know. [*Interviewer: How do the Spaniards do that, for example?*] They've never asked for it, they're not used to it. They ask us 'Could you tell us how this operates'. As Germans we're really spoilt.

On the question as to whether management is cooperative, a German delegate responded: 'Not to the French. They make a real division between the French and us Germans. When the French representatives come along with their stuff they often block them and they just let them go off in their own way'. And a British delegate said complementing this: 'Management definitely finds it easier to do business with the Germans'.

Confidential discussions do take place between the Germans and top management:

> They don't have any reservations towards us, we have good standing with them, good relationships. We have a closer relationship to them than the French [*Interviewer: Are you still welcome guests at the management board in Paris?*] Yes, I must say. They deal with us with respect. It's different with the French unions; they deal with us differently. And that also helps us with our work here in Germany locally, because our local managers also know that we've got good contacts higher up. One example: because of the current social compensation plan we've been negotiating for our side [due to headcount reductions at the German research operation] we've often approached the CEO and said 'Do you have a half an hour for us'. And he said 'Yes, please come by'. And then we're both at the same level and we've had a discussion and we weren't long back from Paris when he sent something to our local HR chief in Frankfurt that there was something for us (raising severance payments). The head of personnel here nearly completely broke down, but we'd threatened him beforehand that if things didn't go as we wanted then we'd go and talk with the big chief. And he laughed at us. Such things are naturally a great help. This is also important for the workforce in Germany as a source of legitimacy, so that the people here see we're not just satellites in this firm but that we, as works councillors, have a network not just to employee representatives in other countries but also to top management in Paris, which is not exactly typical.

4.4.5 The Steering Committee: The protagonists in action

The Sanofi EWC represents a refutation of the hypothesis that frequency of contact alone suffices to promote group cohesion. This EWC has frequent contact – two annual meetings, ten steering committee meetings, a good deal of e-mail traffic and telephone conferences between steering committee members, few language problems – yet despite this its cohesion, its sense of social congeniality, is low. It has the lowest cohesion of all the EWCs in our case studies, and has not emerged as an effective unit with a capacity to take action. This deficiency is so evident that at the end of the interviews we asked steering committee members why they had bothered to meet every month in Paris over so many years if so little emerged as a result, and that there was also no feeling of social togetherness and cohesion. The answer to this is set out at the end of this section.

All our interviewees attributed this failure to an unbridgeable clash of cultures within the forum. They said that the gulf between the different 'trade union cultures', principally the French and the German as a result of its bipolar make-up, was too great. All, including the French, said that the organization, style and operation of the EWC were dominated by French trade union culture. For the non-French union respondents, this dominance and one-sidedness was the reason why no common perspective or path had emerged. This disparity in trade union cultures was also viewed as one of the main differences between the culture of Aventis and of Sanofi-Synthelabo, although in this case the Aventis culture – despite its being incorporated under French law – was seen as more German by the French respondents due to the greater significance of Hoechst within the EWC.

The French delegates, in particular, were surprised by the persistence of such large differences in industrial relations cultures, given the amount of contact over the years. They seemed to assume that other countries would work in much the same way as France, whereas respondents from elsewhere were much more familiar with and conscious of these systemic differences.

One French EWC delegate noted: 'The ways in which the French and the Germans operate is very different. I'm always surprised by this. I didn't imagine it would be like this'.

A French member of the steering committee noted: 'We French have our culture and the Germans have theirs. Within the EWC our culture clearly has priority. And the cultures are not getting any closer. I'd like to be able to tell you something different but I'm certainly not convinced of it. The Germans don't understand how we operate and we don't understand them'.

A long-serving German delegate on the steering committee confirmed this in the following terms: 'Yes, yes, there are very different trade union cultures'. She then added a phrase that explained more than these differences themselves. 'But as yet we have never had a discussion about this'. This lack of discussion about the differences and the lack of a discussion about the unchallenged French dominance was confirmed by a British member of the EWC. He was very disappointed at the lack of fellowship and openness, and angry about the self-absorption of the dominant French delegation.

He also added, self critically: 'I've never actually set out my criticism in the way I'm doing now with you'.

This collision between the industrial relations cultures of Southern and Northern European within EWCs is well attested to from our other case studies. With Unilever, this clash was perhaps even more serious than at Sanofi. But there it was also a topic of ongoing discussion and debate and was placed openly on the table, differences were set out and retained, and there was a growth in cohesion and commonality. Although the development of the EWC into an effective body might have been made more difficult by this, it was not ultimately seriously hampered. In contrast, internal relationships within the Sanofi EWC are categorized by a strong undertow of unrest, underneath a surface appearance of friendly and polite mutual interaction and business as usual. People are, nonetheless, drawing more closely together. The atmosphere was described in the following terms by a British delegate:

> I've been meeting the French on the steering committee every month for six years, but yesterday evening was the first time I've spoken with them, really spoken in the sense of a chat, what hobbies we've got, things like that. Otherwise the meetings are just 'hello are you okay', kiss on both cheeks and then back to my table.

This very late development of close personal relationships came about within the context of a training event scheduled over several days. A non-French member of the steering committee responded to the question as to whether there was cohesion on the steering committee in the following terms: 'I think that we'd like to present this image. We are polite to each other. We promote this image [*Interviewer: Is it actually lived in reality?*] You mean outside the meeting room? [*Interviewer: Yes*] No, I think it's a façade'.

The initial impression gained from the sociogram of the steering committee is that, despite the high frequency of meetings, it is not really a committee that takes executive action, sets a direction and has access to any powers that would enable it to generate a wider dynamism. It is not a strong centre of action, and in this respect is more like the steering committee at Ford. For our respondents, the EWC is, therefore, more associated with the plenary meetings than with the activities of the steering committee. As a consequence, understanding the sociogram of the steering committee means looking at the forum as a whole.

At the centre of this lies the majority consisting of the French members, although these are far from being a solid bloc along the lines of 'the French and the rest'. The four French members of the steering committee originate from four different trade unions. Three are from Sanofi-Synthelabo and only one from Aventis (Rhône Poulenc). Their spokesperson is Ms. Z., the 'First Secretary' of the EWC, who was previously a member of the steering committee of the Sanofi-Synthelabo EWC. She is a member of the CFDT. Her function is that of the EWC chair, in the sense used elsewhere in this study: formally under French law, the forum is chaired by a manager, the CEO for Europe. However, in practical and political terms the 'First Secretary's' role can barely be described as that of a chair. The leadership of the French group, and as a consequence of the EWC as a whole, is not strongly developed and does not match the role played by the EWC chairs at Unilever and Kraft Foods. Differences in status and authority between individuals within the French delegation also seem to have been deliberately compensated for in terms of balancing the relationships between trade unions, obstructing the establishment of a single leadership role. Amongst her duties, the 'First Secretary' takes care of the organization of meetings, is responsible for the minutes, and is the formal addressee for management. She does not have an assistant or secretary – that is, there is no EWC office – but looks after these tasks herself and is supported by the assistant 'secretary' of the EWC, who represents the CGT on the steering committee. Interestingly, none of the four French EWC members on the steering committee can be regarded as representatives of extreme positions or as 'typical French troublemakers'. None of them stood out as calling for protests or militant actions. In fact, since the merger there has not been a strike in any of Sanofi's French operations and neither have there been any protest actions, as was also the case previously at Sanofi-Synthelabo. One reason for this might be related to the nature of the industry, which is characterized by high pay and relatively secure jobs in the pharmaceutical side, and in terms of the employment structure, which is made up primarily of white-collar staff, many of whom are highly qualified.

This French bloc determines the style and manner of operation of the EWC, such as how plenary meetings function and internal communications.

The second largest contingent consists of the Germans. The two German representatives on the steering committee are Herr V., the chair of the works council of the largest German production operation, and Frau W., chair of the works council of the German sales operation. In addition, the German chair of the central works council is the only foreign employee representative with observer status on the company's management board. Other members perceive the Germans as a closed unit and as an elite group with its own way of working, style and mentality – in fact as a group that functions as the real counterpart and alternative to the French bloc. However, since the Germans have their own special access channel to top management they are not really dependent on the EWC. As such, they do not operate in direct competition to the French, which might be expected given the bipolar nature of the forum. They simply do not enter the ring. The Germans were both more well disposed towards, as well as more reticent about, the French bloc than some respondents from other countries. They participate in a cooperative way in meetings and gener- ally play along, but do not fulfil the hopes placed on them by some other national delegates – that is, pressing for a change in the nature of the game to raise the EWC's representative efficiency and effectiveness. In fact, they do not oppose the French bloc and have not pushed for greater influence and scope for the EWC or for a more Germanic approach – because they have the privilege to be treated almost as a German central works council at the company's Paris headquarters.

The British delegate on the steering committee, Ms. C. was previously a steering committee member for the Aventis EWC. As a long-serving delegate, her perspective had been shaped by the EWC's positive effect in enabling national representative arrangements to be established at Sanofi UK (the Sanofi UK Forum). Ms. C. aligned herself with the German posi- tion on the EWC. 'My understanding of the EWC is very close to that of the Germans. I think UK people are close to the Germans, our ways of life are very similar'.

The two other delegates on the steering committee from Spain and Italy were caught between two stools. As far as the modus operandi of the EWC was concerned, they were familiar with the French style of representation from their own countries. As far as outcomes were concerned, the Spanish delegate saw himself in some respects as closer to the critical stance adopted by the Germans and the British. The Italian delegate was seen by the others as being closer to the French bloc.

There was little personal familiarity between members of the steering committee. One reported: 'Not a great deal goes on but we do say to each other "I've heard this and that, how does it look from your viewpoint, or we ought to put that on the agenda, what do you think?"'

Procedure is dominated by the French bloc, whose view of how meetings should be organized has made it difficult to foster informality, networking and closer personal acquaintance. For example, travel and accommodation for plenary sessions and steering committee meetings are not organized collectively, and each delegation has to arrange these individually. One consequence is that foreign delegates are then scattered across several hotels in Paris, with no opportunity for a collective drink at the end of the day's business – a practice which almost all our respondents in every company agreed was vital for building confidence and facilitating networking. One technical reason was that travel costs are not covered by the corporate headquarters but paid for by delegates' own local operations. In addition, no joint meal is organized and there is no social programme (such as a trip on the Seine, sightseeing, or cultural events) during the two days of the plenary meeting. In all the other case study companies, such opportunities and scope for social contacts were regarded as self-evident and, as far as we could ascertain, were always organized in companies based in Germany. We do not have an explanation as to why Sanofi deviates from what would seem to be a tried-and-tested, and indispensable, means for networking, given that these practices were strongly cultivated at Aventis. Even supposing that this approach is one chosen by management, about which we were not entirely certain, the French bloc on the EWC appears to have taken no initiative to counter it. On the contrary, one English delegate brought up this surprising lack of concern for sociability and informality on the part of the French colleagues, who responded as follows: 'They said they weren't responsible for us, we weren't children'. Arguably, such a brusque reaction is more likely to choke off any process of building trust rather than promote it.

A German respondent offered an alternative explanation. He argued that the French members who lived in Paris did not get expenses to cover a collective meal and that local restaurants were expensive. Moreover, they wanted to get back to their families as quickly as possible. An English respondent reported that delegates from 'smaller' countries (in terms of employment in Sanofi), the UK, Spain, Italy, Greece and Austria did organize a joint meal in Paris, and this functioned very well without interpreters as most of those who attended had adequate English. Even if these delegates were to develop slightly closer relations as a result of this initiative, this is arguably more of a dry run as far as EWC work is concerned given the absence of the home-country delegates who are likely to be the best source of news and background about the company's policies. And given the absence of the Germans, that is the bloc whose modus operandi is most respected and from whom one would expect to gain the most from mutual exchange, this would appear to an alliance of satellites. Other notable absentees included the Eastern Europeans. One difficulty in their case has been a degree of suspicion about whether their delegation is entirely legitimate. It was suspected that some delegates had been sent by management and not their trade union.

Even in the case of the frequent meetings of the steering committee, which normally required an overnight stay in Paris, there was no evening programme. The style adopted by the main French protagonists was formal and distanced, and surprisingly uninterested in delegates from elsewhere.

Two events, in particular, in the history of the EWC generated a good deal of mistrust. The first was the attempt by the EWC to conclude a European Framework Agreement with management, which foundered on trade union resistance. The second was the court ruling obtained by two French trade union federations that prohibited management from informing the EWC about corporate decisions *before* it informed national French representative bodies. This constituted a veritable legal assault on the EWC from within the ranks of employee representatives.

Two years after the merger, during a training event that lasted for several days and in a mood of enthusiastic expectation, the EWC had held a discussion to set joint objectives and plans. On a proposal made by the First Secretary, Ms. Z., the German delegation and several other delegates, there was agreement on a plan to conclude a European Framework Agreement on health and safety. In order to skirt around the constraints imposed by the EWC Directive, which limits EWC rights to information and consultation, the promoters of this project suggested establishing a Special Negotiating Body for this purpose based on the legal procedure used to establish an EWC. Management, still led by the former EWC-friendly *patron*, was agreeable to this. However, this was prevented by EMCEF and the national French trade unions. One German interviewee responded as follows:

> This was the only time where we really began to think about the sense and purpose of it all. And we had made a good start. Then EMCEF and French trade unions stepped in: an agreement was national law, they feared that we might weaken free collective bargaining. EMCEF, therefore, wanted to be present at the negotiating table. Management said that it would only negotiate with company level internal negotiators. Since then the whole issue has been on ice. What impressed me was that this was the first time that we were able to agree on something like this, on the EWC's direction, above the level of individual countries. And we also agreed on the issue: identical standards on health and safety. It's a shame and it was frustrating as it took us a long time to get there and we put a good deal of effort into it.

After this no further attempt was made to tackle anything jointly. 'There will also be no more efforts to open up new areas after what happened with health protection. We don't have anything, there is nothing'. And another German EWC member expressed his anger in the following terms: 'The framework agreement was torpedoed by EMCEF, and our own German IG BCE was also involved. I'm still really angry about this'.

This incident also lead to serious conflicts within the French unions, with the 'Europeans' on one side, including the First Secretary herself and some other French delegates, and EMCEF, full-time officials from the French trade unions, and other national trade unions on the other. One of the French 'Europeans' described the affair as follows:

> We felt extremely betrayed by EMCEF, which did not support our approach, and most national unions also did not support us. This loosened our ties and, since after a time our group [the French EWC delegates, who were originally in favour of negotiations, *authors' note*] diverged from the agreed course I was very angry because my words and what I had written had not been correctly quoted. We did not want to put EMCEF in a difficult position, on the contrary. The text was even supported by some members of the European Parliament, but not within our own union. EMCEF consulted national union federations, but the result was negative. This was not honest. I can't be bothered to work any more with EMCEF. Our proposal triggered a real dynamic process and it was knocked down in one blow because someone noticed that there were not many links between the delegates on the EWC and their national organizations. Well for me it's like this, there are people who I just don't want to meet because they betrayed us. *As a consequence there is little trust between the delegates within the EWC.* There's still mistrust. For example, if you just ask for some simple information, such as on the employment situation in individual countries, even that doesn't function.

This French delegate divided his period of office into two equal halves: the first half after the merger up until the failure to conclude the framework agreement, during which matters were moving forward; and the following half, during which what had been the tender plant of a joint approach withered away. He is now frustrated and feels offended, and sees no prospect for change.

The British delegates were also annoyed with the EMCEF official and the French trade unions: 'I didn't ask for him to come, I'm not interested. We are the committee, and he just an observer. I don't want him to make comments. I don't want his guidance. I don't want him to control us'. EMCEF, according to this individual, exercised too much influence over some of the French trade unions.

The framework agreement project was the highlight, the 'dynamic ... the only time when there was a debate about the purpose and role of the EWC'. It was destroyed because the French EWC delegates felt themselves under an obligation to the union federations. The most valuable thing about the EWC, namely the first steps towards practical solidarity, was squandered. More important than the failure of the agreement itself was the fact that this sowed the seeds of mistrust amongst EWC delegates.

The second conflictual event, which had disastrous consequences for internal relationships on the EWC, was the successful trade union legal challenge to the Sanofi management board that culminated in a ruling that prohibited it from informing the EWC *prior* to the competent national French representative body in an internal procedure.

> Management now plays safe and informs the relevant French body first. They are scared of making a mistake. We Germans on the EWC, also the English and some others, wanted to it to be the other way round. We were not successful. No majority was achieved because some delegates from Eastern European countries were against it. There is constant conflict over this on the EWC.

When interviewed on this issue, our French respondents played their cards very close to their chests and did not bring it up spontaneously. However, it was the central critical issue, and a major source of irritation, for the German delegates, who asked themselves why they should go to Paris if management is compelled to sit in meetings wearing a muzzle. The German delegation had complained to their French colleagues in very emotional terms on this issue at a plenary meeting. And they had also defended themselves in formal terms:

> We Germans sent a protest note to management: we would not come to Paris to any more EWC meetings at which we would find out nothing new: we were not going to be treated like idiots. The EWC had to be informed first if a measure affected several countries. *This did not interest our French colleagues at all, they simply carried on as before.* From a German perspective the whole thing went completely off course. Of course, management realized that there had been an internal conflict.

For the Germans, the second most significant force within the body, this meant that the EWC had lost much of its attraction. No other issue highlighted the difference between the French and German modus operandi as clearly as the deep disinclination of the Germans to attend meetings at which nothing was achieved. One German delegate noted: 'The really negative thing about the EWC is the arguing between the trade unions: what harm would it do to give the EWC a right to be the first port of call for information on European matters'.

Ms. Z. the EWC First Secretary, also regretted this event. 'Most of the French trade unions (delegates) did not support the application made by the Germans. This really torpedoed the EWC. It's difficult to come to terms with this'.

The EWC's two internal ordeals share a common root: the unchecked incursion into the EWC of competition between national French trade unions, and their power games, putting it at the mercy of internal French trade union politics. The French bloc on the EWC is obsessed with these issues.

One German interviewee commented as follows:

> The French debate only with each other and not enough with the others. The reason is the large number of trade unions that have to try to reach a consensus. They argue over which union will put its signature to a document or agree on some subject or other. And then they argue again and they carry on doing that in the EWC. Barely any of them feel obliged to use the EWC as a European forum.

According to a British delegate, 'the French are very hard because they are very much unionized in their mindset. So it matters very much what the union wants them to come with'. The intensive e-mail traffic between steering committee members is also largely taken up by this issue: 'I could spend most of the day waiting for e-mails to come through and send them out again, you know, and I could fill them all with union stuff if I would answer all union issues'.

Given these circumstances, the 'First Secretary' had a very difficult task. She had taken on the role of trying to establish a degree of diplomatic balance in an environment dominated by trade union competition and status issues, seeking to cool emotions and ensure that EWC business can be conducted. Her foreign critics accused her of granting too much attention to this national fixation when chairing meetings and of being overly concerned not to fall out with any of the French trade unions instead of directing the EWC to European topics proper. 'She is always wanting to please all the time and not getting on what we need to do. [*Interviewer: wanting to please whom?*] To please their unions and to pacify the French around the table when we know the French unions don't agree to a subject matter. So she wants to keep it all calm'.

This obsession with union affairs was seen as counter-productive and the Achilles' heel of the EWC. One interviewee from Northern Europe had no time for it, as a comment from a British delegate reveals.

> I never use my union badge on the EWC because I'm not representing my union. I'm representing my people. But the French get too tied up in unions and politics around unions, *there is too much union interference with EWC*. But we, as the EWC, are our own. And I think the UK people are strong, but we don't have to use our union influence if you understand me. Our voice as EWC delegates is enough I think.

A German delegate saw that the situation in similar terms: 'We keep trade union matters out. Our delegates in the select committee are heavily engaged in the IG BCE [German chemical industry trade union, *authors' note*] and also keep it informed about our EWC. I think that's enough. We're not competing with the national trade unions. Unlike the French, we can talk about our working conditions both nationally and at European level without trespassing on trade union terrain'.

In the eyes of the German, British, and some of the Spanish and other delegates, the French bloc's obsession with internal French trade union competition and the power balance between them has diverted the EWC from its real responsibilities – genuine representation, dialogue with the employer, and tackling particular common tasks. They are critical of what they see as too much discussion and too little action. One Spanish delegate expressed this in classically diplomatic terms when he said: 'The positive thing about the French is that they are very good at expressing themselves, there is a lot of discussion. I believe generally that we have good intentions on the EWC but we do not implement them so that management also sees that what we say also becomes reality'.

A German delegate responded to the question 'Who are the driving forces of the EWC?' somewhat less diplomatically and more ironically with the comment: 'You mean verbally?'.

Some delegates, and in particular the British, were enormously irritated and expressed their criticism very directly:

> It's very frustrating for the likes of me to come all the way from the UK for a meeting and we end up going off the agenda and not concentrating on what is to do. If you make a comment you are slightly frowned up. You have to make sure that you

can take something back, but it's frustrating when the subject matter changes all the time. It floats and they have no substance. They have a lot of very direct questions to management, wanting lots of answers. But something we don't have is knowing what we are going to go for, the kind of thing where in the UK we would say: right, let's challenge them.

This interviewee was perturbed by the severity of his own criticism and sought to smooth it over by saying that he did not mean it personally: 'We do struggle with pure French people, not like there is a personal issue, it's just the subject matter that floats'.

This tendency to stray off the point, combined with a lack of clear aims and focus, was also painfully evident in discussions with management. Debates were reported as being conducted unprofessionally, with management finding it easy to divide the EWC. 'When we meet management we may discuss things *but then it goes off at a tangent* and talking about other things, so it ends up with no structure. That's what frustrates. And it frustrates other non-French delegates too, you know'.

A German delegate criticized the fixation on trade union matters and the lack of willingness of the French bloc to work together in the context of a specific instance, the closure and contraction of research operations in France and in Germany. 'The French insist on being the first to be informed at national level. But they didn't succeed in any way in mitigating the measures through a social plan. And suddenly we Germans are confronted with a demand to negotiate a social plan for our operation. It's completely ridiculous and did not go well'.

Some French delegates themselves were also critical in some respects about the weaknesses of the EWC. The 'First Secretary' complained that a working party on the employment situation had been established but never really got going, and management had waited for several months for an answer to its document. 'We don't arrive at a point where the EWC finally says – let's get on with it'.

From the standpoint of the Germans, the refusal of the French to deal confidentially with some information provided by management undermines the scope for dialogue and, as a consequence, one of the most important prerequisites for representative effectiveness. 'You can understand why management will often not disclose everything to the EWC, because they

often fall flat on their faces as the meeting has not even finished and everything is already in the newspapers. And they have never experienced that
with us, and therefore they're open with us'.

One element in the complaints made by the others about the
inefficiency of the French bloc also includes a lack of appreciation of the
'useless' culture of obsession with the written word instead of discussions,
and specifically the huge role played by consulting firms and the whole
apparatus of minute-taking. One German member of the steering committee noted on this:

> The French put a great deal of emphasis on the consulting firms that analyse accounts.
> A lot of money is really wasted here. It's a quite different culture. I don't add under-
> stand how one can waste time with such stuff and such a tornado of paperwork.
> Apparently they also read everything. Incredible! If they read in the paper that Sanofi
> is interested in another company they immediately commission a study, and then a
> book. I always think, my God, by the time they've got through all those papers the
> merger would have taken place ages ago. *They just don't look at what eventually happens.*

Another German respondent answered in the following terms:

> The French colleagues write everything down, every word. I sometimes ask myself
> whether they ever read it. What's the point of it. It's a real mentality. There's no real
> reason for it. It's the same with the consultants we got to report on the future of the
> pharmaceutical sales staff. The money is there, and we've got a budget. But personally
> I've never seen any use in any of this and we've had plenty of these expert reports.

Although one of the French interviewees mocked this practice, she ultimately defended it: 'The written text needs three or four months and it can
take a long time. Every participant wants to change a comma, the management, delegates etc. Everyone wants to change a comma or exclamation
mark. Despite that, it can be useful sometimes. You can say, for example,
look I've got the official document, a year ago you committed yourself to
this strategy for this country or Europe or all over the whole world'.

These peculiarities of French 'culture' can only be so prevalent within
the EWC because the French bloc is so self-absorbed. There is no syncre-
tism that draws on other traditions. A German member of the steering
committee noted: 'No, we Germans will not become French. But that has

no significance for the EWC. In the EWC only France has a role, and they find it all quite splendid. The subjects that we talk about, how the meetings are organized, are very French'.

Conversely, the French suspect the German bloc of collaborating with management. One French delegate was quite open about this: 'The Germans think that their way is the best. They sort things out with management and nothing is supposed to reach the outside. And as a result they are quite popular with management. [*Interviewer: Are the Germans less European because of this?*] That's what the French think, yes that's right. It's a shame that the Germans didn't say to the others that they will not pass their information on. It's a pity, but I'm not being judgemental'.

4.4.6 Summary

The establishment of the EWC in the merged group took place under exceptional circumstances, as it was initiated and promoted by Jean-François Deheqc, the *patron*, with the aim of disarming critical voices in Germany (Hoechst works councils, trade unions, politicians). The fact that Deheqc saw the EWC as a catalyst for the merger led to its becoming his 'darling' and was regarded as a kind of protected species from the outset. It was able to obtain a very good installation agreement – the best of the cases considered in this research.

The distribution of seats on the EWC indicates – in line with the national distribution of employment – that the French delegates constitute the largest single bloc, with twelve out of thirty-six places. Within the steering committee, the dominance of the French contingent is even more noticeable, with four of nine seats and a right to appoint the chair. The formal structure of the body is, as a consequence, characterized by a notable home-country effect.

Based on these favourable initial conditions, the EWC soon developed into a well-organized body with high level of interactive density and frequent meetings. These conditions offered favourable prerequisites for a high level of representative effectiveness. Astonishingly, however, this has not been achieved. Neither the steering committee nor the EWC as a whole has, as yet, been able to agree on a set of common issues around which to pursue advances in representation through dialogue with management. The two most outstanding pan-European employment problems have been the closure and contraction of research sites and staff cuts in sales operations. Although these topics were discussed internally, the debate did not focus on achieving a concrete outcome as no specific practical approach emerged that held out the prospect of securing some success through dialogue with management. In the case of plant closures, for example, the action taken by the steering committee has consisted in sending a message of solidarity to the affected site, sometimes in association with a plant visit. It has not taken on any support or coordination roles, such as helping in negotiations for a social compensation plan. The lack of activity directed towards concrete outcomes has meant that this EWC, despite a high frequency of meetings, has not become an effective working body. Although intensely busy, this is more a pre-occupation with itself than engagement with employees' problems.

Solidarity is the subject of lively discussion within the EWC, but this culminates in little more than gestures. Although these can certainly have an emotional impact on the recipients, they are not directed towards any objective. Action is essentially symbolic in nature.

The relationship between the EWC and former CEO, Jean-François Dehecq, was excellent. When he retired in 2010, this benign atmosphere soon dissipated. His successor had neither the intent nor the manner to continue this relationship. He avoids contact with the EWC and does not value dialogue with it – with the exception of the German delegates, who enjoy privileged access to him based on their cooperative approach.

Internal relationships on the forum are characterized by the hegemony of the French 'bloc', which comprises four national trade unions, each of which does not aim to accommodate the other and which are also fixated on the domestic affairs of the French homeland. As a result, the EWC has become preoccupied with internal French union competition and achieving a balance between their respective interests. Against this background, two events occurred that constituted central negative experiences for the EWC, setting in train a downward spiral of trust. In the first, a French trade union took court action to remove the right of the EWC to be informed by management about changes in the company's European strategy *before* national French representative bodies. This was seen as knock-out blow by delegates from other countries, who asked why they should travel to Paris for EWC meetings if European issues had already been appropriated by national bodies. The German and British delegates, who protested about this, reported: 'Our protest did not interest the French colleagues at all. They simply carried on'.

The second negative experience was the efforts of the EWC to conclude a first European Framework Agreement with management on health and safety. These were quite far advanced, but were then torpedoed by some French trade unions together with EMCEF – a step also applauded by trade unions in some other countries. This also exposed the French EWC chair, who had invested a good deal of energy in this project. The cause was identified by a British EWC member in the following terms: 'What's really negative are the trade union disputes'.

Group solidarity between the 'French bloc' and other delegates is low. For example, this is the only one of our case studies in which there is no provision for informal contacts between members, and in particular between those from the homeland and other countries. No attempt is made to cultivate personal connections and no such connections have been formed. Dealings are formal and distanced. The Sanofi EWC illustrates particularly clearly that it is difficult for other forms of solidarity to take root in the absence of group solidarity and personal trust as this also means that there is a lack of the solidarity, as well as the requisite discipline, needed to constitute an institution. Steps towards strengthening group identity were vitiated by negative key events. The French national system of representation at company level militates against building the EWC into a capable actor. What is surprising in this case, however, is that there has been no hint of the genuine and specific strength of the French system of representation, namely militant solidarity (protest, acts of resistance), but merely rhetorical expressions and ritual gestures of proletarian solidarity.

One general conclusion from this is that the EWC is highly constrained by the home-country effect. Those members who had hoped to build it into a participative force within the company feel extremely let down. In its initial years, when it was favoured by the *patron*, it represented a fairweather EWC that subsequently lost its bearings when buffeted by headwinds.

CHAPTER 5

Comparing patterns of solidarity:
Varieties of constellations for interest representation

Our research has unearthed four patterns of EWC solidarity:

- Solidarity as an extension of the status of 'workplace citizen'.
- Subsidiary solidarity.
- Protest solidarity versus participative solidarity.
- Solidarity as a gesture of sympathy.

We now propose to compare these patterns using the research dimensions of group solidarity, calculus of self-interest, activity, group constitution, and effectiveness. Our hypothesis as to the relationship between these dimensions is as follows. The aim and objective of the EWC is the effective representation of interests at European level. Effectiveness presupposes activity, in the sense of a high frequency of meetings, internal communication and joint work. Successful activity, in turn, presupposes the internal organization of a steering committee, which constitutes the capacity and discipline enabling it to act as a cooperative and integrated group. In turn, and crucially, becoming constituted as an organized group with the capacity to take action (an 'association') depends on trust, which, for its part, is the outcome of familiarity, mutual acquaintance and a sense of cohesion, but is (also) a function of the fact that EWC delegates believe that the EWC can be of use for their own countries.

Table 6: Research dimensions – overview

	Activity		Effectiveness		Group constitution		Group solidarity	
	High	Low	High	Low	High	Low	High	Low
Unilever	x		x		x		x	
Kraft Foods	x		x		x		x	
Ford		x	x			x		x
Burger-Miller	x			x	x		x	
Sanofi	x			x		x		x

Accordingly, we consider solidarity in terms of its relationship to representative effectiveness: that is, as a form of activity which raises cooperation in order to achieve a common aim. It embraces those perceptions and activities that enable a pressing and challenging problem for interest representation to be resolved. We do not include in this that type of solidarity that offers no more than symbols and rhetoric, although we do register this as an indicator of support and concern.

The pattern of 'solidarity as an extension of workplace citizenship' (Unilever and Kraft Foods) is ranked as 'high' in all four dimensions. These EWCs have both high effectiveness and high levels of activity. Their steering committees operate in a way that corresponds with the model of a 'participative working forum'. They exercise ongoing transnational representative activity by raising employee interests in dialogue with central management. Management, which initially took a negative stance towards them, now fully acknowledges them as a partner for dialogue and, increasingly, as a negotiating party. They exercise a participative function at European level that is moving towards the status of a German group works council. This does not mean that they have reached this standard, but rather that they aspire to such a role. We already made an initial assessment of their function and effectiveness in an earlier study (Kotthoff, 2006a). It is now possible to see from a position of closer proximity what has facilitated such effectiveness and how such EWCs have acquired their capacity for action. This is primarily the result of an impressive process of group formation enabled by a comparatively high level of group solidarity.

Social proximity that builds trust has not emerged spontaneously, but has been the product of a step-by-step process extending over the decade-and-a-half of these forums' lives. Additional significant factors that have contributed to this have been individual stability in the composition of the groups, the development of an internal division of labour and exercise of group discipline, and, in particular, the legitimation of leadership authority exercised by an acknowledged chair.

Group cohesion has grown as a result of engaging in, and surviving, a number of internal conflicts, and coming to terms with defeats. This also did not occur through a straightline and predetermined path: in fact, it was a protracted and difficult route, with ample frictions, setbacks and disappointments. What is clear is that a major contribution was made by a willingness to be tolerant, and a determination to try again and carry on 'in spite of all'. At Unilever, a permanent fault-line was constituted by the 'North–South' conflict. In terms of ideology and general political approach, it remains unresolved but no longer poses a threat to the institution's stability and capacity to act following the growth of interpersonal familiarity in the group, which is now able to contain and absorb this conflict and deal with it pragmatically as an internal matter. At Unilever, one key experience was a training event, at which the function and strategic direction of the EWC was intensively discussed, leading to the decision to set up the feedback group. At Kraft Foods, no single experience is remembered as a major inflection point, although the close and reliable cooperation established between the Norwegian chair and the German adviser, together, in particular, with the cohesiveness of a group of confident and strong women on the steering committee, are recalled as significant and critical elements in the life of the forum.

The central issue in the cases of Unilever and Kraft Foods is then to explain how the change in central management's stance from rejection to recognition of the EWC came about.

In the case of the pattern of *'subsidiary solidarity'* (Ford), we observed a comparatively low level of activity (the lowest of all the case studies).

The EWC adopted a narrow definition of its European remit, but in one significant sub-area of representation – responding to threats to employment security that equally affected all European plants – it achieved a high level of effectiveness. The effect of this in terms of the social constitution of the EWC as a functioning association is meagre, as the EWC or steering committee has not evolved into a closely cooperating group with its own distinct institutional impact and capacity to initiate activity. It is not a working body with a daily operational agenda. There is also a low level of interpersonal, social and group solidarity amongst the members. In view of that, it is pertinent to ask how this EWC achieved its effectiveness. Its efficacy in concluding European Framework Agreements is a product of its close attachment to national trade unions. Its remaining effectiveness is principally a product of the fact that it was attached to the powerful German central works council at the corporate headquarters in Cologne through the personal union of the chair of both bodies. This then constitutes an example of the EWC type that we have denoted as 'Advocate of the Diaspora' in which the German works council chair intercedes on behalf of the others. This is a home-country model, in which the works council at the headquarters is engaged both as mediator and supporter for the interests of other countries, based on its privileged access to central management, and is made use of by the others in this capacity. The dynamic within the group is a clientelist model centred on an influential advocate. This represents a quite different type of group to a participative working body with a capacity to shape management decisions.

One key event for the Ford EWC was the separation of Visteon, as the way in which the EWC functioned in this case set the pattern for future operations. The key question in this instance is then: what explains the habitually restrictive stance of the EWC towards European issues?

In the case of the pattern of development we have termed *'protest solidarity: dominance of the Southern European model of representation'* (Burger-Miller), we saw, as at Unilever and Kraft Foods, that there was a high level of activity and strong process of group formation, together with group solidarity on the part of some of the non-German members. However, in contrast to these other cases there was a low level of effectiveness. The origin of this was that the EWC was not recognized as a partner for dialogue by central management. Despite its aspiration to be a 'participative working body', it has failed to become participative. Based on the pattern of home-country centred industrial relations at the company, this type of EWC might have been predestined for the path already trodden by Ford – namely an EWC as 'Advocate for the Diaspora'. However, because the central works council and trade union have rejected any linkage between the EWC and codetermination arrangements at the corporate centre, in contrast to the central works council at Ford, the EWC has set about building itself autonomously as a significant representative body, albeit as yet unsuccessfully. As such, it would appear to be the obverse of Ford: that is, high activity – low effectiveness. Group solidarity, which is especially strong amongst the non-German members, is expressed here in a high level of cooperation, with high engagement and idealism for a common cause, and a high degree of tolerance for others despite differences and conflicts.

The key phenomena in this case are the anti-German sentiments of the Southern European delegates and the unexpected disappointment about the flagrant disregard of the EWC's rights to information and consultation by management, even on decisions with major impacts on the workforce and despite the generous installation agreement, together with the impression this prompted that, in representative terms, the EWC was being accorded 'Third World' status.

In this case, the key analytical question is: what caused this EWC to fail in terms of the model 'Advocate for the Diaspora'.

The pattern of *'solidarity as a gesture of sympathy'* (Sanofi) exhibited a low level of effectiveness, despite high activity – a characteristic shared with the EWC at Burger-Miller – as well as a weak process of group formation and low level of group solidarity – an attribute shared with Ford. Sanofi represents the one instance in our case studies that was ranked as 'low' on all three of these latter research dimensions. As such, it shares the narrowest interface with the other four case studies. Neither the steering committee nor the forum as a whole have become socially integrated. The two principal national groupings continue to have a national focus. The dominant French country contingent has expressly obstructed the emergence of European perspectives and practical approaches. The second largest country grouping, the German, also continues to draw primarily on national approaches to representation, with which it has been able to trump the French contingent, as it were, in its own backyard, at the corporate centre. The case of Sanofi represents a type of EWC that remains strongly focused on the corporate headquarters, but which does not correspond with the model in which the headquarters EWC acts an 'Advocate for the Diaspora'. The reason for this is that it is neither able nor willing to exercise the role of advocate as, following the departure of its sponsor, the former *patron*, it no longer enjoys privileged access to corporate management. In order to retain any prospect of becoming an effective institution for interest representation, it would have to depart from the path of the homeland model, which is strongly reinforced by the structure of the company, and reconfigure itself as a 'participative working body'. In turn, this would require a high level of internal constitutive capacity that it currently does not possess as a result of French inter-union competition at the corporate centre.

The three central experiences in this case are the 'wooing' of the forum by the *patron*, Jean-François Dehecq, the original instigator of the merger, its abandonment by his successor, and the torpedoing of the body by the trade unions active at the French corporate centre.

The central analytical questions for Sanofi are: why did an EWC that is dominated to such an extent by the French home-country, and which had such an auspicious start, fail to develop any form of protest solidarity or solidarity-in-struggle at the moment when the new CEO demonstrated his disregard for the institution? Why did the characteristic strengths of the French model not deliver any gains in this area? One further riddle is: what might impel this EWC to a higher level of activity, given its low level of capacity for action and effectiveness?

One important affinity between the EWC at Burger-Miller and the Sanofi EWC consists in the fact that, in both cases, the trade union(s) that set the tone at the corporate centre have not promoted the development of the EWC into an effective organ of interest representation. One further factor in common is that a generous EWC installation agreement and initial enthusiasm were not sufficient to form an effective anchor for a subsequently effective EWC.

The contribution made by individual cooperation and solidarity in establishing an effective steering committee, together with the emergence of group solidarity, go hand in hand with a cognitive process in which the benefits for an organization's own clientele are balanced against awareness of the need and urgency to extend employee representation within the group at a European level. This assessment turns on what one of our respondent termed 'grasping the connection'. What arguments, interpretations and scenarios will suggest this and help form the corresponding motivation? This principally addresses what we have termed 'solidarity based on enlightened self-interest' (category 1 in the Introduction). Logically, this process of balancing and reflecting on self-interest will precede action. In practice, however, as well as temporally, these two elements are very closely intertwined. There are a range of types of calculation and notions of rationality that are relevant to this pattern of solidarity.

In the case of some of the protagonists at Unilever and Kraft Foods, who have continued to be active up until the present, developing a European awareness was a process that had already taken place in the period prior to these EWCs' being established: more precisely, it was closely linked with the immediate pre-history of the process of establishment. Some national unions in the food sector – including the German NGG – and the European branch-level trade union federation made a major contribution to this. A number of the key figures that we interviewed had attended some of the early European trade union meetings that had been financed by the European Commission. One particularly important element in this was the high level of internationalization in this branch, which had led trade unions into becoming pioneers in calling for an EWC Directive. While some companies had long been active in a large number of countries, what was new was the centralization and standardization of marketing, distribution systems, management structures. Although the consequences of these changes were often not directly evident at local operational level, as personnel management remained national and local, more insightful employee representatives who took an interest in long-term corporate strategies realized that this represented an irreversible change. These included the long-serving chair of the Unilever EWC, G. By creating European product markets, and hence standardising production, firms would be able to reduce the large number of brands oriented to national tastes and secure substantial cost savings. New transnational brands were created and nationally successful brands internationalized.

The Norwegian chair of the Kraft Foods EWC, B., also participated in the first international meetings prior to the adoption of the Directive. She reported on her assessment of what would be in Norway's interest in such an arrangement: 'I saw that the decisions were made outside Norway and that we must follow the management structures in the company. I saw very clearly that workers must work together when we have a lot of factories in a lot of countries'. For her, the clinching argument was the need to secure a correspondence between these levels, in line with the approach that she was familiar with from Norwegian works councils: that is, employee representation should be located at the level of management at which decisions are actually made ('follow the management structures'). The sectoral trade unions viewed the company at that stage, when it was still Kraft Jacobs Suchard, as a test case for establishing an EWC on a voluntary basis under Article 13 of the Directive.

It was rare to hear arguments at Unilever and Kraft Foods that questioned the need for interest representation to be Europeanized. Although reality clearly lagged behind the argument, this was attributed to human inertia and the abstract nature of the overall issue. There were calls for European-level protagonists to become better known at plant level. Typical of this was a comment by a local works council chair: 'In principle, the EWC should be important for us – especially because of the centralization of production management in Switzerland. There's no getting round this. The idea is right. But for me, it's not close enough to make it something I can really get hold of'.

The long-term aim of the protagonists was that the EWC should have comprehensive and far-reaching scope for participation in as many fields of interest representation as possible. As far as current practical policy was concerned, a consensus had emerged within the forum that the most pressing challenges for the EWC were the numerous plant closures and disposals, rationalization projects imposed across the whole of Europe, transfers of production to other European plants (not only in Eastern Europe), and securing investment for the European region in competition with other

world regions. It might be argued that the growing European consciousness of employee representatives was being pulled along by strong forces in
the real economy. However, this would only be half the truth, as, had this
process been a surefire one, the small elite of EWC protagonists would not
have had such difficulties in persuading others. As we show below, other
facilitating conditions were required to ensure that a European rationality
was able to gain a foothold.

Although Ford in Europe had been strongly internationalized and
increasingly centralized from the mid-1960s, the linkages between works
councils and plant-based trade unionists, in many ways comparable with
those at Unilever and Kraft Foods, have continued to be viewed differently to those cases. The national level continues to take priority over the
European level, with the latter understood as strongly subsidiary in the
sense that the higher level is only invoked when the national level is unable
to secure a resolution. Europeanising interest representation is not an issue
that has excited a wave of enthusiasm; rather, it is a project viewed coolly
and tackled in a sober and pragmatic fashion. The key issue is that a consensus exists between employee representatives from different countries
on such an understanding of the European space. It is generally accepted
that European matters that touch on interest representation should be
defined restrictively. The EWC is undoubtedly the focus of enlightened
self-interest. This relates primarily to joint defence in the event of unusual
threats. Above and beyond this, non-German delegates have an interest
in benefitting from the advocate role of the chair of the EWC and central
works council that is founded on the latter's privileged access to central
management via German codetermination arrangements. But what interest
do the Germans have in taking on this advocate role? Their interest is that
of enhancing the legitimacy of their own dominance through exercising
accommodative behaviour. Givers need the acknowledgement of recipients
in order to retain the initiative.

The fact that such profound reservations about Europe could prevail
in such a strongly Europeanized company as a specific 'in-house' form of
rationality, as common sense, is not an automatic product of this situation, and must, therefore, be the result of other factors that we turn to
further below.

At Burger-Miller, the topic of Europeanization arrived both late and rather abruptly with the acquisition of Miller. It was clear to all concerned that the company needed an EWC. The project was taken up with enthusiasm by the non-German delegates from the newly-acquired acquired units, whose main perception was that they would be embraced by the competent German industry union and powerful system of codetermination at the corporate centre and then progressively raise their – poor – working conditions up to German standards. We can only suppose that, even right from the outset and despite the German union's support for establishing the EWC, concerns about over-ambitious expectations meant that this interpretation of what Europeanization implied was not wholly shared by those located within the codetermination system at the corporate centre. This led to a collision between two different notions of self-interested reason concerning Europe within the company: an assertive one on the part of the non-Germans and a defensive one on the part of the Germans who inhabited the system of codetermination. The representatives of codetermination at the corporate centre acted out of fear of the spread of a less skilled, lower paid, and largely unorganized sphere of employment, characterized by generally precarious conditions. The non-German members of the EWC basically represent this group of workers. They are eager for their sector to experience an upgrade through linkage with the benefits and advantages of German codetermination. This not only represents a meeting point for different strategies of representation but also two divergent patterns of life and work.

At Sanofi, it is difficult to perceive any consciousness of a European rationality. Few arguments based on self-interest were advanced that might have constituted reasons for establishing a strong European network of employee representatives. Those members that originated from Hoechst were initially vehemently opposed to the merger: that is, they saw no advantage for themselves in a 'Sanofi Europa'. Following completion of the hostile takeover, their self-interest consisted in defending and preserving their national style as much as possible within the new corporate setting. The acquiring and the acquired parts of the new group were then engaged in a struggle for identity and for who would determine how the forum would be perceived. However, this struggle was not played out openly within the

EWC but rather in a covert code that remained hidden behind a screen of neutral or amicable interpersonal conduct. For representatives from Sanofi-Synthelabo, Europeanising interest representation was associated with a fear of being overwhelmed by the Germans; for representatives from Hoechst, in contrast, it was fear of enforced conformity, a compulsion to adapt. For them, the key issue was what would survive in the new French group of the system of interest representation that had previously prevailed at the once proud – and German – Hoechst. We have seen that in the field of interest representation, and in contrast to other functional areas, a surprisingly large number of key elements were retained. Within the EWC there has been no debate about which fields of interest and areas of representation should be assigned to the new institution. As a consequence, the EWC does not really know what it is for, especially in view of the fact that the French trade unions represented at the company see it as unwanted competition and have acted to curtail its development. There is no discernible perspective on what the specific role of the EWC should be.

The key preconditions for the emergence of solidaristic behaviour on the part of the actors can be drawn together as follows.

(1) *Personal and human social cohesion*
This turns on the type of social contact that extends beyond work-based relationships into the personal sphere, and a zone – if only perhaps a small tract – that allows common lifeworlds to emerge through such forms of behaviour as collegiality, hospitality, interest in the lives of others, openness to difference, participation in social events, and a willingness to embrace the unfamiliar. The essence of this is that there should be a growth of personal closeness and familiarity, in which credibility and reliability can flourish, and through which the risks of being disappointed can be lowered. Familiarity is the basis of trust. And trust is the mother of solidarity. This is the 'natural law' of solidarity identified by the founding fathers of sociology (Durkheim, Tönnies, Weber). It is the social glue that emerged as the most important dimension in our research. Building mutual familiarity and trust takes places through communication. As a consequence, surmounting language barriers, or at least sufficient competence in a lingua franca,

is a key performative condition for the successful practice of solidarity (cf. Stirling and Tully, 2004).

Cohesion is the product of frequent contact – that is repeated encounters. Frequency of meetings of the steering committee and the EWC as a whole is, therefore, an important indicator of this. However, cohesion does not follow automatically from frequency of contact. One example is that of the Sanofi EWC, whose members did not develop mutual warmth despite their frequent meetings. Frequency will only have a socially integrative effect if it associated with encounters that enthuse the participants, an openness to difference, and a willingness to become involved with others.

One obstacle to this in many EWCs is the low level of knowledge of delegates about the rules and practices of employee representation in other countries, and hence an insufficient understanding of the exigencies that they are subject to, both cultural and situational. This did not apply to the bulk of the steering committee members that we interviewed in the five case studies, chosen for their status as being amongst the 'best cases', who were well aware of the main cultural and structural aspects of interest representation of others as a result of their typically long and intensive activity on the EWC. They have long got past the stage in which training programmes on general national characteristics, such as styles of address and manners, or fundamental systemic differences in interest representation could offer much more help. However, this does not apply for knowledge of the situation in Central and Eastern Europe.

In our study two features stood out as being especially relevant in fostering personal trust and familiarity: the perceived fairness and integrity of the other party, and their openness to the needs of others and willingness to discuss these. On the issue of integrity, EWC members are particularly concerned that the other party communicates honestly and correctly, and does not hold back important information or behave deceptively, and that they are reliable and consistent – for example, they keep to commitments. As far as openness to others is concerned, the expectation is that they should show good will and understanding, and be friendly and interested in their dealings.

(2) *The associative impact of organizational citizenship*

This precondition for solidaristic behaviour deals with the motivation and engagement that leads individuals to contribute to creating and consolidating a body with a capacity to act and in a position to realise in practice the legally-enshrined status of 'workplace citizen'. The capacity to act signifies a collectively organized and coordinated presence in consultative and participative activity as a counterpart to European central management. This requires the internal structuring of the body into a group that can act purposefully as a unit. The praxeology of this process of group formation is amongst the most difficult challenges for the emergence of effective EWCs, as it presupposes a division of labour, discipline, and the legitimation of leadership roles. Our detailed descriptions of the social processes taking place within steering committees in the firms under consideration convey an impression both of considerable progress as well as the fragility of this dimension.

It is evident too that the individual personalities of the protagonists, and in particular of leaders, play a crucial role. The constitutive processes of the EWCs at Unilever and Kraft Foods cannot be understood without reference to the significant impact of long-serving chairs. And at Unilever it was noticeable what great hopes were pinned on the person of the new EWC chair when managing the succession issue. Similarly, but in a different context, the EWC chair at Ford as head of codetermination at the company's headquarters, took the responsibility for his European office very seriously, and was careful to ensure that a balance was maintained within that particular pattern of solidarity between countries and plants. In these three cases, the positive stage of development of the EWC was explicitly attributed to a considerable extent to the individual involved by the steering committee and EWC members who we interviewed with the formulation: 'We've been lucky with our chair'. Even at Burger-Miller, again in a different context, the German chair acted as an engaged European, although the codetermination system from which he originated had largely abandoned the EWC project. Conversely, at Sanofi the failure of the process of group formation hindered the emergence of a recognized leader: far from being legitimized, the engaged EWC chair was undermined and ultimately resigned from the position.

The epitome of this form of solidarity is civic virtue, which consists in engagement in the political life of a group or association, and in this dealing with annoyances and adversity with tolerance and resilience. This is especially significant if the group is in the process of development and some pioneer work needs to be accomplished in this task. Organizational psychology has encapsulated this type of behaviour in the notion of 'organizational citizenship' (Organ et al., 2005).

(3) *Enlightened self-interest*

Actors must be convinced that their contribution to and engagement in constructing a European union of employee representatives at company level is rational from the standpoint of the interests of their own country or operation, and that it offers an added-value. Put in general terms, the added-value consists in minimising the prospects of employees being played off against each other: that is, reducing the advantage that management enjoys through its knowledge of the whole and its ability to benefit from this in practical terms. This capacity is a result of understanding the context and internal linkages in the company. However, conceived in such abstract terms, this is not sufficient to inspire action. In reality, this is a very concrete task, as circumstances vary from company to company and are interpreted differently by the actors. At Ford, these connections were interpreted restrictively in that the EWC only offered added-value within a narrow spectrum of activity. At Unilever, Kraft Foods and Burger-Miller they were interpreted in a much broader way, leading to a wider conception of the EWC's scope. At Sanofi, no majority view that the EWC offered an added-value had emerged.

This emphasis on the interests of delegates' own plans should not be confused with the narrow 'parish pump' mentality that prevails in many EWCs nor be equated with free-riding – simply pursuing an individual gain without contributing to the functioning of the whole. Rather, the issue is one of an 'enlightened' self-interest that fosters cooperation in the wider union because it enshrines the common good, which in turn generates added-value (also) for delegates' own operations. The aspiration to bring something back home for one's own immediate constituency is entirely natural, and should not stand in the way of establishing a representative union provided that delegates also make substantive contributions to constructing the overall edifice. Our case study reports indicate what a difficult balancing act this is in practice. However, the scope for performing this exercise, the foundation for subsequent success, lies in the fact that interpreting self-interest is not simply a matter of calculus and cannot be statistically determined but rather depends on the overall perceptual horizon, into which flow values, ideals and experiences. The greater the growth of social cohesion and credibility, the wider this horizon will be. The prospects of a gain in one's own interests are raised to the extent that there is an investment in the whole.

In particular, the question of utility is posed for protagonists in EWCs dominated by the home-country as they often do not see themselves as dependent on others but rather as donors. However, the representatives of our two home-country dominated EWCs (Ford, Burger-Miller) did act in a solidaristic way. Why did they do this? There are good arguments for the case that this was not due to selflessness but rather, among other things, that it was in the interest of maintaining their dominant status or anticipating a position in which the headquarters might come to rely on the others. Looking into the future and judiciously reading the signs was a characteristic of most of the protagonists.

This tension – working towards a 'not yet' – is underpinned in the case of very many protagonists, and not only those from the home-country of the company, by an idealism rooted in their trade union backgrounds. One example is the Norwegian EWC chair at Kraft Foods – an individual held in high regards by her EWC colleagues, and also ultimately by management.

(4) *Solidarity-in-struggle*
The classic forms of this type of solidarity are mass actions involving large sections of the workforce. No such action had taken place in

any of our case studies. Smaller scale action had, however, occurred in two instances in the form of symbolic protests: a symbolic walk-out during a meeting with management, undertaken by the EWC steering committee at Burger-Miller, and a demonstration by office-holders from a variety of countries that marched around the company head-quarters at Unilever.

Nonetheless, this form of solidarity is one that retains a central place in the imaginations of our interviewees as mass action remains an indispensable tool at national level, and unions would lack credible strength without the capacity to deploy or plausibly threaten it from time to time. Initiating and organising such action belongs within the scope of trade unions, not workplace representation, in countries with dual systems of representation, such as the Netherlands and Germany. It also applies in Southern Europe, where workplace representative bodies have a right to take industrial action but where successful mass action relies on the support and coordination of national trade union confederations. The lack of support for European mass action through coordinated activity by national trade unions is, as a consequence, one of the main reasons why such action is almost non-existent both in our case studies but also in EWCs more generally, and why it remains a desiderata.

Solidarity-in-struggle also exists in a close relationship with civic solidarity, in particular where the issue is one of promoting and instill-ing the cohesiveness of the forum. Such EWC action is analogous to the work of maintaining party discipline within a parliamentary con-text, where the issue is to counter an opponent's strength by effectively deploying one's own forces. In the context of an EWC, this includes how the first day of the annual meeting is organized at which, as a rule, the employee side meets alone and prepares for the next day's session with management, offering an opportunity to draw together resources, practice various roles, and rehearse strategy. It also includes preparing for joint meetings between the steering committee and management. The issue is always one of finding a line to take, sharpening arguments, practising unity, and closing ranks. Success is highly dependent on the preparation of such meetings, and subsequent public performance, by the EWC chair and steering committee. It is the quiet process of steering undertaken beforehand and in the background that produces success. This calls for competences such as those possessed by a capable leader of a parliamentary party group.

Meeting these four preconditions of solidarity would enable an EWC to have the capacity of a body in line with the first pattern of solidarity (solidarity based on enlightened self-interest). However, this is not a stage model. Types of solidarity do not have to follow each other in sequence. Awareness of 'enlightened self-interest' does not have to be at the beginning – indeed such a position would be far too intellectualized. However, what is central is that there is an enduring foundation of group solidarity, without which the other dimensions will remain fragile and fleeting.

We now shift attention from the level of the actor to that of structure and pose the question: is there a connection between the four patterns of solidarity and how companies are organized?

Drawing on Marginson (2004) and our own work (Kotthoff, 2006a), our hypothesis has been that the scope for EWCs to become an institution with a capacity to take action and acquire a relatively autonomous and high impact in relation to national structures of representation – that is, an EWC of the type 'participative working body' – was greatest where there was a high level of corporate internationalization (sites in many countries, relatively low proportion of employment in the home country) effected through a centralized management structure, an internationally constituted cadre of top management, an integrated production structure, and a rationalization strategy imposed from the centre. These are the characteristic features of a Eurocompany.

Of our case studies, Unilever, Kraft Foods, and Ford correspond best with this type of structure. Unilever and Kraft Foods represent a very convincing confirmation of this hypothesis. However, Ford does not. If one compares each of the structural variables individually, it is apparent that having a centralized organizational structure and integrated production arrangements are more marked at Ford than at the other two companies: however, the characteristic of having a low proportion of the total workforce in the biggest country is less pronounced. Whereas the share of total employment at Unilever and Kraft Foods in the country with the largest employment is only 17 per cent in each case, it is 45 per cent at Ford (Germany). And since Germany is also the headquarters of Ford's European management, combining this with the share of employment generates a marked homeland effect for interest representation: that is, a dominance of (quasi) home-country national representation arrangements. This constitutes the major difference between Ford and the other two companies.

Table 7: Share of employment EWC seats in the largest country

Company/country	Share of employment	Share of EWC seats
Unilever/Germany	17%	11%
Kraft Foods/Germany	17.5%	11%
Ford/Germany	45% (UK 13%)	26% (UK 26%)
Burger-Miller	60%	15%
Sanofi/France	45% (Germany 18%)	33% (Germany 18%)

Table 7 illustrates the significance of the distribution of shares of employment. In those case-study companies with the highest shares of employment in the home country, there is a strong homeland effect (Ford, Sanofi) or a tendency towards this.

The significance of the home-country effect has been dealt with frequently in the EWC literature. As a rule, it is identified with the typical national model of industrial relations, which then generates country specific types of EWC and patterns of solidarity: Southern European plant-based trade unionism, North European dual system. Our results suggest that such an analysis is both formal and over-simplistic. In addition to Ford, there is also a home-country effect at Burger-Miller and Sanofi, but in the latter two cases is associated with other patterns of solidarity. This difference evidently calls for some explanation, in particular if the home-country effect for the same country (Germany) has different impacts, as at Ford and Burger-Miller.

In the variant of the home-country effect that one would expect in companies with German corporate headquarters, as at Ford, an influential national system of interest representation at headquarters, usually with a social partnership approach, will integrate and protect those smaller countries represented on the EWC and, if needed, intercede on their behalf with central management as an advocate. This constitutes the EWC type 'Advocate of the Diaspora' identified in the 2006 study, in which the chair of the works council takes on the advocate role. The EWC functions as an appendix to or client of interest representation in the home country and is dominated by this. Frequently, the individual leading interest representation arrangements at the home country will also hold the role of EWC chair. The EWC itself does not develop any significant or autonomous impact and does not engage in a high level of independent activity: it is not a working body and does not have a distinct agenda. However, it is effective because it can selectively attend to the problems of other countries through this subsidiary path. Other countries are able to obtain support and acquire 'voice' via the medium of the home country works council.

Many researchers do not regard this as an effective type of EWC because it does not have a specific common European orientation and continues to be focused on the dominant country, and therefore, as a consequence, is not organized in an egalitarian way but has inbuilt disparities. However, our case studies indicate that such an EWC is entirely capable of delivering a common European perspective and can practice European solidarity, if albeit not to the extent and intensity that applies in the case of the 'EWCs as participative working body'. Nonetheless, it still has a clearly noticeable effect. It is a different type of effective EWC, adapted to its specific context. Many EWCs in large German companies probably correspond to this type and, despite their growing internationalization, continue to have their main focus in Germany. The sheer weight of the home country means that it would not be realistic to expect EWCs in such companies to develop into the type of EWC that we have designated as a 'participative working body'. At the same time, it would also be inappropriate and unrealistic to deprecate the representative effectiveness of such EWCs. As a consequence, we would argue that the 'EWC as advocate' should be regarded as one of the two effective variants of EWCs in addition to the

EWC as 'participative working body'. The key criterion for this is that the EWC offers a real added-value for other countries.

One such instance in our research is the *Ford* EWC. In this case, the positive effects of the advocate role are clearly evident, and the EWC generates an added-value for the others.

In the case of *Burger-Miller*, the same homeland, Germany, had a quite different effect. In this case, other countries were not looked after by employee representatives at the corporate centre in an integrated way, but rather were left to their own devices and gained no added value from its resources and privileges. The reasons for this are that, firstly, central management rejected any integration of other countries into the culture of the corporate centre; and, secondly, the system of employee representation at the corporate centre did not take on the role of advocate for the Miller operations in other countries. The company was divided into two very different parts with very distinctive and unaligned corporate cultures and approaches to employee representation. Employee representatives at the corporate centre felt themselves under too much pressure to adopt the role of advocate, given the tough stance adopted by Miller's top management. The trade union at the corporate centre kept its distance from the Miller culture, with its low pay, precarious working conditions, and low level of trade union organization, and concentrated on defending German employment standards. The customary identity of the company had become very diluted in a painful breach with corporate traditions. Paradoxically, rapid internationalization led to a greater emphasis on national ways of thinking on the part of employee representatives at the corporate centre.

At *Sanofi*, the dominant French system of employee representation at the corporate centre was preoccupied with internal union competition and did not look more broadly at the prospects for cross-border co-operation. One further reason is that it was uncertain about the large-scale merger that had formed the company. Fears of competition and being overwhelmed by foreign influence were so great in the case of some French trade union organizations that they torpedoed the EWC by resorting to the law and undermined any initiatives towards solidarity that might have enabled to the EWC to be constituted as an effective group.

Our observation that corporate structures and typical national patterns of industrial relations might exercise an influence on patterns of solidarity, but that different patterns of solidarity can emerge despite similar initial structural conditions, has led on to the proposition that these objective structures are not transposed into reality unfiltered but only operate via the perceptions and interpretations of human subjects. A principally structure-based theorization is too static as it underplays actors' interpretative and innovative performance as well as their prior history. However, the fact that structures are interpreted subjectively does not imply that this process is voluntaristic, individual, or possibly arbitrary: rather, within each company subjective processes are shaped by collective patterns of interpretation, and their tradition. As such, they involve crystallized structures of consciousness that have emerged as a 'condensate' over long periods of time as a result of seminal experiences both in the area of corporate strategy and interest representation. We denote this mutual interaction of objective and subjective factors as configuring the *constellation for interest representation* of the company in question. This constellation serves both to define problems and indicate the corridor of possibilities within which solutions might be found. It is closely linked with the social order of the workplace within the company, and constitutes those dimensions of this that are concerned with actors' interests.

The constellation of interests at *Unilever* was characterized by the conditions and experiences that favoured establishing a relationship of equality between plants and their representatives. The company has never been entirely at home in any European country. For example, neither the UK nor the Netherlands has accounted for the dominant share of employment in the group. And neither have employee representatives from one of these countries enjoyed a special relationship to top management. Most European operations are small to medium-sized. There is no dominant employee representation at the corporate centre and there is no bipolarity between two equally strong competing groups. This means that the preconditions are not present either for a unilateral concentration of power or for competitive struggles. Unhampered by either a dominant national or competitive situation, the idea of Europeanization interest representation emerged relatively swiftly at the point at which the rapid European centralization of the group had become a central concern both for trade unions and workplace employee representatives. As such, the soil was already well prepared for the influx of a transnational logic in a step that was supported by the trade unions. One contributing factor was that the debate about the EWC Directive and the accelerated restructuring of the company took place at the same time. And since the personnel management policies of the company continued to be decentralized up to that point, national plant-based employee representatives had previously had little contact with each other and were then able to meet unencumbered by prejudgements and the burden of history. The key psychological effect of this was that no national employee representatives were seen as having a special relationship to central management or being particularly favoured by it as a consequence.

The takeover in 1993 of the Swiss-German company Jacobs Suchard by the highly centralized US company *Kraft*, part of the Phillip Morris tobacco group, was the dominant event both in terms of corporate history and the practice of interest representation. Quite suddenly, the level of management at which decisions were taken became remote – in the USA – prompting the idea of establishing a single level of interest representation to match that of European management. As with Unilever, there was also a coincidence in this case between this central corporate event and the decisive phase in discussions around the EWC Directive, adoption of which was imminent. The proactive role of the German foodworkers' union NGG and European union federation represented further favourable preconditions that made this company into one of the EWC pioneers. As a result of the takeover of the biscuits division LU of Danone, the European part of the group became considerably larger and with that the number of seats on the EWC. As with Unilever, in this case too, no country is dominant.

One factor promoting a commonality of experience at Kraft Foods is that important decisions are taken outside Europe – in the USA. A sense of all being subject to a form of externally imposed domination is one that customarily draws people together. Representatives from the LU factories were unhappy about the merger as they feared that their French organizational culture would become Americanized. This group solidarity, and a willingness to come to a consensus that this generated, is one of the reasons why the large proportion of Southern European delegates (45 per cent combined) has not led to the abandonment of the Northern European approach to dealing with European management that prevailed at LU before the takeover. In this instance, major acquisitions are interpreted in a way that has not provoked internal competition but rather generated a solidaristic response that has helped in the constitution of employee groups.

One significant element in the overall constellation of interest representation is the stance that central management adopts towards the EWC. At Unilever and Kraft Foods, this changed over time from one of rejecting the EWC to recognising it as a partner for dialogue. This constituted the key precondition for what had become a working body being transformed into a *participative* working body. The change took place in response to the constitution of the EWC as a group with a capacity to take action and which sought participative dialogue with management. From this it is evident that in both cases constructing the capacity of the EWC to act and willingness on the part of central management to engage in dialogue is a recursive procedure. Both condition and reinforce each other.

The constellation of interest representation at *Ford* is characterized by the bipolarity of the UK and Germany based on the circumstance that each had a similar scale of production and employment, with large plants and employee representatives who were aware of their power. The competitive relationship implicit in this structure was not mitigated by the establishment of Ford of Europe in the 1960s. In fact, it gave it an additional twist. Far from diminishing national patterns of thinking on the part of employee representatives in the two countries during the 1970s and 1980s, the growing Europeanization of corporate structures reinforced these. Because London was the headquarters of Ford of Europe, and its management was British, German representatives enviously suspected that the British side was enjoying preferential treatment from management. And because more investment flowed to the Continent, and not Britain, British representatives felt themselves increasingly disadvantaged. This was a constellation designed to foster rivalry and strife as it led to a perspective in which each saw Europeanization as prejudicial to its interests and clinging to nationality as a means of defending prior gains. Corporate realities and the perceptions of employee representatives were heading in opposite directions.

At a very late stage, realising that the tensions had simply become too great, a small number of senior representatives on both sides suddenly woke up to this and embarked on a rapprochement, in which the individual vision and determination of a small number of individuals, in particular the German chair of the central works council and the leading English full-time official, were very evident. Curbing this competition and achieving greater transnational corporate cooperation at the trade union level was also in the interests of European management, which consequently supported the establishment of the EWC. The outcome of this constellation has been consensus on a cautious and defensive approach to resolving the issue of the Europeanization of employee interest representation. The basic national orientation has been retained, but now linked with the realization of the necessity, based on enlightened self-interest, of not taking from others and working together on specific matters. This has created a marriage of convenience, or defensive alliance, in relation to external threats. The subsequent emergence of the German operation as a de facto headquarters has meant that its representative has taken on the role of both leading and acting as advocate in a delicately balanced relationship.

At Ford there is also a link between the patterns of solidarity that characterize the EWC and the stance of central management towards it, with management in this case exercising a strong initiating role in shaping the relationship through the fact that it recognized the EWC from the outset and reinforced its more restrictive position on Europeanization.

The constellation for interest representation at *Burger-Miller* was centrally shaped by the acquisition of Miller – a company with a very different business model and structure of employment – in which two parts, each incompatible with the other in terms of their social structures, were fused into a whole. Employee representatives at Miller operations outside Germany had great expectations of Europeanization as they hoped that it would lead to an improvement in their employment conditions via the central works council and the German trade union. However, both the union and central employee representatives were sceptical about Europeanization and closed off the option of active participation in the EWC, which was obliged to stand on its own two feet. The key element in this constellation of interests consists in the fact that central management, which has pursued a strategy of downgrading employment conditions, has not been willing to accommodate Miller employee representatives' aspirations for improvement and saw no benefit in engaging in dialogue with the EWC.

Also in the case of *Sanofi*, the constellation for interest representation was determined by a large-scale acquisition (Aventis). In this case, however, central management took quite a different position. Rather than refusing to communicate, it both promoted but also made use of the EWC as it is saw that such a body could prove helpful. The EWC was a goodwill project undertaken by management, a wedding gift to the Germans to put a friendly face on what was, in fact, a hostile takeover of Hoechst. Employee representatives from both the main countries, France and Germany, did not expect anything very positive from Europeanization (that is, the takeover). Following the retirement of the sponsoring CEO, dialogue with the EWC was abandoned by his successor, and the delegates from the two central countries proved unable to develop group solidarity and transform the EWC into an institution with a capacity to initiate action. As previously at Ford, Sanofi became the site of a collision between two rivalrous principals – but which were not engaged in an open conflict with each other.

The starting points for constellations of interests are companies' internationalization strategies and practices, together with key corporate decisions on mergers, acquisitions and transfers of production, new marketing strategies, and extensive organizational changes. However, these economic and organizational facts, which intervene into the status hierarchy of the various operations and influence their perspectives, are not transposed mechanically into social factors. Rather, they constitute the raw material for discussion and debate, for interpretation and in which emotional investment by EWC delegates from different countries takes place against the background of their prior experience, national cultures of representation, specific factors in their own situations, management's strategic communications, and their own aspirations to exert power. One example of the significance of a complex situation can be seen in the case of Sanofi. The merger of Hoechst and Rhône Poulenc to form Aventis took place in the context of an optimistic and positive constellation of interests (see Kädtler, 2006: 112ff). The German head became the new CEO, so that there was an expectation from the German side that the accustomed culture of representation would continue; at the same time, the French side saw the potential benefits in participation in established German representative arrangements. In contrast, the merger of Aventis with Sanofi-Synthelabo took on a negative aspect from the outset, as the political context suggested more of a hostile takeover than a merger of equals.

These constellations of interest representation have exercised a profound influence on relationships between EWC members, and with this on which patterns of solidarity will emerge. Dominant individuals within the EWC also have a major effect, as our analyses of the role of the key actors in the case studies highlighted at many points. These factors have proved to be the most influential in determining the pattern of solidarity.

At a deeper level of analysis, therefore, buried in the historical underground of the relationship between representatives from different countries, a few key aspects and core experiences have proved critical in shaping, over the course of time, the dynamics of the process of Europeanization within the EWC. Mutual perceptions and interpretations have become entrenched over time into a valid narrative with which all subsequent delegates have grown up.

At Ford, such a narrative has become 'rivalry'. Over a long phase of serious status competition, a bipolarity between employee representatives from the two main countries, the UK and Germany, has emerged. In the case of Burger-Miller and Sanofi, it was anxiety about loss and identity prompted by a large-scale merger which, far from drawing countries and business divisions together, led employee representatives at the corporate centre to abandon any role in offering assistance to others. And in the cases of Unilever and Kraft Foods, it was long experience with relationships of equality that fostered group solidarity and group formation. In both of these cases, it would be appropriate to make some reference to the political philosophy of the Enlightenment, in which equality and solidarity are seen as mutually supportive.

The historical material that solidarity has to work through, and against, consists of rivalry between colleagues, the competitive pursuit of status, and anxiety about identity, not related in a generalized way to national patterns of behaviour but to the particular context in which workforces and their representatives come together and collide as parts of one and the same company. And the historical material on which solidarity can grow is a constellation for interest representation characterized either by the socio-dynamic of 'the strong helping the weak' or of 'equal amongst equals'.

EWC and Trade Union Relations

6.1 A complicated but necessary arrangement?

In their study of 'EWCs in Practice', which encompassed fifty-four bodies in total (Eurofound, 2004), Eurofound outlined the necessity of conceptualizing the notion of 'insider-outsider' relations. Although the Eurofound research applied the concept to the role of management within EWCs, management here being the outsider, we contend, based on our empirical findings, that this approach is equally applicable to the role trade unions play or do not play within this European institution. If nothing else, it denotes that there exists, either directly or indirectly, a relationship between EWCs and trade unions. Implicit in our use of this concept is the belief that trade union status might have consequences for the way an EWC functions, a point that occupies centre-stage throughout this section.

Certainly, EWC literature to different degrees has thought it necessary to discuss EWC and trade union relations. For example, a key issue raised by both Lucio and Weston (2000) and Royle (1999) concerns what is commonly referred to as 'management capture and isolation' of EWCs. In short, trade unions are perceived as a guarantor against EWCs' becoming a managerial tool for country benchmarking, a threat posed by EWCs that has been addressed in a number of studies (Wills, 2000; Hancké, 2000; Tuckmann and Whittall, 2002). In addition, such a presence also ensures delegates possess the right competencies at this European level (Lecher et al., 1998) – trade unions are not only an invaluable source of European expertise but equally members of a European trade union network.

Of course, we have to recognize that legally trade unions continue to be denied access to EWCs. 'The Directive makes no mention of trade unions whatsoever, and regards workplace employee representatives as the agents of the employees' side and as those who should be informed and consulted' (Waddington, 2010: 28). Even the recent recasting of the Directive failed, to the annoyance of trade unions, to address this delicate issue. However, as most empirical studies indicate, the EWC does not necessarily represent a 'union-free zone' (Lecher et al., 1998, 2001; Whittall, 2000, 2009; Kotthoff, 2006; Telljohann, 2005), and certain backdoors to EWC meetings have been left open to trade union officials. These include the existence of an already recognized trade union presence within the company, plus the notion of 'external expert' embedded in the Directive. Furthermore, trade unions, often by default it should be noted, also have access to EWCs. This is due to the fact that many EWC delegates are trade union members and in some cases directly delegated by their trade union to attend EWC meetings. Hence, it would be short-sighted not to assume, especially in companies in which managerial decisions are increasingly being centralized (Marginson, 2000, Marginson et al., 2005), that trade unions are not interested in trying to utilize this source to influence the EWC/managerial agenda.

Certainly, irrespective of their legal status, our five case studies confirm that trade unions have contact to EWCs via one of the three access forms discussed above. This fact raises important questions about the nature of this contact and what bearing such relations have on the inner workings of the EWC. This takes the issue of trade union presence a step further, beyond the mere notion of an EWC's independence. There exists an assumption that access alone is not the key issue, rather that the character of this involvement can shape the contours of EWCs.

In trying to answer these questions, we confirm the proposition made by both Telljohann (2005) and Lecher et al. (1998) that the EWC trade union relationship is extremely complex, problematical even. Hence, although an EWC's independence might be guaranteed by a trade union presence, such involvement will not necessarily improve the way the EWC functions, in particular measured against the yardstick of transnational solidarity. On the contrary, a number of variables, in particular two discussed in the literature, suggest that a trade union presence is restrictive rather than progressive in this respect.

The first concerns the nature of trade unionism within this European sphere. The key point to recognize here is that 'trade unionism', often a catch-all phrase, incorporates ideological, political and structural differences, which, as Pulignano (2005) and Whittall (2000, 2010) note, are played out within EWCs. Unions, therefore, compete to impose their interpretation of the world (Whittall, 2010; Waddington, 2010), a fact that can have consequences for the role that trade unions play and potentially the way this European institution functions. Certainly, these cultural differences could be observed in all five case studies. Delegates spoke of the different roles played by trade union officers at Ford, for example. German officials exercised a far more observatory role compared to their British counterparts. While in the case of Unilever, delegates from Latin countries tended to veer towards each other, delegates not only found it easier to communicate but they recognized the existence of a similar value system too. In sum, EWC research has long contended that cultural differences – that is, a preference for direct action over social dialogue as practiced in southern and northern European countries respectively – could paralyze the EWC as EWC delegates become sidetracked by internal battles.

Secondly, another factor that appears in the literature and is considered to have a great bearing on these two representative levels, potentially the most challenging obstacle of all, concerns conflict over the issue of representation. As Waddington (2010) rightly notes, the EWC is a 'contested institution'. It involves what Lecher et al. term the 'strategic orientation' of EWCs (1998) and Waddington (2010) the 'issues of purpose and efficacy'. In short, what this involves is whether EWCs have a remit to negotiate agreements. While trade unions lobbied hard on behalf of the EWCs and have often played an influential role in founding EWCs, lurking in the shadows of these developments is a fear, one which generally unites trade unions irrespective of their national heritage, that the EWC could 'encroach on the domain' of collective bargaining undertaken by trade unions (EMF, 2000a). This implies that the EWC and trade union relationship is potentially very combustive. Certainly, a review of trade union policy documents, particularly those of the European Trade Union Federations such as the European Metalworkers' Federation (EMF) (2000a, 2000b, 2000c, 2006), demonstrate that an important aspect of trade union involvement in EWCs

concerns control, and specifically controlling the latter's agenda by steering
it away from entering into negotiations with management or, at least where
this cannot be avoided, co-signing any such agreements. To summarize, it
is an undisputed fact that trade unions either directly or indirectly have
a presence within EWCs. After having played a decisive role in both lobbying on behalf of the EWC Directive and supporting, certainly in the
so-called 'pioneer phase', the foundation of EWCs, EWCs continue to be
closely associated with trade unions. Of course, this raises a whole array
of questions about the nature of this association, some of which we have
touched on above and which we return to throughout the rest of this section. The most pressing questions can be whittled down to the following:
What degree and form of involvement can be observed? How does this
influence the functioning of the EWC, and specifically does it promote or
hinder transnational solidarity? In turn, these questions, certainly according
to EWC literature, are influenced by an EWC's independence, ideological battles over the best form of employee representation, and the right to
negotiate. Before turning to these key issues more closely, we offer a brief
overview of the trade union presence in the five case studies.

6.2 Case studies – trade union presence

UNILEVER

Unilever respondents portray trade union involvement in the EWC as
no more than peripheral. It was noted that a Dutch union officer had
been given responsibility by the European Mine, Chemical and Energy
Workers (EMCEF) and European Federation of Trade Unions in the Food,
Agriculture and Tourism (EFFAT) to co-ordinate relations, but that the
individual in question 'no longer comes and was totally' uninterested in
EWC affairs, according to a delegate from Germany. It was implied that
the Federation's involvement was hampered by a co-ordination problem

between EMCEF and EFFAT. Lower down the representative structure, national unions demonstrated very little initiative in shadowing events and issues undertaken by the EWC, too. Discussing the situation in Spain, an EWC member from that country pointed out that they attempted to keep the national federations informed of European developments within Unilever, but lamented that no systematic method was in place to facilitate such an information flow. Moreover, this was not a problem encountered solely by the Spanish delegate. Although in Germany, the Netherlands, the UK and France the unions are well organized at plant level, they showed very little interest in the European level. Generally, EWC delegates could draw on the different national and European trade unions for support whenever and wherever required, but any initiative had to come from European employee representatives as the EWC remains an issue that is still not on the formers' 'radar'.

KRAFT FOODS

In contrast to Unilever, the trade unions, at least on the surface, have a greater presence within the Kraft Foods EWC. The chairperson was keen to outline how the German foodworkers' union Gewerkschaft Nahrung-Genuss-Gaststätten (NGG) and EFFAT had played an instrumental role in the foundation process during 1995/1996. More tellingly, the EWC has an adviser; this is a union official from NGG who negotiated the EWC agreement and who, in addition, is EFFAT's designated Kraft EWC co-ordinator. The individual in question is recognized as a key actor within the EWC. When questioned about the adviser's involvement, however, respondents strangely played down his role as a union official. An expert on European affairs, he was evidently viewed as invaluable to the EWC chairperson, but he represents much more of a union figurehead than serving as the active voice of either NGG or EFFAT. Discussing the union officer's role the respondent noted: 'He is always at the meetings, but he cannot make up for the lack of general trade union influence in the EWC. How can he do this?' A further aspect that would suggest greater trade union involvement concerns the chairperson. Since the late-1980s, the person in question has been a convenor of a Norwegian trade union. Clearly, the trade union presence on the EWC is a deceptive one, though. It is more one that has come about by default rather than active design, and is dependent on an individual's biography, where there is a spillover effect between national and European responsibilities. Moreover, biographies often indicate that the 'here and now' is of major importance for actors. For our respondents, certainly those on the steering committee, the here and now is increasingly governed by a European agenda, which has consequently raised the EWC aspect of their work, so much so that the Kraft Foods EWC appears to have taken on the form of a German joint work council.

BURGER-MILLER

Of all the five case studies the German industrial company Burger-Miller[1] proved to be the most complex in terms of relations between the EWC and trade unions. This complexity is directly linked to the company itself, which consists of two distinct worlds: the world of Burger, characterized by high-tech products and based on a highly-skilled and strongly union-ized workforce with robust codetermination arrangements, and the world of Miller, based in its foreign operations on low-tech products, low skills and very low levels of trade union organization. Although the competent German trade union played a key role in setting up the EWC, a year after Burger went global following its takeover of Miller, the position of the German union within the EWC is extremely contentious. It has tradition-ally seen no value in this European institution. Instead, it has continued to focus its energies on representing its core members in its German area of operation through established arrangements within the German model of industrial relations. As a consequence of the German union's stance, in particular the fact that it failed to attend many EWC meetings, delegates from Italy, France, and Spain, all with a strong trade union connection, have acquired a greater say in determining the direction of the EWC. However, the emergence of a parallel trade union network, in which some

---

1   Burger-Miller is a pseudonym for this company, which employee representatives wished to keep anonymous.

EWC delegates play a leading role, indicates that reservations amongst trade unionists persist.

FORD

The Ford EWC is the one case study in which the various levels of trade union representation are most conspicuous. National trade unions from the UK, Germany, Spain and Belgium, countries in which Ford has key production sites, have access to the EWC. In addition, the European Metal Workers' Federation has a union coordinator, in the form of an IG Metall delegate, on the EWC. Furthermore, there is an emphasis placed on trade unions' delegating members to the EWC. In the case of Romania, for example, the EWC chair insisted that such a principle also apply to this new member of the European Union. This represents a move to stop the company delegating management missionaries – a problem often associated with accession countries. However, the strong trade union presence, one that has also seeped through to the steering committee that meets three times a year, is portrayed as essentially symbolic.

Our respondents played down the role of the EWC and the strong trade union involvement of the UK union official is portrayed as that of a German works council chair. More generally, respondents were keen to point out, similar in some respects to the Kraft Foods EWC, that the trade unions' involvement was more symbolic than real – except in the process of negotiating European framework agreements.

SANOFI

In some respects the Sanofi EWC parallels that of Burger-Miller. Formed in 2004 after acquiring Aventis, Sanofi remains to all intents and purposes a global company with a very French character. As a consequence, and like the German union at Burger-Miller, French unions have displayed a lack of interest in EWC affairs. Although respondents noted that in the foundation phase a meeting was held in Brussels that allowed delegates the opportunity to discern which trade unions were represented as well as how unions differed in structure and responsibility, this coming together of trade union interests was short lived. Even the German trade union, the Industriegewerkschaft Bergbau, Chemie, Energie (IG BCE), a body of significant influence within Sanofi Germany, has abstained from attending EWC meetings.

6.3 Analysing the trade union presence

6.3.1 Trade union presence and management control

In all five case studies, a trade union presence could be observed to varying degrees. This was guaranteed either directly through a trade union official attending an EWC meeting or indirectly by reporting back through national union structures. However, the quality of this 'presence', measured in terms of involvement and influence, would appear to be limited. In the one case where trade unions had the potential to play a key role, the Ford EWC, reluctance to influence the agenda prevailed even on the part of the IG Metall/EMF delegate. Over a decade since Lecher et al. (1998) undertook their first systematic study of EWCs, one in which they suggested trade unions played a peripheral role within this European institution, the trade union landscape appears to be virtually unchanged. EWCs continue to sit uneasily within the trade union portfolio. Interviews with union officers from Germany and other countries indicated that Europe is quite low in trade unions' 'pecking order', with collective bargaining and representing the interests of national members remaining their cardinal concern.

In short, trade union EWC involvement is not unproblematic. For example, contrary to Pulignano's (2005: 395) findings on the role of ETUF officials, there was no evidence, even in the best case scenario of Ford, that such individuals assert their authority 'to build bridges between workplace representatives of multinational companies and the development of trade union policies'. Nor was their any evidence to imply that such union officers play a strategic role 'in facilitating the exchange of information and practices among employees' (Pulignano, 2005: 400). If anything trade union involvement in our five case studies drastically declined after they initially facilitated the foundation process. Even the much referenced training and expertise that trade unions were expected to provide was not very much in evidence (Lecher et al., 1998, 2001; Hancké, 2000; Huzzard and Docherty, 2005; ETUC, 1999). In fact, a picture emerges, certainly in the cases of Unilever, Ford and Kraft Foods, that EWC members, especially those who meet on a regular basis within the steering committee, possess expertise that does not require them to seek trade union support.

Close working relations with management, but more importantly cooperation between EWC delegates, which as Whittall et al. (2009) show is increasingly helped by ICT, mean that EWC delegates are well informed about company strategy and possible responses. Moreover, there was no evidence to support Hancké's assertion (2000: 104) that 'it is difficult to imagine workers ever being able to respond to the contemporary economic challenges posed by the Europeanization and globalization of capital' without the involvement of trade unions. Or for that matter, as Telljohann (2005) suggests, that an inadequate level of involvement leads to the demotivation of EWC delegates. On the contrary, in spite of a lack of trade union presence, a core group of European activists are bringing this European institution to 'life'. In most cases, dispersed EWC delegates, specifically the steering committee members, are in weekly if not daily contact with each other. Quite clearly the EWC is becoming an integral part of their employee representative arsenal.

However, has the peripheral role played by trade unions, as observed in other case studies (Royle, 1999; Wills, 2000), led to management hijacking the EWCs in question? A number of researchers have argued that this represents a real threat to the functioning of EWCs. Hancké (2000: 55), for example, noted: 'And as a result of this relative lack of interest by unions, this ongoing, and indeed accelerating Europeanization of industrial relations in the car industry is increasingly taking place on management's terms, with the EWCs as a critical part of that process. The political implications of this analysis are clear: the future of EWCs lies to a large extent in the hands of the unions themselves'. Royle (1999: 344) came to a similar conclusion when studying the McDonalds EWC: 'McDonald's has been able to take advantage of loopholes in national European labour legislation (and in some cases utilize dubious election processes) to minimize trade union presence in the EWC. [Furthermore] international trade union organizations have been kept out of the process ...' Quite simply, and in contrast to these claims, the answer to this question is a definitive 'no'. None of the case studies observed demonstrated any degree of either 'management capture' or 'isolation'. In the case of Burger-Miller, a company with a strong tradition of German corporatism, where employee representatives traditionally benefiting from management's open-door policy, an 'us and them' culture could be observed. The fact remains, a point taken up by Knudsen et al. (2007) and Timming and Veersma (2007), that EWC delegates' identity is defined within their relationships with management, the 'other' as they call it, rather than by management unilaterally.

A number of factors contribute to the independence of EWCs, even where the involvement of trade unions is not as developed as researchers have suggested is necessary and as national, as well as international, federations would possibly prefer. Firstly, the works councils in question were by no stretch of the imagination a managerial construct. Not only was the original decision to found the EWC employee and not management led, but more importantly the ground work provided by trade unions in shadowing in the foundation process secured a strong sense of independence that was sustained, irrespective of weak trade union participation in subsequent years. Secondly, delegates on the whole were not handpicked by management. The majority of delegates came with strong trade union credentials, credentials which by default would appear to guard against management manipulation. Thirdly, even in cases where management proposes certain EWC delegates, this is no guarantee that such individuals will abide by managerial demands. A number of factors appear to be at play here. EWC delegates we interviewed with a traditional trade union biography are aware of this problem and have subsequently taken appropriate precautions to neutralize such a threat. As in the case of Burger-Miller, this involved the presence of an informal mentoring scheme in which trade union delegates have gone out of their way to include non-trade union delegates in the decision making processes. This helped cultivate friendships and a mutual sense of responsibility. Furthermore, as the work of

Tuckman and Whittall (2010) on works councils set up by management has demonstrated, managerial nominees after a certain period of time often feel obliged to exhibit a sense of independence. In the case of one of the leading Unilever EWC figures, for example, this was a person with a clearly defined managerial background, someone who went out his way to outline how they had initially been very wary of trade union organizations. Over the years, however, their involvement within the EWC resulted in their becoming a member of a white-collar union, but more importantly working very closely with shop stewards from more traditional organizations within their national environment.

Traditionally trade unions have feared that their lack of involvement in EWCs could lead to management hijacking the EWC and subsequently using this European institution to promote social dumping. Irrespective of whether such involvement is a guarantee against social dumping, our research uncovered no real evidence to corroborate such a position. Even given the lack of a strong trade union presence within the EWC, delegates retained a strong notion of autonomy, where either their role as an employee representative at the national level or their interaction with European management proved defining factors. A trade union official from IG BCE who we interviewed even went as far confirming this finding when noting that:

> The first generation created the organizational preconditions, and had to struggle to be recognized by management, and that was a very important step.

Certainly, in the cases of Kraft Foods, Unilever and Ford management were increasingly being forced to recognize that the EWC is an important source of employee representation.

6.3.2 What explains trade unions' lack of involvement in EWCs?

Ironically, it could be argued that trade unions are not required to be more assertive in their involvement with EWCs as, at a latent level, they have in fact prevailed in this area. As suggested above, trade unions arguably helped set the tone initially through their support for establishing

EWCs, and many EWC delegates are, by default, the custodians of trade union values due to their close association with organized labour, and as such are, as it were, guilty by association. However, as we shall see in the next section, neither of these facts, something underlined in the work of both Telljohann (2009) and Waddington (2010), are a safeguard against a potential decoupling of EWCs and trade union interests. Just because management has not been successful in controlling the EWC does not automatically ensure that EWC delegates might choose a developmental path that is not necessarily desired by trade unions.

Why then have trade unions failed to play a more prominent role in EWC affairs, even in cases where they have legally been guaranteed access to EWCs as in the case of Ford and Burger-Miller? Is it simply due to either dominance of a 'single' or 'dual' tier of representation, as argued by Telljohann (2005)? For Telljohann (2005: 37) this explains why it is that only Italian trade unions are so active in EWCs, so much so that 'it seems possible to talk of a fully-fledged Italian model of the EWC that differs from the two kinds of EWC which are generally referred to in the litera- ture ... The Italian model is characterized by the leading role of the external trade unions that is typical of the one-tier system of interest representa- tion'. Certainly, this might explain the reluctance of German trade unions to increase their EWC profile, given that the German system of codeter- mination provides a clear division of labour between works councils and trade unions, with the former assigned responsibility for company-related issues. A member of the Burger-Miller EWC, for example, felt that this was the reason why the German union had failed to play the strong role in the EWC that would have befitted its influence and size. Discussing this issue a German delegate on the Unilever EWC noted:

> Exactly, and what I had to learn was that the good cooperation that exists between the works council and trade unions in Germany, where it's clear who does what and we get along, with a few exceptions, that this doesn't apply everywhere in Europe. Some areas are clearly out of bounds, and there is already some distrust towards works councils.

Equally such a situation describes why the trade union official leading the British delegation on the Ford EWC went out of his way to emphasize the amount of time that he invested in this European structure: 'I mean, the easiest thing for me to do would say "I'm sorry, I'm too busy, I mean I've got more pressing business". I mean that's the easiest thing in the world for a National Officer to say. But I'm doing the job that I've been employed to do'. However, such a conceptual understanding, we contend, has certain limitations. Firstly, the dual system is underpinned by a mutual trust that has developed within particular national settings – the EWC, certainly at this stage in its development, cannot be compared with its national counterpart in, say, Germany. The division of labour within the German system is based on high-trust relationships that are reflected in the fact that the majority of works council chairs in Germany are trade union members. Unlike within the national environment, unions have no influence over delegates emanating from other European countries. The EWC is a Pandora's box for trade unions, unpredictable and difficult to guide from the outside. Next, in the case of the 'single tier' argument, the importance attached to attending every EWC and steering committee meeting by the British union official responsible for Ford was the 'exception rather than the rule'. In none of the other four case studies was any such engagement to be observed. The activity at Ford reflected more than anything else the continued importance of the American car producer in the UK and the fact that UNITE remains very present within the UK plants.

Quite clearly, irrespective of the policy commitments towards EWCs on the part of both national and international federations, the latter developing clear policy guidelines to encourage greater trade union involvement in this European institution, such endeavours are likely to prove futile if the actors in question neither posses the resources nor what is best described as the European 'normative constitution' needed to exercise this function. Beginning with resources, both interviews with trade union officials at all levels of the representative spectrum, together with an array of literature on this subject (Waddington, 2001; Platzer, 2010), confirm that unions' Achilles heel remains not only a lack of personnel but also of personnel with the necessary training to serve or serve on EWCs. Speaking on behalf of the chemical sector an official from IG BCE summed up the problems faced by trade unions generally:

> The problem is, firstly, that we have a lot of EWCs, as distinct from at the begin-
> ning when we only a had a few and when we were involved in the negotiations, and,
> secondly, it's a much bigger effort to give proper support to processes inside EWCs
> than to support a single negotiation ... That is, we just need a hell of a lot more people
> who are capable of actually meaningfully fulfilling the ideal of coordinating EWCs,
> that we always swear we should.

The respondent touches here on something that also goes to the heart of European Trade Union Federations' (ETUF) EWC endeavours: the coordination of EWC activities. For example: 'Develop common strategies. Speak with one voice. It is important because if you don't speak with one voice then you cannot be successful' (EMF official). But as Waddington (2010) and Platzer (2010) note, ETUF budgets are limited, to say the least. Waddington (2010: 31), someone who has had unparalleled access to the ETUF documents, tellingly states; 'the income of the EMF from the affiliated unions was €4,326,873 and it employed seventeen people. The corresponding figures for the EMCEF were €891,560 and eight employees and for UNI-Europa €1,668,766 and 16.5 employees ... The situation amongst the national confederations, however, remains far superior. The Norwegian Landsorganisasjonen, for example, was €29,952,000 and it employed 270 people ...' Hence, even though ETUFs now have at their disposal a network of EWC coordinators, when questioned about the role of ETUFs, our respondents indicated that the European federations lacked the necessary means either to send officials to EWC meetings or ensure that nationally nominated coordinators, usually an official from the largest union within the company, abided by the guidelines outlined in the ETUFs' EWC policies. The current dilemma of the ETUFs is summed up excellently by a member of the Sanofi EWC:

> We are supported by a representative from EMCEF on the European Works Council.
> The problem is simply that, if you are familiar with the structure of EMCEF you'll
> know that there is hardly any money, and hardly any people, and that one single
> individual coordinates several EWCs, which sometimes have their meetings at the
> same time, and as far their personal side is concerned, this individual has some major
> health problems.

The EMF (2000a) has also noted that its coordinator policy is faced by a number of obstacles. These include the following:

1. Different countries interpret the role of a coordinator in different ways.
2. Some countries do not send their coordinators to EWC meetings.
3. Coordinators do not always have the necessary skills to fulfill this role.
4. In some countries the level of local autonomy restricts trade union involvement.

The question of resources leads on to our next point, the importance placed on European policy by national unions. Resource allocation is highly political as it reflects those areas conceived as important by organizations. The lack of resources, for example, available to European officials at a national and European level, and all our respondents indicated this was a problem, is symptomatic, we would argue, of unions' continued inability to make Europe a key agenda issue. For example, a German trade union official responsible for EWCs noted that a key part of their remit concerned servicing existing national works councils. This involved: producing materials for works councils' election, organizational work prior to works council elections and analysing the results of the election. These time-consuming responsibilities leave very little time left for EWC matters. Other union officials confirmed this. Various respondents acknowledged that trade unions were struggling to Europeanize their structures:

> I've got the feeling that the trade union has been so handicapped in the past ten years that it has done nothing, taken no initiative. I can't see anything, no progress, also not at the NGG. Perhaps I'm complaining at too high a level. What I'm missing is any keeping up with the pace. Europe is moving so fast that there are completely new dimensions, and I can't see how the trade union is responding to that (German works council member at Kraft Foods).

> I'd like to see more presence there ... There's this load of experts that travels from country to country, and they always meet at the nicest places, and sometimes I get invited – they are off doing their high-falutin' European stuff, but I don't see this in

our forums. They're trade unionists, lawyers – these are academic events ... (Chair of EWC Unilever EWC).

I'm on the executive board of IG Metall here, and I would say that we don't do enough internationally. The way we deal with European lobbying – we're treated like the poor relations, and we have to get through with very few people in Brussels (Chair of Ford EWC).

A key issue here, one widely discussed in the literature on trade unions and referred to above (Offe and Wiesenthal, 1982; Knudsen et al., 2007; Hyman, 2001), is the continued 'centrifugal' character of trade union organizations. By their very nature they posses an organizational structure which is not only the product of a national environment (Hyman, 2001), with unions a historical product of emerging modern national states in the nineteenth century, but, moreover, their main task is to support local interests – that is, the people who pay their monthly union membership fees. Interviews with trade unions demonstrate that EWCs are not seen as part of national officers' 'core business' (IG BCE European official), and that the EWC only becomes an issue 'when there's big problem'. Interviews revealed that parochialism is not a phenomenon specific to German trade unions. A Belgian delegate on the Ford EWC argued, 'each trade union is occupied with their own affairs'. According to a delegate on the Burger-Miller EWC, this represented a general conservatism on the part of national trade unions:

I will use a very bad word here because of ... they are conservative, just to say. And everybody is normally afraid of losing their influence, their power and so on. And they are conservative in that way. Not ... everything they do ... they are ... they do support the ... European market and things like that, okay, okay, but 'We would like ...' and so on and so on ... In my opinion it's quite clear that they are very slow and they are very cautious and conservative in their way of thinking about these institutes, EWC (Burger-Miller EWC member)

The widespread reluctance on the part of trade unions that was prevalent in our five case studies confirms Armingeon's (1998) critical assessment of trade unions' ability to internationalize. According to Armingeon (1998: 74) this involves institutional inertia, a failure to 'resist pressures to adjust for a long time, even where these are growing stronger'. For example, although the process of centralization could be observed to different degrees in all five case studies, and was especially prominent at Kraft Foods and Unilever, unions continue to remain very much embedded within the nation state.

A mixture of a lack of resources and a continued focus on what union officials refer to as the concerns of the 'national membership', national collective bargaining, would appear to explain what can only be described as the peripheral role played by trade unions within our five case studies. Certainly, the rationale offered by Armingeon (1998) goes some way to understanding such a reluctance. However, it also needs to be recognized that the industrial landscape of many European countries has changed dramatically since the 1990s. The huge decline in membership experienced by European trade unions and the general decentralization of collective bargaining has undoubtedly hampered attempts to widen organizational responsibilities. However, as Lucio and Weston (1998) noted over a decade ago, such inertia could have the potential to lead to multinational collective bargaining outside of existing national arrangements – that is, to micro-corporatism.

6.4 Encroachment – Micro-corporatism

At different times in this section we have touched on the issue of 'encroachment', a term used to define the possible development of a negotiation modus within the EWC structure. In short, EWCs threaten to usurp trade unions. How real is this development, though? As we know, Marginson et al. (1993, 2006) and Kotthoff (2006 a.) have discussed what is now widely referred to as the Eurocompany, a phenomenon in which 'international companies develop distinct European dimensions to their forms of (management) organization and coordination of production and market servicing' (Marginson, 2000: 10). More to the point, such a development is seen as a catalyst for European micro-corporatism, in which 'EWCs are likely to provide a focal point for further developments in European industrial relations, especially European collective bargaining' (Marginson, 2000: 11). Discussing wider developments in industrial relations Brewster et al. (2007: 51) come to the core of this issue when they note that micro-corporatism involves a shrinking market for employee representation:

> [A]ll forms of collective representation – whether union based or not – are likely to be eroded in favour of more direct, manager-centred forms of participation. If this is indeed the case it suggests that a shrinking market for such services might intensify competition between different representative practices.

As the literature pertaining to EWCs indicates, this represents a nightmare scenario for trade unions (Lucio and Martinez, 2000), one which unions have been aware ever since the EWC Directive was passed in 1994. Of course, trade unions concerns were alleviated to a certain extent by the fact that the Directive only empowers EWCs with information and consultation rights, a restriction the ETUC did not deem it necessary to address when negotiating the 'recasting' of the Directive in 2008. In fact, we would argue that a general trade union approach can be observed; irrespective of whether they originate in dualist or monist systems, trade unions have sought to restrict EWCs in order to maintain their collective bargaining prerogative. Huzzard and Docherty (2005) note, for example, that the so-called 'Network for Union Democracy', described as loose group of unions on continental Europe, categorically prohibits EWCs from touching issues relating to pay and conditions. In a similar vein, ETUFs have used various congresses to adopt policies designed to steer EWCs away from becoming an active negotiator. Discussing the EWC Directive, the EMF (2000b: 6) argued:

> [The legislator] should stipulate where their competency ends (in our view where collective bargaining, wage negotiations and discussions about labour conditions and similar issues begin), for these have always been – and should remain – the responsibility of trade unions at European level ... Within such a framework, EWCs would become legally defined information and consultation bodies ... Our feeling is that the right to negotiate within the community-scale companies should remain with European trade union organizations. At a later date EWCs could secure negotiation rights, but only in connection with specific soft issues, like equal opportunities, vocational training and the fight against discrimination.

However, the likes of the EMF (2000d) are aware of the possibility of EWCs developing a negotiation strand to their remit. Even given the restrictions imposed by the Directive and trade unions themselves, although in the case of the latter this is highly problematical due to the fact that EWCs are not legally dependent of a union mandate, the EMF concedes that the question of collective bargaining is not 'clear cut'. This issue has also been taken up by Telljohann (2009) when studying the role of EWCs in signing European Framework Agreements. Firstly, he notes, that many EWCs are no longer content with receiving and commenting on information. On the contrary, he argues that we should not 'exclude an evolution of the bargaining practices of parties towards transnational collective bargaining at the company level on a voluntary basis' (Telljohann, 2009: 20). Furthermore, Telljohann (2009: 56) suggest that framework agreements, specifically those signed pertaining to Europe, are evidence of a process in which trade unions and EWCs are becoming decoupled:

> The differences between IFAs [International Framework Agreements] and European-level framework agreements [is that they differ] procedurally in terms of the role played by different actors. In this case of European-level framework agreements, transnational company level employee representation structures (i.e. EWCs) play a much stronger role in initiating, negotiating and signing the agreements.

Certainly, the case studies presented here confirm many of the developments, fears and conflicts between EWCs and trade unions outlined above. Although the speed of change might be different, all five case studies have either gone or are going through a process of centralization, a process that has seen them evolve into a Eurocompany as outlined by Marginson (2000) and Kotthoff (2006a). In particular, Unilever and Kraft have a strong central management structure, while it should be noted that Ford was one of the case studies that initially inspired Marginson's work. Referring to the situation at Kraft a member of the EWC steering committee noted:

> The significance will continue to grow as a result of the concentration of the company in Europe, [with] unchanged conditions for competition. If trade unions do not succeed in focusing more on this, the process will decouple and there will be more EWCs that are incorporated into the business – that is, workplace alliances detached from the trade union movement, that's what will happen.

In the case of Unilever, for example, the EWC has negotiated a new agreement that not only provides it with more rights but also procedures to be adhered to in periods of restructuring. A member of the EWC takes up the story:

> We put forward some points on restructuring, especially in cases where it is better to sell a plant than close it; we need three-year employment guarantees in the event of a takeover, in the event of restructuring and transfers, or if [output] is transferred, all this sort of thing. We have got some principles, and we succeeded ... I wouldn't say we got our way entirely but we have established principles, and they're generally complied with.

However, as a Burger-Miller EWC member noted, unions are wary of such developments: 'I think they [unions] are simply afraid of losing the bargaining rights. That is the key point'. As an official of the European federation indicated, such agreements would contradict their guidelines and hence represent the potential for conflict:

> Our position is clear. We are not ... We will not recognize [international] framework or European framework agreements which have not followed the procedure which we have decided on here internally, because we don't want trade unions to be bypassed.

Although conflict between EWCs and trade unions over 'representative rights' was not widespread, due if nothing else to a current lack of interaction between these two levels, respondents did refer to a few occasions when this had occurred. At Ford, for example, a German EWC respondent explained in some detail how their British colleague, a convenor, had been reprimanded by a union official for taking decisions that usually fell within the realm of trade union responsibility:

> He [the British convenor] understood that completely, and he had had a big row with his trade union official – it was Tony at the time – who then became general secretary of the T&G, and has just retired ... They had a big row, because that was the first time that a convenor, who doesn't have a lot of power in England – that's always the full-time official who does everything – said to his full-time official, watch out mate, this is a completely different tradition in another country, and that's a good tradition and we should follow it. But the trade union – the full-time official – had not played along, and they regarded it as interference in their affairs etc. And then

Richie retired, and then after that most of the other English colleagues in quick succession, and they had understood what it was possible to build up strategically in European terms, but when they went – retired – this knowledge was lost in England. The full-time officials got the power back in their hands.

When questioned about collective bargaining rights, the British official on the Ford EWC categorically opposed such a development:

> Do I see a ... Ford of Europe EWC as the bargaining instrument for Ford of Europe employees? No, I don't, I don't. That's too complex, it's too complicated, there's different structures ... there's legally binding agreements ... there's a whole mish-mash if you like ... everybody is different ... [Y]ou know, ultimately if I'm asked the question: 'Is the EWC the for that? [collective bargaining]' – 'No, of course, it is not'. But what it does it allows us to exchange information. It allows us to debate with colleagues who are predominantly in the same situation as we are in.

Such a discrepancy could also be observed at Sanofi. Here the role of the EWC, and in particular whether the EWC should be empowered with a mandate to negotiate, led to conflict between EWC delegates and EMCEF, the European federation. As the following respondent outlined, this conflict continues to hinder relations between these two representative levels:

> We felt extremely betrayed by EMCEF, which had not supported our approach, and the national organizations had also not supported [us]. Most of them did not support our approach and that also loosened ties ... I was really angry. Good, with EMCEF there will be another meeting, but it will be more difficult because of what happened. For me, it's that there are people that I don't really want to meet. Because I think that they betrayed us. Although it was us that had advanced the right of the EWCs at the company, and the right to negotiate in the company.

In summary, our case studies in the main corroborate Marginson's and Kotthoff's assertion that within Eurocompanies – that is, with a centralization of the managerial-decision-making process – a European industrial relations sphere is emerging. At its heart is the EWC. Constituted by employees of the company, this European body has begun to surpass the legal and the organizational constraints imposed by legislators and also by the trade unions. What does this mean for the relations between EWCs and trade unions in the future? It is this question that we consider more directly in the next and final section.

6.5 Summary

Having fought for over three decades on behalf employee rights within the
European Union (formerly European Community), and in particular to
secure the EWC Directive, trade unions continue to struggle to develop a
European perspective, as our research confirms. We uncovered no evidence
to corroborate Lecher et al.'s (2001) assertion that national unions have
been forced away from a policy in which Europe, particularly EWCs, is a
niche issue, to one where Europe is integrated into union policy generally.
On the contrary, EWC delegates and union officials noted that Europe
generally and EWCs specifically remain peripheral issues for trade unions.
It would be an exaggeration to say that the EWC represents a 'union-free
zone', but equally it would be an overstatement to suggest that they play a
role in steering the inner workings of this European institution. Alarmingly
for trade unions, EWCs, certainly in the cases of Unilever and Kraft Foods,
appear able to guide company policy irrespective of trade unions' ability
to be more present within this European institution. In short, EWCs have
become an independent employee body that is responding to management's
strategy to centralize decision-making processes – in short, to shadow the
emergence of a Eurocompany.

According to Telljohann (2009: 58) 'for the trade unions this situation presents a strategic dilemma ... European-level negotiations by EWCs
represent, on one hand, a useful strategy to handle the consequences of
and to counter the increasing transnational economic activities of TNCs.
On the other hand, trade unions need to ensure that they stay involved in
company-level negotiations at European company-level because if EWCs
decide to enter into negotiations without involving trade unions, then
unions risk being marginalized'. This raises of course the question as to
whether EWC delegates actively desire the marginalization of trade unions.
We found no evidence to support such a position. On the contrary, EWC
delegates indicated they would welcome an increase in union involvement.
Many respondents referred to their trade union membership, partly out of
sympathy for trade unions but more importantly because they envisaged

that trade unions had an important role to play in EWCs. The main input that respondents referred to concerned: union's knowledge of developments across sectors, expertise in legal issues and the ability to organize industrial action.

> Yes. Good, it's of course important that there will be some input from the trade union side as the representatives from the individual countries have a broader perspective, not only in the car industry but something of the competition in the individual countries. I think that it is important that they are there, because it generates a wider view of things in discussions (Ford EWC delegate).

> For me, we need the trade unions that are more militant than they are now (Unilever EWC delegate, Spain).

> I think that union involvement is a positive thing because it helps guide the individuals in terms of legislation. They understand better what's going on ... So there are an awful lot of things that they learn about ... (Unilever EWC delegate UK).

Trade unions, though, remain prisoners of what one union officer called 'parish pump politics'. They are the product of an historical period which, seen from an organizational perspective, is increasingly less suited to face the challenges posed by Europeanization. As a consequence, national unions are unwilling either to shift resources to support EWCs or to empower ETUFs with greater representative rights. However, there is a silver lining here. Irrespective of this inertia, our findings suggest that a group of committed EWC activists, actors with a clear European outlook, are promoting an agenda which is potentially laying the foundations for a European system of industrial relations. This emerging developmental path is not only a challenge to management prerogatives, but equally to trade unions' 'containment' policies. Seen from this perspective one might be optimistically led to conclude that this represents a potential route for trade union revitalization from below. After all, none of EWC respondents demonstrated an interest in questioning the principles of trade unionism. Rather they argued that such principles, which are currently anchored within a national environment, be complemented by a European perspective.

CHAPTER 7

Conclusion

The central problematic in this study was that of the construction of Europe as a space for perception, experience and cooperation on the part of members of EWCs. Is Europe a relevant point of reference for employee interest representation at corporate level? Has a transformation taken place in the categories in which this is thought about? This presupposes changed structures of consciousness and a changed conception of those who are deemed to belong, of group identity, of how one should behave in relation to others, and what binds people together. The nature and intensity of this experience of the European space is manifested in a readiness and capacity for solidarity – that is, for cooperation and mutual support aimed at developing a strategy for representation that is more effective for all.

We relate solidarity to the behaviour of EWC members and in particular to members of the steering committee. This is *influenced* by their assessment of the scope and limits of solidarity on the part of workforces and their local representatives, but is not *determined* by it. Workforce solidarity consists in making perceptible sacrifices for employees in other national operations, as well as participation in protest and strike actions aimed at supporting them. Unquestionably, both these theatres of solidarity are closely related. However, in our view, one should distinguish that type of solidarity between EWC members that is needed to constitute an EWC into a body with a capacity for activity from protest solidarity and a preparedness to make sacrifices demonstrated by workers. The reason for this is that these latter two will only succeed if the former is in place and effective. Opening a space for perception and cooperation between workforces more generally requires a capable cadre of representatives with a European consciousness and experience. As a consequence, we do not wholly concur with Richard Hyman's gloomy diagnosis that 'internationalism is largely the preserve of professional trade union diplomats' (Hyman, 2001: 67), as our study shows that, in the field of company-based European transnationalism, numerous semi-professional members of EWC steering committees can work in a solidarity with each other. At the same time, we also have to note that the demand that 'employees at the grass roots need to actively participate in this process' (ibid.: 70) is far from being met.

Our research results suggest that such a space of perception and cooperation has not generally been opened up and exists only embryonically. As a consequence, we have concentrated primarily on the process of how *EWC members* who are initially unfamiliar with each other then become acquainted, grow more familiar, and draw closer together to initiate and promote a new space of joint interest representation. Our research also looked at solidarity on the part of *workforces* and their local representatives. However, we had few results: as yet, there is relatively little European activity to report on. Had we measured the progress of EWCs solely by this yardstick, this study would have been a very brief one. The only – individual – examples of the inclusion of sections of the workforce was at Burger-Miller.

The idea that greater European consciousness and European solidarity in employee representation is a movement driven from below, pressed upwards, as it were, from the grass-roots is, at least based on our research, largely an illusory one. The reverse would appear to be the case. Where we have discerned initial steps towards a change in consciousness on the part of workforces, the impetus has come from those protagonists on EWCs, and in trade unions, who have become aware of and acquired experience in European matters: that is, from European pioneers, both in terms of theory and practice, amongst elected workforce office holders. It is also clear that the progress that we have been able to discern from our reports of European protagonists and cadres runs up against its limits wherever these individuals have been unable to generate a comparable change in awareness on the part of their constituents – that is, workforces and local representatives.

Our method consisted in choosing five EWCs, which, based on our own knowledge and the judgement of other experts, appeared to number among those EWCs that had made some progress towards transnational cooperation. As such, this is a selection of the best, gauged on a wide range of indicators. They are EWCs that stand out because of successes in representation, such as concluding good EWC installation agreements, European Framework Agreements and/or a high level of activity (such as frequent meetings or intensive internal communication).

In four of the five cases (Unilever, Kraft Foods, Ford and Burger-Miller) our first impression was confirmed. We were able to identify an extension of the field of interest representation into the European space, and we considered this to be the product of cooperative and mutually supportive behaviour. We found numerous and impressive examples that demonstrated the presence of solidaristic behaviour, albeit in different forms and with varying characteristics.

The evidence for this consisted principally in the dedication of large amounts of time and energy to building the EWC into a body with the capacity to engage in activity: taking on the perspectives of other countries and local operations; open information about local strategies for representation; a willingness to assume some shared responsibility for solving the problems of other plants and operations; a mutual moral commitment (code of conduct) to delay transfers of production to one's own location until the relinquishing plant has concluded an acceptable social compensation plan; and solidarity actions by the EWC in protest against management decisions. In contrast, in our case studies we encountered no instance of where an EWC had organized cross-national protest action on the part of large sections of the workforce.

Also in the fifth case, the EWC at Sanofi, developments were initially promising, but this process then broke down and went into reverse in a downward spiral of mistrust.

If we consider the EWC as an actor, our research indicates that the real agents are the members of the steering committee. Our focus on those individuals who sit at the head of the forum looks beyond the roles familiar, for example, from German works councils (taken as a yardstick for institutionalized national employee representation). In contrast to these, ordinary EWC members meet only once a year, or twice at the most, involve an encounter between people who are unfamiliar with each other, who never encounter other in the normal course of their work, and, because of language barriers, have barely exchanged a direct word. Even where there is scope for members to become better acquainted over time, the rhythm of meetings is very different to that of a well-functioning national representative body. For example, members are likely to meet only five times over the course of five years, and possibly even less if individuals, with whom a close relationship might have been built, leave and are replaced by others. In some EWCs, attempts have been made to counter such transience by establishing rules for continuity, such as not permitting the principle of rotating trade union delegates customary in Southern Europe. In particular, training events that last for several days (where these are organized, they usually take place every two years) have proved very useful in fostering relationships between EWC members. However, even that cannot fundamentally change the situation.

It is important for the work of the steering committee, and the link between it and the forum as a whole, that there is a guaranteed flow of information between annual meetings and – at the least – between significant countries and plants: that is, at least one EWC member in each country should serve as a reliable point of contact and relay for information to local operations.

The role played by trade unions in the EWC process varies from case to case, but in general has been peripheral. EWC members convey the impression that union organizations remain only marginally engaged with, and often distant towards, EWC work – an aversion, in part, due to fear of competition. Members would like trade unions to make a greater commitment. One by no means unrealistic path of development has been for EWCs and trade unions to become increasingly alienated, with a concomitant independence of the institution of the EWC, for example in the form of micro-corporatism.

One key factor in the emergence of solidarity within the EWC are behaviours that enable it to constitute itself as an effective association: that is, a stable process of group formation, group discipline, the establishment of leadership authority and a coordinated internal division of roles. The emergence of a capable and socially integrated group presupposes the interaction of two, apparently counterposed, basic forms of solidarity: group solidarity that generates trust; and utilitarian solidarity based on enlightened self-interest. The latter consists in understanding the implications for employment participation at group level of the significant transformations in corporate administration – namely the transnational centralization of strategic decisions. That is, it requires grasping the changed contexts and drawing the consequences from this for the representation of employee interests that also operates at the level of the corporate centre. Specific practices of representation then vary between extending the status of industrial citizenship through dialogue with management and a more adversarial approach at transnational level.

For us, the concept of a 'constellation for interest representation' is associated, in historical perspective, with the levels of both structure and agent. Whether and to what degree the link between group solidarity and solidarity based on self-interest can be successfully established depends, first and foremost, on the nature of this constellation within the group. For its part, this constitutes the current reflection of the transnational history of industrial relations at the company. The EWC then is presented with an aggregate of psycho-social material to process that is the product of the primary qualities of these relationships operating over the long term within this constellation.

Whether the EWC simply reproduces this material or whether it changes it – at any event, it will have an impact on its approach. In the cases of Unilever and Kraft Foods, this primary quality was one of equality; in the case of Ford, bipolarity. At Burger-Miller and Sanofi, the history of transnational interest representation has been strongly determined by recent mega-mergers, which, in the first of these cases, led to disappointed hopes for advocacy, and in the second to anxiety about a loss of identity and being swamped by an alien entity. For the EWC, the main demand placed on it is to work and deal with the specific qualities of these relationships in each case.

References

Andersson, M. and Thörnqvist, C. (2007). 'Regional Clusters of Communication: between National and European Identities'. In Whittall, M., Knudsen, H. and Huijgen, F. (eds), *Towards a European Labour Identity. The Case of the European Works Council*, pp. 94–110. Abingdon: Routledge.

Armingeon, K.(1998). 'The Persistence of Differences between National Industrial Relations Systems in Europe'. In Lecher, W. and Platzer, H-W. (eds), *European Union – European Industrial Relations?*, pp. 72–80. London: Routledge.

Bach, M. (2008). *Europa ohne Gesellschaft. Politische Soziologie der Europäischen Integration.* Wiesbaden.

Baum, R. C. (1975). 'The System of Solidarities: a Working Paper in General Action Analysis', *Indian Journal of Sociology*, Vol. 16, 306–353.

Baurmann, M. (1998). 'Solidarität als soziale Norm und als Norm der Verfassung'. In Bayertz, K. (ed.), *Solidarität. Begriff und Problem*, pp. 345–388. Frankfurt am Main: Suhrkamp.

Bayertz, K. (ed.) (1998). *Solidarität. Begriff und Problem.* Frankfurt am Main: Suhrkamp.

Bayertz, K. (1999). 'Four Uses of Solidarity'. In: idem (ed.) *Solidarity*, pp. 3–28.

Bayertz, K. (1999). *Solidarity.* Dordrecht: Kluwer.

Beckert, J., Eckert, J., Kohli, M., and Streeck, W. (eds) (2004). *Transnationale Solidarität. Chancen und Grenzen.* Frankfurt am Main/New York.

Bleses, P. and Rose, E. (2009). *Europäische Betriebsräte: Ergebnisse sozialwissenschaftlicher Forschung 2004–2009*, Hans-Böckler-Stiftung, Düsseldorf, <www.boeckler. de/pdf/mbf_ebr_sozialforschung_2009.pdf>

Bonin, H., Lung, Y. and Tolliday, S. (eds) (2003). *Ford. The European History.* Paris.

Bordenave, G. (2003). 'Ford in Europe, 1967–2003'. In: Bonin et al. (eds) *Ford. The European History*, pp. 243–317. Also online at <www.gres-so.org>

Brewster, C., Wood, G., Croucher, R. and Brookes, M. (2007). 'Are Works Councils and Joint Consultative Committees a Threat to Trade Unions? A Comparative Analysis', *Economic and Industrial Democracy*, Vol. 28:1, 49–77.

Bronfenbrenner, K. (ed.) (2007). *Global Unions: Challenging Transnational Capital Through Cross-Border Campaigns.* Ithaca N.Y.

Brunkhorst, H. (2001). *Solidarität unter Fremden*, Frankfurt a.M.

Brunkhorst, H. (2008). 'Demokratische Solidarität in der Weltgesellschaft', *Aus Politik und Zeitgeschichte* (ApuZ) 21/2008, 3–8.

Dallinger, U. (2008). 'Rationale Kooperation oder Moral? Der Wohlfahrtsstaat aus der Sicht der ökonomischen Institutionentheorie', *Soziale Welt*, 2/2008, 157–180.

Delhey, J. (2004). 'Nationales und transnationales Vertrauen in der europäischen Union', *Leviathan*, 1/2004, 15–45.

Durkheim, E. (1984). *The Division of Labour in Society* [1893/1984] Trans. W.D Halls. Basingstoke and London.

Ebbinghaus, B., and Visser, J. (1994). 'Barrieren und Wege grenzenloser Solidarität: Gewerkschaften und europäische Integration'. In: Streeck, W. (ed.) *Staat und Verbände*, Opladen.

Ebbinghaus, B. and Visser, J. (eds) (2000). *Trade Unions in Western Europe since 1945*. Basingstoke.

Eigenmüller, M. and Mau, S. (eds) (2010). *Gesellschaftstheorie und Europapolitik*, Wiesbaden.

EMF (2000a). *Policy Paper on the Future Role for EWCs and Trade Unions in a Community-Scale Company.*

EMF (2000b). *The 'European Works Council' project. Evaluation Report.*

EMF (2001). *Co-ordination on European Works Councils: Binding Guidelines for procedures and contents, including abridged version for wider circulation.*

EMF (2010). 'EMF Internal procedure for negotiations at multinational company level – Adopted by the 102nd EMF Executive Committee, Luxembourg, 13th and 14th June 2006'. In EMF (2010), *Milestones: From Rome to Madrid, Supplement 2005–2009*. Brussels: EMF.

Fetzer, T. (1980). 'Walking out of the national workplace. Industrial disputes and Union Politics at Ford in Britain and Germany in the 1970s and 1980s'. In Bonin, H. et al. (eds) (2003), *Ford. The European History*, pp. 393–415. Paris.

Fetzer, T. (2009). 'Europäisierung und Nationalisierung. Deutsche Gewerkschaftspolitik bei Ford (1967–1989)'. In Friedrich-Ebert-Stiftung (ed.), *Archiv für Sozialgeschichte*, Bd. 49, Bonn, 283–302.

Fligstein, N. (2008). *Euro-Clash: The EU, European Identity and the Future of Europe*. Oxford.

Flodell, C. (1988). *Miteinander oder gegeneinander? Eine sozialpsychologische Untersuchung über Solidarität und Konkurrenz in der Arbeitswelt*. Wiesbaden.

Fortune, 'Can Ford save Ford?' 18 November 2002.

Goffee, R. and Jones, G. (1996). 'What holds the Modern Company together', *Harvard Business Review*, 11/12 1996, 133–148.

Guest, D. E. (1987). 'Human Resource Management and industrial relations', *Journal of Management Studies*, Vol. 24:5, 503–521.

Habermas, Jürgen (2008). *Ach, Europa*, Frankfurt am Main.

Habermas, J. (2004). 'Solidarität jenseits des Nationalstaates. Notizen zu einer Diskussion'. In Beckert, *Transnationale Solidarität. Chancen und Grenzen*, pp. 225–235.

Haipeter, T. (2006). 'Der Europäische Betriebsrat bei General Motors Auf dem Weg zur europäischen Mitbestimmung?', *WSI-Mitteilungen*, 11/2006, 617–623.

Haipeter, T. and Banyuls, J. (2007). 'Arbeit in der Defensive? Globalisierung und die Beziehungen zwischen Arbeit und Kapital in der Automobilindustrie', *Leviathan*, 3/2007, 373–400.

Hancké, B. (2000). 'European Works Councils and Industrial Restructuring in the European Motor Industry', *European Journal of Industrial Relations*, Vol. 6:1, 35–59.

Hauser-Ditz, A., Hertwig, M., Pries, L., and Rampeltshammer, L. (2010). *Transnationale Mitbestimmung? Zur Praxis Europäischer Betriebsräte in der Automobilindustrie*. Frankfurt/New York.

Hauser-Ditz, A., Hertwig, M., Pries, L., Rampeltshammer, L. (2009). 'European Works Councils as International Non-profit-organisations: an Organizational Research Approach to a Crucial Element of Europeanisation'. In idem (eds) *European Works Councils in Complementary Perspectives*. ETUI, Brussels.

Hettlage, R. and Müller, H-P. (eds) (2006). *Die europäische Gesellschaft*. Constance.

Hirschmann, A. O. (1982). *Shifting Involvements. Private Interest and Public Action*. Oxford: Basil Blackwell.

Hondrich, K. O. and Koch-Arzberger, C. (1994). *Solidarität in der modernen Gesellschaft*. Frankfurt am Main.

Hürtgen, S. (2011). 'Europäische Interessenvertretung – eine Frage der nationalen Kultur?', *Industrielle Beziehungen*, 18(4)2011, 315–335.

Huzzard, T. and Docherty, P. (2005). 'Between Global and Local: Eight European Works Councils in Retrospect and Prospect', *Economic and Industrial Democracy*, Vol. 26:4, 541–568.

Hyman, R. (2001). *Understanding European Trade Unionism: Between Market, Class and Society*. London.

Hyman, Richard (2011). 'Gewerkschaftliche Strategien und Solidaritätspolitik unter globalen Konkurrenzbedingungen'. In Gerlach, F., et al. (eds): *Solidarität über Grenzen. Gewerkschaften vor neuer Standortkonkurrenz*, pp. 51–72. Berlin.

Jones, G. (2005). *Renewing Unilever. Transformation and Tradition*. Oxford.

Kädtler, J. (2006). *Sozialpartnerschaft im Umbruch. Industrielle Beziehungen unter den Bedingungen von Globalisierung und Finanzkapitalismus*. Hamburg.

Keller, B. (2001). *Europäische Arbeits- und Sozialpolitik*. Munich.

Keutel, A. (2011). 'Die Soziologie der europäischen Integration', *Berliner Journal für Soziologie*, 1/2011, 147–165.

Klemm, M., Kraetsch, C., and Weyand, J. (2011). 'Solidarität in der europäischen betrieblichen Mitbestimmung als theoretische Herausforderung – ein kultursoziologischer Lösungsvorschlag', *Industrielle Beziehungen*, 4/2011, 292–314.

Knudsen, H., Whittall, M. and Huijgen, F. (2007). 'European Works Councils and the Problem of Identity'. In: Whittall, M., Knudsen, H. and Huijgen, F. (eds) 2007. *Towards a European Labour Identity. The Case of the European Works Council.* pp. 5–18.

Kotthoff, H. (1994). *Betriebsräte und Bürgerstatus. Wandel und Kontinuität betrieblicher Mitbestimmung.* Munich and Mering.

Kotthoff, H. (2006a). *Lehrjahre des Europäischen Betriebsrats: Zehn Jahre transnationale Arbeitnehmervertretung.* Berlin: edition sigma.

Kotthoff, H. (2006b). *Ten Years General Motors European Employee Forum (EEF).* Hans-Böckler-Stiftung. <http://www.boeckler.de/pdf_fof/S-2006-919-2-1.pdf> accessed 18 September 2012.

Kotthoff, H. (2007). 'The European Works Council and the Feeling of Interdependence'. In Whittall, Whittall, M., Knudsen, H. and Huijgen, F. (eds) 2007. *Towards a European Labour Identity. The Case of the European Works Council*, pp. 169–181. Abingdon: Routledge.

Kotthoff, H. (2011). 'A. Schütz oder A. Gramsci? Kommentar zur Kontroverse Klemm/ Kraetsch/ Weyand vs. Hürtgen', *Industrielle Beziehungen*, 2/2011, 346–351.

Lecher, W., Nagel, B., and Platzer, H.-W. (1999). *The Establishment of European Works Councils. From Information Committee to Social Actor.* Aldershot: Ashgate.

Lecher, W., Platzer, H.-W., Rüb, S. and Weiner, K.-P. (2002). *European Works Councils: Negotiated Europeanisation. Between Statutory Framework and Social Dynamics.* Aldershot: Ashgate.

Lucio, M. and Weston, S. (2000). '"European" Works Councils and "Flexible Regulation": the Politics of Intervention', *European Journal of Industrial Relations*, Vol. 6:2, 203–216.

Mählmeyer, V. (2011). *Vom Informations- und Konsultationsgremium zum Verhandlungspartner? Der Europäische Ford-Betriebsrat im Verselbständigungsprozess der Visteon Komponentensparte bei Ford of Europe.* Universitätsverlag des Saarlandes, Saarbrücken.

Maljers, F. A. (1992) [1966]. 'Inside Unilever: the Evolving Transnational Company', *Harvard Business Review*, 11/12, 133–148.

manager magazin 6/2007. 'Unilever. Die Zentralgewalt'.

manager magazin 12/1998. 'Unilever. Der provinzielle Multi'.

Marginson, P. (2000). 'The Eurocompany and Euro Industrial Relations', *European Journal of Industrial Relations*, Vol. 6:1, 9–34.

Marginson, P. and Sisson, K. (1996). 'European Works Councils. Opening the Door to European Bargaining', *Industrielle Beziehungen*, No.3, 229–236.

Marginson, P. and Hall, M. (2004). 'The Impact of European Works Councils on Management Decision-making in UK- and US-based Multinationals: a Case Study Comparison', *British Journal of Industrial Relations*, Vol. 42, 209–233.

Marginson, P., Buitendam, A., Deutschmann, C. and Perulli, P. (1993). 'The Emergence of the Euro-company. Towards a European Industrial Relations', *Industrial Relations Journal*, 24(3), 182–190.

Marshall, T. H. (1950). *Citizenship and Social Class: And Other Essays*. Cambridge.

Mau, S. (2009). 'Europäische Solidarität: Erkundung eines schwierigen Geländes'. In Harnisch, S., Maull, H. W., and Schieder, S. (eds), *Solidarität und internationale Gemeinschaftsbildung*, Frankfurt am Main/New York, pp. 63–88.

Mau, S. (2007). *Transnationale Vergesellschaftung. Die Entgrenzung sozialer Lebenswelten*. Frankfurt a. Main.

Miller, D. (1999). 'Towards a "European" Works Council', *Transfer*, Vol. 5:3, 344–365.

Moore, B. (1978). *Injustice: The Social Bases of Obedience and Revolt*, M. E. Sharpe, White Plains, NY.

Müller, T.; Platzer, H-W. and Rüb, S. (2004). *Globale Arbeitsbeziehungen in globalen Konzernen? Zur Transnationalisierung betrieblicher und gewerkschaftlicher Politik?*. Wiesbaden.

Müller, T. and Hoffmann, A. (2001). 'Euro-Betriebsräte unter der Lupe. Zusammenfassender Bericht über die Forschungsliteratur', *Industrielle Beziehungen*, 1/200, 103–111.

Müller-Jentsch, W. (2007). *Strukturwandel der industriellen Beziehungen*. Wiesbaden.

Münch, R. (2008). *Die Konstruktion der europäischen Gesellschaft. Zur Dialektik von transnationaler Integration und nationaler Desintegration*. Frankfurt.

Nevins, A. and Hill, F. E. (1957). *Ford: Expansion and Challenge, 1915–1933*. Bloomington.

Nuissl, H. (2002). 'Bausteine des Vertrauens – eine Begriffsanalyse', *Berliner Journal für Soziologie*, 12 (1), 87–108.

Offe, C. and Wiesenthal, H. (1980). 'The Two Logics of Collective Action: Theoretical Notes on Social Class and Organizational Form'. In *Political Power and Social Theory* 1: 67–115.

Offe, Claus (2007). 'Obligations Versus Costs: Types and Contexts of Solidary Action'. In: Karagiannis, N. (ed.) *European Solidarity*, 113–128.

Olson, M. (1965). *The Logic of Collective Action*. Cambridge (Mass.)/London.

Organ, D. W., Podsakoff, PhD, and MacKenzie, S. B. (2005). *Organizational Citizenship Behavior*. Thousand Oaks.

Platzer, H-W. (2010). *Europäisierung der Gewerkschaften. Gewerkschaftliche Herausforderungen und Handlungsoptionen auf europäischer Ebene. Perspektiven gemeinsamer Politik mit der Sozialdemokratie*, Internationale Politikanalyse, Friedrich-Ebert-Stiftung <http://library.fes.de/pdf-files/id/ipa/07178.pdf> accessed 19 September 2012.

Platzer, H.-W., Müller, T. (2011). *Global and European Trade Union Federations* (with Rüb, S., Oetgen, T. R., Helmer, M.) Oxford/Berne.

Pulignano, V. (2005). 'Europeanization and Organised Labour: An Unsolved Dilemma?', International Workshop, Warwick University, 18–19 November, <http://www.fafo.no/Oestforum/Kunnskapsbase/Seminarer/workshop_nov05.pdf> accessed 19 September 2012.

Rampeltshammer, L. and Wachendorf, N. M. (2009). 'European Works Councils in Germany'. In: Hertwig, M. et al., *European Works Councils in Complementary Perspectives*. pp. 261–279.

Rawls, J. (1971). *A Theory of Justice*. Cambridge (Mass.)/London.

Rorty, R. (1989). *Contingency, Irony, and Solidarity*. Cambridge.

Royle, T. (1999). 'Where's the Beef? McDonald's and its European Works Council', *European Journal of Industrial Relations*, Vol. 5:3, 327–347.

Rüb, S. (2009). *Transnationalisierung der Gewerkschaften. Eine empirische Untersuchung am Beispiel der IG Metall*. Berlin.

Rüb, S.; Platzer, H-W. and Müller, T. (2012). *Transnational Company bargaining and the Europeanization of Industrial Relations: Prospects for a Negotiated Order*. Oxford.

Seidman, G. W. (2007). *Beyond the Boycott: Labour Rights, Human Rights, and Transnational Activism*. New York.

Stichweh, R. (2000). *Die Weltgesellschaft: Soziologische Analysen*. Frankfurt.

Stirling, J. and Tully, B. (2004). 'Power, Process and Practice: Communications in European Works Councils', *European Journal of Industrial Relations* 10(1): 73–89.

Stöger, H. (2011). *Abstieg oder Aufbruch? Europäische Betriebsräte zwischen Marginalisierung und transnationalem Einfluss*. Münster.

Streeck, W. (1999). 'Social Citizenship under Regime Competition. The case of their European Works Council'. In idem. (ed.), *Korporatismus in Deutschland*, pp. 124–158. Frankfurt am Main.

Telljohann, V. (2005). 'The European Works Council – a Role beyond the Directive?', *Transfer*, 11 (1) 2005, 81–96.

Telljohann, V. (2005). 'The Operation of EWCs'. In Fulton, L. and Telljohann, V. (eds), *Quality Inventories on the Operation of European Works Councils*, pp. 29–55. Bologna.

Telljohann, Volker; da Costa, I.; Müller, T.; Rehfeldt, U.; Zimmer, R. (2009). *European and International Framework Agreements: Practical Experiences and Strategic Approaches*, Luxembourg, Office for Official Publications of the European Communities.

Thome, H. (1998). 'Soziologie und Solidarität. Theoretische Perspektiven für die empirische Forschung'. In Bayertz, Kurt (ed.) *Solidarität. Begriff und Problem*, pp. 217–262. Frankfurt am Main: Suhrkamp.

Timming, A. R. and Veersma, U. (2007). 'Living Apart Together? A Chorus of Multiple Identities'. In Whittall, M., Knudsen, H. and Huijgen, F. (eds) 2007. *Towards a European Labour Identity. The Case of the European Works Council*. pp. 41–54. Abingdon: Routledge.

Tolliday, S. (2003). 'The Decline of Ford in Britain: Marketing and Production in Retreat'. In: Bonin, H., Lung, Y. and Tolliday, S. (eds) (2003). *Ford. The European History*.

Tuckman, A. and Whittall, M. (2002). 'Affirmation, Games and Increasing Insecurity: Cultivating Consent within a New Workplace Regime', *Capital and Class*, No. 76, 64–94.

Tuckman, A. and Whittall, M. (2010). 'Giving employees a voice? Lesson from the New Employee Forums in the UK'. In Garibaldo, F. and Telljohann, V. (eds): *Labour, Education and Society*, Issue on 'The Ambivalent Character of Participation. New Tendencies in Worker Participation in Europe', 269–284, Brussels.

Ullrich, C. G.(1996). 'Solidarität und Sicherheit. Zur sozialen Akzeptanz der Gesetzlichen Krankenversicherung', *Zeitschrift für Soziologie*, Vol. 25, 171–189.

Waddington, J. (2010). *European Works Councils: A Transnational Industrial Relations Institution in the Making*. New York, Abingdon.

Waddington, J. (2006). 'Was leisten Europäische Betriebsräte?', *WSI-Mitteilungen*, 10/2006, 560–567.

Weiler, A. (2004). *European Works Councils in Practice*. Luxembourg.

Whittall, M. (2000). 'The BMW European Works Council: A Cause for European Industrial Relations Optimism?', *European Journal of Industrial Relations*, Vol. 6:1, 61–83.

Whittall, M. (2003). 'European Works Councils. A Path to European Industrial Relations? The Case of BMW and Rover'. (Unpublished PhD thesis, Nottingham Trent University).

Whittall, M. (2010). 'The Problem of National Industrial Relations Traditions in European Works Councils: The Example of BMW', *Economic and Industrial Democracy*, Vol. 3:4, 70–85.

Whittall, M., Knudsen, H. and Huijgen, F. (2009). 'European Works Councils: Identity and the Role of Information and Communication Technology', *European Journal of Industrial Relations*, Volume 15 (2), 167–186.

Whittall, M., Knudsen, H. and Huijgen, F. (eds) 2007. *Towards a European Labour Identity. The Case of the European Works Council.* Abingdon: Routledge.

Whittall, M., and Kotthoff, H. (2011). 'Les comités d'entreprise européens, des zones libres de syndicats?', *La Revue de L'Ires*, Sommaire N° 68, 2011/1, 207–236.

Wilkins, M. and Hill, F. E. (1964). *American Business Abroad: Ford on Six Continents.* Cambridge.

Wills, J. (2000). 'Great Expectations: Three Years in the Life of a European Works Council', *European Journal of Industrial Relations*, Vol. 6:1, 85–107.

Zoll, R. (2000). *Was ist Solidarität heute?* Frankfurt am Main.

Index

Trade Unions Past, Present and Future

EDITED BY CRAIG PHELAN

This series publishes monographs and edited collections on the history, present condition and possible future role of organised labour around the world. Multi-disciplinary in approach, geographically and chronologically diverse, this series is dedicated to the study of trade unionism and the undeniably significant role it has played in modern society. Topics include the historical development of organised labour in a variety of national and regional settings; the political, economic and legal contexts in which trade unionism functions; trade union internationalism past and present; comparative and cross-border studies; trade unions' role in promoting economic equality and social justice; and trade union revitalisation and future prospects. The aims of the series are to promote an appreciation of the diversity of trade union experience worldwide and to provide an international forum for lively debate on all aspects of the subject.